ADDITIONAL PRAISE FOR *The Girl from Purple Mountain*

"Together May-lee and Winberg Chai have created a testament that reads like a compelling and rich novel, full of incident, soul, and fire."

—LUIS ALBERTO URREA, AUTHOR OF *GHOST SICKNESS* AND *IN SEARCH OF SNOW*

"This is the fascinating story of a Chinese family, covering three generations and the entire twentieth century. With a strong woman often at the forefront as mother and grandmother, the Chai family struggled to surmount political repression, conflict, and economic misery. . . . To read this work is to understand the drama of China—and its people—in revolutionary times."

—ROBERT A. SCALAPINO, ROBSON RESEARCH PROFESSOR OF GOVERNMENT EMERITUS, INSTITUTE OF EAST ASIAN STUDIES, U.C. BERKELEY

"The Chais, father and daughter, are a good team as they alternate in writing episodes about the vicissitudes and triumphs of two Chinese families who come together in a marriage and create an American one. A poignant and delightful memoir."

—HENRY LUCE III, FORMER PUBLISHER OF *TIME* MAGAZINE

"This stirring memoir written by a father-daughter team is graced with masterful writing and keen observations. The authors deftly move in and out of colorful anecdotes by means of flashbacks while never stalling the forward motion of their narrative. In telling a moving story of Chinese immigrants who suffer the hardships of war and political strife, the authors also give a succinct account of modern Chinese history. *The Girl from Purple Mountain* should be on the must-read list of anyone interested in Chinese culture and history."

—TAO-TAI HSIA, CHIEF OF THE EASTERN LAW DIVISION, LIBRARY OF CONGRESS

"The writing in this book is adept and bold-spirited, savvy in its perspective on history, unflinching in its revelation. The authors' compelling rendering of our human proclivity for both tenderness and cruelty distinguishes them as ardent laborers in the fields of the word. This is a work that smolders and sings."

—MARILYN KRYSL, AUTHOR OF *WARSCAPE WITH LOVERS, SOULSKIN,* AND *DIANA LUCIFERA*

THE GIRL

FROM PURPLE MOUNTAIN

~ *Love, Honor, War, and One Family's*
Journey from China to America ~

MAY-LEE CHAI
AND WINBERG CHAI

THOMAS DUNNE BOOKS
ST. MARTIN'S PRESS
NEW YORK

THOMAS DUNNE BOOKS.
An imprint of St. Martin's Press.

THE GIRL FROM PURPLE MOUNTAIN: LOVE, HONOR, WAR, AND ONE FAMILY'S JOURNEY
FROM CHINA TO AMERICA. Copyright © 2001 by May-lee Chai and Winberg Chai. All
rights reserved. Printed in the United States of America. No part of this book may be used
or reproduced in any manner whatsoever without written permission except in the case of
brief quotations embodied in critical articles or reviews. For information, address St. Martin's Press, 175 Fifth Avenue, New York, N.Y. 10010.

www.stmartins.com

BOOK DESIGN BY CASEY HAMPTON

Library of Congress Cataloging-in-Publication Data

Chai, May-Lee and Winberg Chai
    The girl from Purple Mountain: love, honor, war, and one family's journey from
China to America / May-lee Chai and Winberg Chai.—1st ed.
        p. cm.
    ISBN 0-312-26808-4
    1. Chai, Ruth Tsao. 2. Chinese Americans—Biography. 3. China—
Biography. I. Chai, Winberg. II. Title.

E184.C5 C42 2001
973'.04951'0092—dc21   2001017425
[B]

First Edition: June 2001

10 9 8 7 6 5 4 3 2 1

For Ariel Lien Chai,
first of the fourth generation in America

CONTENTS

Love is of source unknown, yet it grows ever deeper.
The living may die of it, by its power the dead live again.

—Tang Xianzu (1598), from the preface to
Peony Pavilion (Translation by Cyril Birch)

A NOTE TO THE READER

We have decided to tell this story in two voices, that of my father, Winberg, and myself, May-lee. Originally we thought we could write this memoir in a single voice, that of my father, as he was a participant in and witness to many of the events we describe. However, we discovered that his voice alone was insufficient. My father experienced the wars in China—the Sino-Japanese War (1937–1945) and the Civil War (1945–1949)—in his childhood, which was highly traumatic and resulted in the repression of these memories for most of his adult life. As we began work on the memoir, I came to discover that the story of my family, and my grandmother, was not only what actually happened to them in China, but also how these events were later both remembered and repressed in America. No one else wanted to recall the wars or the family fights that accompanied them, yet my grandmother refused to let anyone forget. As a child, I found this tension between remembering the past and ignoring it extremely frustrating. Why couldn't my family just tell me what had happened? But now, as an adult, I realize that there is no single version of the past in a family history.

For example, after the 1937 invasion of Nanjing by the Japanese Army, the family was forced to flee to Hunan province where they lived in a village in the countryside. These years were terrifying to my grandmother because of the precarious nature of their lives, never knowing when the Japanese would arrive. However, to my father, living in the countryside from the ages of four to nine was terribly fun and exciting. He found country living to be filled with more adventures for a boy than his structured life in the city had ever allowed. He could run barefoot all year round. He remembered seeing the traveling folk performances that visited the village. If we were to tell the story of our family, I realized, we had to encompass both perspectives, as these differences accounted for the confusion in the way these stories were passed down to me, and to my brother and cousins.

Ultimately, we decided that I would have to tell part of the story as well. My frustration at not understanding was, in part, the impetus for writing this memoir. In college I started studying Chinese so that I could translate family documents, as if they might tell me what had happened during the war years. However, I discovered that the answers I sought were more complicated and the documents only raised more questions. I have spent more than ten years researching this memoir—traveling to China frequently, living in Nanjing for nearly two years, and also convincing my father to return to some of the cities and sites of his family's wartime experiences. By describing my efforts to understand the past and my father, I am trying to show how these stories pass imperfectly from one generation to the next yet how important it is to make the attempt to understand them.

We have benefited from the research of numerous scholars and the assistance of many individuals in writing this memoir. Their names follow at the end of the book.

Finally, we want to explain the romanization system that we have used. The Chinese names in this book reflect several spelling systems, including the Wade-Giles system, which was popular before 1949 (including Yangtze River, Chiang Kai-shek); the pinyin system, currently in use in mainland China (such as Nanjing, Zhou Enlai); and Americanized spellings that no longer use diacritical marks (such as Tsao instead of Ts'ao and Chu instead of Ch'u). Names of historical figures are spelled as they are best known in America. Some names of nonhistorical figures have been altered for privacy reasons.

—May-lee Chai

THE GIRL FROM PURPLE MOUNTAIN

I

THE BETRAYAL

Ruth Mei-en Tsao Chai, circa early 1970s.

~ *Winberg* ~

My mother was buried alone, surrounded by strangers, the way she wished, in a New York mausoleum auspiciously bearing the name of her college dorm. Ferncliff. She had changed her burial plans secretly, with the help of my youngest brother. A decade earlier, my parents had bought side-by-side plots. My father had thought the matter was all settled.

When she inquired into the mausoleum, price was not an issue, nor the "neighborhood"—the race and religion of the occupants of the surrounding tombs. My mother was concerned with only one thing: she wanted a single spot for her coffin, a space where all the surrounding plots had been taken. She wanted a spot where she would be encircled by strangers, where my father could not be buried beside her.

After her sudden and unexpected death, after the discovery of her change of heart and my youngest brother's complicity, my father went to the mausoleum and argued with the overseer. Couldn't something be done? A neighboring space bought from its owner? His wife's body moved? But the forms she had signed, forms that my youngest brother had cosigned, were legal and binding. It had been my mother's wish to be buried in this manner; there was nothing my father could do.

My father eventually bought a plot on the grounds outside the mausoleum. "I will be her guardian. I will stand outside for eternity and guard her body."

He convinced himself that this new setup was just what my mother had anticipated. She had sent him a secret message from the grave. He could prove his devotion and his love in this final way. Just as he had proven his devotion and love while she was alive, now his bones would lie in respect and devotion for eternity.

In classical Chinese, the writer leaves a space before a name to show respect. Every time my father wrote of my mother in a letter, he left a space before her name. He saw this physical separation of their coffins as his last sign of respect for my mother.

In one of his last letters to me, my father wrote of his continuing sadness at the absence of my mother, his inability to go through her things. They lay as she had left them throughout their tiny apartment in Manhattan. Chinese dresses made decades earlier in Taiwan and Shanghai. Jewelry hidden in McDonald's Styrofoam boxes. A box of mildewed *Life* magazines, dollar bills rotting between the pages, where she had glued them. She'd been saving these magazines for nearly a decade, a memento of her failed attempt to send money to her brothers in China. During the Cultural Revolution, they had been sent down to the countryside by Mao, two German-educated surgeons, to "learn from the peasants." They did not know how to plant rice. The peasants didn't know how they would feed all these useless intellectuals sent from the cities. Scholars now estimate more than 30 million Chinese died of starvation or illness stemming from deprivation and exposure during Mao's experiments with restructuring society.

My mother began receiving letters that looked like chessboards they were so heavily edited by censors, entire lines blackened, every other character blotted out. But she understood that her brothers were now living in the countryside, in poverty. And she remembered from her refugee days how the people in the countryside had liked to hang on their walls as decor the glossy pictures from Shanghai movie star magazines and especially exotic Western-style advertisements. She had this idea, how to help her brothers. She would send them a box of *Life* magazines. She would enclose a cheerful letter, telling her brothers that they should give out the pictures to their "farmer friends"; she would not let on that she had understood their complaints, that she had understood exactly what kind of hell they had fallen into; it would be the kind of generic family letter a censor could read and pass on, thinking nothing was there. But her brothers would understand. Then the censors would open the box and see an innocent pile of old magazines, they could flip through a few she would put on the top which would have no money, and the rest would then be passed to her brothers. Her brothers would understand that their sister would not be so foolish as to send them magazines when they were starving, and they would carefully search through the *Life*s until they realized she had carefully, cleverly glued together x-number of pages per issue and there they would find the dollar bills. The dollars would help them to bribe officials, to bribe the farmers, to get something to eat.

Using such cunning, my mother had survived the Japanese invasion of China, the era of the warlords, and the Chinese civil war.

Unfortunately, my mother had not anticipated that the Communist customs officials did not allow Western bourgeois propaganda to enter their socialist paradise. The first box of *Life* magazines was returned to her, unopened. They stayed in a corner of her bedroom then near the radiator, first baking, then mildewing after the pipes above the ceiling sprang a leak. By the time she died, my father had forgotten about the dollar bills and threw away the box of magazines.

I remember the morning of her death. It was still early. My children had not yet left for school. My wife was making breakfast, the kitchen sizzled with eggs and bacon. I had a headache. I wasn't hungry. I may have fussed at my wife, saying: "Why go to all this bother? Cereal's good enough. I'm not even hungry."

The phone rang. I remember thinking that it was odd to have a call early in the morning. It was my father.

"Winberg, Mother is gone!" he shouted into the receiver. "She's gone! She's gone!"

"What do you mean?" For a few seconds, I thought my mother had left him, gone off in a pique of anger, the way she had when I was a child.

"The paramedics came. I thought she was sleeping late. I got up.

I always get up at the same time. I went to the kitchen to make breakfast for Mother and she wasn't up yet. She always gets up early, before me, she was never lazy. She wasn't in the living room watching television. She always likes to watch the television in the morning. So I went to see what she wanted for breakfast. I opened the door to her bedroom and called to her, 'You're not up yet! It's morning! What do you want for breakfast?' And she didn't respond. I couldn't wake her." My father said he went to get my younger brother, who lived in an apartment in the same building, and my brother came up and couldn't wake her either. They called the paramedics who then came and told them she was dead. My brother, hysterical, had refused to let the paramedics take her body. She was still there.

"I'll come as soon as I can." My father was still crying when I hung up.

It didn't seem real yet. I told my wife and she looked shocked, then sad, but I couldn't share her emotions. I couldn't feel anything. Not until my mother's funeral, when I had to reach out and touch her pale, cold corpse with one finger, because I still couldn't imagine her dead even though she lay before me in an open casket, her face done up in ghost-white powder and rouge from the Chinatown mortuary, her steel-gray hair braided and piled like a pagoda on the top of her head. It was a traditional hairstyle for a woman of her generation, but she had never worn her hair like that, never worn makeup like that. I looked at her corpse and could not imagine that this had been my mother. But when I touched her, I knew.

"She had a premonition," my father said. "She knew. But I wouldn't listen."

He was sitting in the near-dark of his room in my youngest brother's house, where he had moved after my mother's death a week earlier. He could not bear the Manhattan apartment they had shared for twenty-six years. In his bedroom in the suburbs of New Jersey, my father had constructed a makeshift shrine for my mother, in the Buddhist tradition, although he had converted to Christianity long ago in order to marry her. He had framed a picture of her. It was black-and-white. In it, she wears a shiny black satin dress with embroidery of flowers and leaves in a diagonal across her shoulder, a white silk shawl and tiny dangling earrings. She is looking directly into the camera, smiling with her lips pursed as if she had just finished speaking when someone took the picture. She is still in her fifties in the photograph, and I know that my father had chosen this picture because she is still young enough to look healthy and vigorous, as though she will never die. My father had plugged in two large red and yellow plastic Christmas candles, the kind people in the suburbs like to put on their front porches for the holiday, one on either side of the photograph, which was set on a small nightstand. My father must have found them somewhere, in my youngest brother's garage perhaps, because it was April. There was also a bowl of strawberries that he had placed as an offering in front of the picture, but in the semidarkness of his room I didn't see the bowl at first. I didn't notice them for days, until the strawberries had already begun to rot, and I turned on the light to see what that smell was and found the bowl of moldy fruit.

He was kneeling before his shrine and he was still crying.

"She came to me in the middle of the night. The light woke me up. She tried to tell me but I wouldn't listen."

This is how I imagine my parents' final exchange:

Light like old yellowed newspapers fell across the room from the slightly open door of the bathroom, over the mountain range of rumpled blankets, brushing against the high cheekbones and flat nose of my father before falling onto the cluttered bureau top. The bulb of the night-light in the bathroom flickered once then glowed tremulously. It was an old bulb and needed to be changed. Surely it would go out soon.

My father stirred in his sleep.

My mother stood in the doorway of the bathroom. She may or may not have been looking at him. It had been years since they slept in the same room, much less the same bed. It was more comfortable alone. All the aches and pains that had settled in her body. And besides, my father snored.

The light did not fall upon the glass holding my father's false teeth. They floated in the dark corner of the bureau behind his heavy digital watch—a Christmas gift from one of my brothers—and a once-white handkerchief. There were plastic photo cubes on the dresser. The face with the three of us, his sons, lined up in a row in front of my parents' house in Taiwan was partially illuminated. We are smiling. The neighboring face also caught the light—a picture of my parents at their forty-fifth wedding anniversary party. A big cake with the blue and silver candle shaped like a "45" is clearly visible on the table. My father is wearing his dark gray pin-striped suit and my mother wears a royal blue embroidered silk dress. Her white arms are at her sides. Her jade bracelet has slipped down to her wrist and cannot be seen in the photograph because of the table edge. She is wearing her black curly wig and is not smiling because she did not like her false teeth. My father is smiling, even though she had said his false teeth looked like the teeth of a laughing horse. He is holding her hand, but the picture does not show that either—the cake blocks their hands.

My mother stood in the bathroom, a glass of water in one hand. She surveyed my father now. She called out to him. Loudly.

He stirred in his sleep. His puffy eyelids fluttered.

"Father!"

He was awake now. He squinted without his glasses. His wife was standing in the doorway of the bathroom, splashing light all over his face. "Go back to bed, Mother," he mumbled. He was hard to understand without his teeth. "It's night."

She stood there annoyed for another minute, then took her medicine and shuffled back to her bed.

When my father woke up the next morning, my mother was already dead. He would spend the rest of his life wondering what she had wanted to tell him.

"She was trying to tell me. She knew!" he moans, kneeling before her shrine. The red glow of the Christmas candles makes his face appear to flicker. His mouth gapes open, a toothless black hole. He is howling.

My youngest brother thinks she took too much medicine and killed herself. Forgot how much she took and died.

We don't talk about the change in the burial arrangements. She'd asked him to do it and so he did. He'd done it many, many years before she died. Maybe he thought she'd change her mind in time. None of us expected her to die when she did.

My parents believed in eternity, in heaven and hell, God and Jesus. It is quite possible this affair with the mausoleum, the secret pact with my youngest brother to change her grave site, all this was an elaborate plan to give my father one more chance to show his love. A message for him to decode. And if he succeeded, she would be more than happy to spend eternity with him, husband and wife, in heaven forever and ever. This is what my father believed.

But it's also possible that my mother was not leaving a message for him at all. After a lifetime of betrayals and tragedies and heart-break, perhaps she could not imagine anything but more betrayal and tragedy and heartache, and this plot was her way of heading off more disappointment.

My father never remarried after my mother died and instead de-voted the last years of his life trying to understand what her death and burial meant, how he could continue to prove his love to her now that she had departed from their earthly existence, and how he could continue to understand the messages she sent to him when he dreamed.

For many years, I acted as though none of this mattered. Because I did not understand how my parents' lives could end this way, I sim-ply ignored what I did not like and cared only to remember their life together. In my mind's eye, my parents were neither young nor old, they were neither sickly nor in pain, they had their worries but noth-ing seemed insurmountable. They were forever the way they had been when we first immigrated to New York in the 1950s. They were my parents, immortal. And I was their son, beloved.

Now that nearly twenty years have passed since my mother's death, fifteen since my father's, I have had time to reflect upon their actions and my own. I see now that I was wrong. It is my duty to try to understand my mother, to seek answers. To ignore the past is too much like forgetting. And to forget the past would be to dishonor my parents.

I owe my *entire* life as a man to my parents. I owe my life as an American, with a good education, a good career, a free life, to my mother. Without her foresight, her sacrifices, I would not have had anything. I know this now, even though when I was a young man—a bold, even arrogant man—I would never have admitted as much.

I must now try to remember what I can, what I have tried to forget about my family, about our lives in China during the wars and our

2

THE BOOK OF SECRETS

Charles and Ruth in California visiting their grandchildren, 1968.

~ *May-lee* ~

Growing up, I didn't know much about my grandmother's life in China, or my grandfather's for that matter, except the most academic details, their scholarly achievements, the moments that coincided with what school taught me about the history of China and America. I knew only the official story of my grandparents' lives, the story reserved for formal occasions, for introductions to strangers, the glittering details chosen for their ability to cast their lives in the most glamorous terms.

I didn't know exactly when my grandparents were born, my grandmother in Nanjing, my grandfather in a small town in Anhui province, just that they were both born sometime near the very beginning of the twentieth century, which meant that they had the great misfortune of living through interesting times. They witnessed the fall of the Qing dynasty and the birth of the Republic of China. They then saw the promise of democracy dashed as their country disintegrated into regions controlled by warlords. They survived the Japanese invasion of China, fleeing the Rape of Nanjing in 1937, moving from city to city, one step ahead of the Japanese army. After the Com-

munists won the civil war, they fled to Taiwan then finally immigrated to New York in 1955.

My grandmother, "Ruth" Mei-en Tsao, was one of the first
women admitted into a national university in China when the government finally allowed women to attend in 1920. She was invited
by the Japanese Ministry of Education to tour Japan. Educated by
missionaries, she was a devout Christian and had insisted that my
grandfather convert as well before she agreed to marry him. In her
youth she'd memorized the entire Bible. At a time when many Chinese women still had bound feet and were illiterate, she'd been a
professor of English. During World War II, she served as Lady
Mountbatten's interpreter in China. A woman of strong convictions,
she was always credited by her family with saving their lives because
she'd had the foresight to insist that the family immigrate to America
after the Communists won the civil war.

My grandfather, "Charles" Chu Chai, although he was a scholar
in his own right, considered himself the luckiest man on earth to
have married such a woman. He had been awarded the most prestigious academic prize in China for his generation, an American
Boxer Indemnity Fund scholarship, which enabled him to study at
the American-run Qinghua College in Beijing then come to America
to study through a Ph.D. at the school of his choice. In 1927 he
chose to go to Stanford to complete his B.A., because ever since he'd
been a little boy and had heard tales of "Gold Mountain," he had
always wanted to see California. After he became engaged to my
grandmother, he decided to attend Northwestern University Law
School in Chicago so that he could be closer to his fiancée who had
been awarded a scholarship to study at Wittenberg College in Ohio.
In China, he held many important government positions, working in
the Legislative Yuan to draft the new Chinese constitution and later
training army officers under the warlord of Hunan province. He was
the founding dean of National Chongqing University Law School.
After immigrating to America, he cowrote nine books on China with
my father, several of which became best-sellers. But he always considered marrying my grandmother his greatest achievement. She'd
had many suitors, after all.

"She was the most beautiful woman in China," Ye-ye would say
proudly, "the most intelligent." Then he would smile like a young
boy about to set off a string of firecrackers at New Year's.

But nothing in the official version of the story of their lives helped me to understand my grandmother—not when Nai-nai was alive and intimidated me, certainly not after she had died and her decision to be buried alone mystified me.

Unlike the affection I felt for my grandfather, I always found my grandmother a little frightening.

While Ye-ye knew how to entertain his grandchildren with magic tricks, my grandmother would look at me and say to my mother in her most commanding voice, "Don't dress her in pretty clothes. Only plain clothes. Or someone will kidnap her!"

Nai-nai liked to disrupt our family gatherings in New Jersey with dramatic tales of horror experienced during the war. "He gave away all the children's milk!" she sighed on more than one occasion, pointing a finger at my grandfather's nose. "How will we live? There's nothing to eat!" Because I had no idea what she was talking about, I thought she was losing her mind.

By the time I knew her, in the 1970s, Nai-nai wore only decades-old Chinese silk *qipaos,* which she'd purchased in Shanghai and Taiwan before emigrating to New York. Their high-necked collars and intricately patterned embroidery gave her a formal, somewhat imposing appearance. Because her teeth had gone bad in the war, she'd had them all removed and replaced by dentures, which she never wore because they hurt. She never smiled. She seemed never able to remember my name and referred to both my brother and me as "the boys." I never knew if this was a bad translation of the Chinese term *haizi,* meaning "children," during the era of the universal male pronoun, or a habit she had acquired as the mother of three sons and no daughters.

I knew that it had been my grandmother's idea to go back to China in 1932, the year of my father's birth. Both my grandparents were living in Chicago at the time, my grandfather finishing his law degree, my grandmother her master's. They could have stayed in the United States. My grandfather was offered a teaching position at Northwestern University, but after my grandmother had discovered her pregnancy, she insisted they return home to China, to Nanjing, so that their first son would be born Chinese, and so that she could see her mother who was ill.

But nothing turned out as she'd imagined. Her mother died before

Nai-nai arrived home, and her father immediately remarried. Five years later the Japanese invaded in the infamous Rape of Nanjing, and my father's family became refugees in their own country.

I knew from family stories, the ones told after dinners among friends, that my grandmother had nearly gotten Ye-ye killed during the war. As refugees, the family had been forced to flee on the Yangtze River, from city to city, and once they'd been aboard a boat along with a battalion of soldiers who were very drunk and sang obscene songs all night long.

My grandmother insisted that my grandfather leave the cabin and tell the soldiers to be quiet. "The children cannot sleep!" Very religious, she felt this was what God wanted to be done. Ye-ye didn't want to go out, but she insisted so he dressed in his soldier's uniform—at the time he was employed by the warlord of Hunan, running a military academy for officers—and with a male servant to accompany him, he went out to tell the soldiers to quiet down.

They responded by grabbing him and trying to throw him overboard.

Because he was obviously a rich man, a rich man with connections, with his whole family in their own cabin with many servants, some of the soldiers warned that it would cause too much trouble to kill him and urged their comrades not to drop him into the swirling river. While the soldiers debated what to do, my grandfather escaped, dashing back to the cabin with his servant. They hastily barricaded the door with heavy furniture while Nai-nai and my father and uncles sat crouched under a sturdy table, praying, as the soldiers pounded on the door.

But I also knew that everyone in the family credited Nai-nai with saving them, with getting them out of China before the Communist takeover. Her own brothers and their children had not been so lucky.

"Nai-nai was smart, she knew," my father always said, the only thing he'd say about the war when I was a child. "Ye-ye was offered a very good job at the end of the war, but she said, no, we had to go, we had to leave. Go to America."

Nothing was ever this simple, of course.

Initially, Ye-ye had been awarded a grant by the U.S. State Department to catalog Chinese art at the National Gallery in Washington, D.C., but Nai-nai thought he shouldn't go—there was only one visa for him, none for the rest of the family. She'd heard too many sad stories of husbands and wives separated for years in different cities, in different countries because of the war, because of careers, and even if they didn't divorce—because Chinese couples of a certain generation rarely did—the man too often started a second family and the old wife was left with the children and a paper husband. While in exile in Taiwan, Nai-nai pulled every connection, wrote every missionary she'd ever known, letting them know their prodigy was still alive, had survived the war, and now her eldest son was ready to go to college in America, too. Because of her letter campaign, my father and his brothers were all eventually awarded scholarships to study in America. She and my grandfather came later when Ye-ye was offered a teaching job at the New School for Social Research in New York. In this way, she kept the family together.

Whenever they discussed her contribution to the family's salvation, her sons shook their heads in admiration but also a little aggravation. In the second half of her life, in her life lived after the war, she pursued her goals with a single-mindedness that ranged from pushy to overbearing. Did it make it better, easier to bear, because she was usually right?

Or did it make it worse?

When I was a little girl whenever I did something my father didn't like, he would say, "Just like Nai-nai!" Then he would sigh in exasperation. But I never knew what he meant by that.

I did not particularly want to be just like Nai-nai.

Even when I was a teenager, my father would periodically explode in anger at something I had done and I would shout too, refusing to back down, until finally he'd conclude, a little sadly, "You're really Nai-nai's granddaughter."

I still didn't know what he meant.

I always thought that I'd been named after my grandmother, but after she died when I was thirteen, I discovered that I had been mistaken.

As I was the first Chai grandchild, the first Chai daughter in two generations, and the first Chai born in America, my parents wanted to name me after my grandmother, who had always wanted a daughter and whose hard work during the war they said had made it possible for the family to come to the United States. My grandmother's Chinese name was Mei-en, "Beautiful Blessing," and so I was to be May-lee, which also meant "Beautiful," with an Americanized spelling.

However, my parents later explained that Nai-nai had objected. It was not traditionally done to name a granddaughter after her grandmother. She refused to allow me to use the same character for "Mei."

"She should have her own name," she'd said firmly.

Ye-ye thought of a compromise. I would be named May-lee in English after my grandmother, but he selected a different character for "Mei," so that in Chinese my name means "Plum Blossoms" instead of "Beautiful." Nothing like my grandmother's name.

I thought that meant she hadn't liked me.

A few weeks after my grandmother's funeral, Ye-ye called my father to say that Nai-nai had appeared to him one night. She stood before him, before his bed, light suddenly streaming from behind, crashing over Nai-nai's body like breakers on the coast, splashing white light over her head and foaming around her ankles. She spoke without words, opening and closing her mouth like a fish underwater, but this time my grandfather understood everything. He called my father immediately. She wanted her middle son to marry. He'd been the filial son, despite his birth order, living in the same building as my grandparents, looking after them, shopping with them, a good son, but now it was time for him to start his own family.

It was 1981 and China's paramount leader Deng Xiaoping had only recently, in the past couple years, begun to enact his open-door policies. Letters from our relatives were arriving with more frequency and this was how my grandfather heard from the elder of his two sisters, now living in a remote part of western China, the dusty railroad city of Lanzhou. She and her engineer husband had been sent there during the Cultural Revolution but they hadn't suffered terribly: she'd had to denounce her family—her brothers for leaving the motherland after the revolution, her sister in Taiwan—and then things had settled down. Her husband was a professor at an engineering college now and her son a member of the Communist party. Her husband, always very organized, had kept track of the family. When Ye-ye wrote of his desire to find a bride for his son, she said her husband would write to the relatives in Beijing and see if they knew anyone with an unmarried daughter for my uncle, a suitable family, a good match.

When just such a bride was found, my uncle, ebullient, invited both my brother and me to be in his wedding party, as well as my cousins, my aunt, and seven of his colleagues from work.

Gu Mu and Gu Fu, as my grandfather's sister and her husband introduced themselves to me, arrived in New York in December of 1981, just in time for the wedding they'd helped to arrange.

"Why can't you speak Chinese?" Gu Fu demanded upon meeting me. He spoke with a startlingly perfect British accent. He hadn't spoken English in more than three decades, not since the Communist revolution in 1949, but he explained that he'd kept up by secretly listening to the BBC.

"We wanted to learn Chinese," I said, "but he wouldn't teach us!" I pointed an accusatory finger at my father.

Gu Fu turned to him. "What on earth is the matter with you? You don't teach them a bloody thing!" He shook his head. Then he taught my brother and me three useful phrases to help us through any Chinese conversation: *Wo bu dong,* I don't understand; *Wo bu zhi-dao,* I don't know; and, *xie xie,* thank you.

"They should be able to say *something.*" He clicked his tongue against the roof of his mouth. "What were you thinking?" But if my father heard, he ignored his uncle.

Unlike her husband, Gu Mu spoke no English, but she smiled at my brother and me through thick, black-rimmed glasses that swallowed her features, then said something in rapid-fire Chinese in a surprisingly shrill and loud voice.

No one would translate a thing she said.

Nai-nai had always complained about my grandfather's family, what scoundrels they were, how wily, but my grandfather's sister seemed anything but threatening. Gu Mu came only to my shoulder and seemed so slender that we were afraid she would blow away when traffic passed too close.

As we walked in midtown Manhattan admiring the ornate holiday decorations in the department store windows, she fell behind. Her tiny legs, moving double time, could only carry her so fast. My brother and I walked on either side of Ye-ye and Gu Fu, holding them by the arms, as my father had instructed.

"Shouldn't we wait for Gu Mu?" I asked in concern as we rapidly outpaced her. Because my father had decided to relocate to the Midwest two years earlier, I was experiencing New York again as if for the first time in my life, a grand hustle-bustle city, but a little intimidating, a little frightening with its fast-moving crowds.

"Oh, she's fine," Gu Fu insisted, smiling.

I watched Gu Mu over his shoulder as we walked on, and she smiled cheerily, waving.

My uncles, aunt, aunt-to-be, and cousins arrived later for dinner at Happy Family, my grandparents' favorite restaurant. The proprietors, the Lee family, came to America from Taiwan on the same boat as my grandparents. The synchronicity had sealed the friendship for nearly thirty years. That, and the fact that Mr. Lee always gave them a special price, as well as dishes that weren't on the menu. As my uncle's wedding banquet was going to be held at Happy Family, when we arrived that evening, my grandfather and Mr. Lee conferred for some time about the menu. When he was still a teenager, my grandfather had studied cooking under a former imperial chef who'd been expelled from the Forbidden City after the fall of the Qing dynasty in 1911. My grandfather had discovered the man working in his college cafeteria. Because of this experience, Ye-ye always liked to order very fancy dishes.

The five colds, the three hots, the jellyfish noodles and ginger strips arrived and we began to eat.

I was acutely aware of Gu Fu's staring. His black eyes were focused directly on me. He was watching me eat, I was sure. At fourteen years old, I was highly self-conscious.

"He's staring at me." I nudged my brother.

"Stop it," he said, pushing me away.

I tried to ignore my great-uncle. The waiters brought the next series of courses, including chicken for me, beef for my brother, sea slug, pigeon, lion head meatballs, *xiao long baozi,* and an unidentifiable tureen that contained, among other things, tentacles. As the lazy Susan spun like a top, I dared a glance across the table. Sure enough, Gu Fu was still staring. I thought perhaps as I was the eldest grandchild, I was being measured against some internal family standards that I had not known existed.

In my nervousness, one of my chopsticks slipped and I dropped a *baozi* onto my lap.

Gu Fu winced and looked away.

I wished then that I knew how to eat like a Chinese person, instead of an American. For example, my father could peel grapes with his teeth, spitting out the perfect whole skin, inside out and unbroken, while continuing to chew the fruit. My grandparents had been able to debone chicken in their mouths—despite their ill-fitting dentures. When I tried such a thing, I choked. They could sip piping hot soup that burned my tongue. They knew what was edible inside a crab whereas I couldn't tell the poison gills from the sweet meat. My grandparents had always been very proud of my American ways, as if I were the living proof of the family's assimilation: Look what those Chais can do, just like everyone else in America.

But now when I looked up, I caught a glimpse of horror on Gu Fu's face: his grandniece, so awkward at the table, like a functionally retarded person. I hunched down into my seat.

Gu Mu smiled and trilled something at me, but again, no one would translate.

While my uncle's fiancée—a beautiful woman from Beijing, as tall and slender as a model—sat demurely between Gu Mu and Gu Fu, my father and his brothers were shouting loudly in Chinese, about all manner of things. As was our custom, we had a room to ourselves, partitioned from the other patrons by sliding vinyl panels. As a child, I never knew if the primary purpose of these special room dividers was to provide privacy or to protect the rest of the restaurant from the volume of conversation that accompanied any large family gathering. But tonight my grandfather was uncharacteristically quiet; he slumped in his chair, barely eating. He'd lost a lot of weight since my grandmother's funeral. For the first time in my life, I thought of my grandfather as an old man.

The day before my uncle's wedding, we went to visit my grandmother's mausoleum. It was larger than I had imagined, with lighting like a school gymnasium, harsh and flat, amplified by the shiny tile floor. Each aisle was lined with marble tomb markers, rows and rows, each bearing a name and date in tasteful gold lettering. The placards rose so high toward the ceiling that near the top I could no longer read the names.

Nai-nai's tomb was ground level, however. Her names, in Chinese and English, easy for all to read.

"She always liked modern things," my father said.

My grandfather gestured for us to kneel before her tomb, and my brother and I complied, the floor cold against my tights. He leaned against us. We knelt for some time.

"She liked the flowers in the middle," my father said, chattering now. He gestured toward the containers attached to vases on the walls. "Everyone can share this way. Have flowers all the time. She thought if no one brings her flowers, at least she can share everyone else's flowers."

"How do you know?" I asked, curious.

My father paced nervously behind us, his shoes tapping on the floor, a hollow sound. He laughed awkwardly. "Yep. She always liked modern."

My mother took a picture, my brother and I kneeling with my grandfather, and then it was time to go. We had the wedding rehearsal to attend.

Years later when I looked at the pictures taken that day, I was surprised to see Ye-ye's gaunt face, his cheekbones sharp like glass beneath his skin. I hadn't remembered him looking like that at all. Whenever I thought of Ye-ye, I thought of him the way he had looked when I was a child and we lived in New Jersey and visited my grandparents every weekend. In my mind's eye, he had a large, round face, an easy smile, a smooth forehead that extended over the top of his head. Because I had never known him when he'd had hair, I never thought of him as bald.

How could this fragile man in the photograph be Ye-ye?

Sometime after my grandmother's death and my middle uncle's marriage, my father put together an album about Nai-nai's life. Photos from the war, official-looking documents made of thick rice paper stamped with large red seals. But when I asked him to translate them for me, he'd take off his glasses and hold the book close to his nose, squinting, then say, "No, no, no. It's just Chinese, just Chinese," and refuse to translate anything.

There were pictures of a young girl, shyly demure, her features even and pleasing. Later during the war, the photos revealed an older woman with shadowed eyes, nearly defiant before the camera, with her sons gathered around her like a shield. In these later pictures, she was almost the woman that I'd known, the survivor.

I would pore over the album of my grandmother's life, looking for clues to understand her, to understand me, to understand my family, which was always both so familiar and strange to me, with its secrets and vexing silences, its closeness and closedness, its deep fierce love and undercurrents of even deeper resentments.

How could I be just like Nai-nai if I hardly knew her at all?

After I went to college, I decided to study Chinese language and history, and after six years, I was able to read and speak, albeit with a very strong American accent. And so finally, with the aid of my dictionaries, I was ready to tackle the album that my father had put together about my grandmother's life. What I discovered was that most of the documents had nothing to do with her: they were Ye-ye's work certificates, receipts for building supplies, property deeds.

I despaired of ever understanding anything.

3

UNBOUND FEET

Ruth in her late teens.

~ *Winberg* ~

My own wife has passed away, a little more than four years ago. I am myself a grandfather. Does this help me to understand my parents? I am now in life where they once were.

I never imagined myself this way. A grandfather, a widower. An *older* man. I cannot think of myself as *old*.

At my age, I am supposed to be wise. This is a joke, the idea that wisdom comes automatically with age, like the AARP card in the mail.

I was born in the year of the water monkey, 1932. That means I am supposed to be exceptionally clever, prone to mischief, a teller of tales, a child who tends to be spoiled, a young man who is inclined to be arrogant, an old man who is bound to be regretful, perhaps. But perhaps not.

I was the firstborn son. In the Chinese tradition at the time of the republic, firstborn sons were treated like young emperors. I could do no wrong, I wore the best American-style bomber caps and double-breasted coats. I was the first in Nanjing to own an American-made bicycle even though we lived in the midst of war and the money used to buy the bicycle could have bought rice for a year if that much rice had been available, as rice was rationed. I could boss my two younger brothers mercilessly, which I did, and I could order the servants about, and if I caused something to break as I ran through the house in my hand-knitted underwear or if I refused to eat my dinner or if I were upset because I was not allowed to accompany my father to meetings with his friends and cried loudly, the servants were punished instead of me. In other words, I was a spoiled brat, a living terror, a feudal tyrant (if you prefer the Communists' terminology).

But I'm getting ahead of myself. It is in my nature to wish to speak of myself first even when I should be talking about my parents.

I do not know for certain when my parents were born. Perhaps my mother in the year of the fire horse and my father the year of the wood snake, for these are the years my father wrote in my wedding book, 1906 and 1905, and he assured me that these were the true dates. But my mother seemed more the snake, clearheaded with a sense of history, than my father, and we always believed growing up that she was the older of the two. Now everyone who would know for certain is dead. It was just like him to be chivalrous enough to change birth dates with my mother so that she would appear to be younger. However, when my mother died, five years before my father, they added years to her age in the Chinese funerary tradition so that it seemed as though she had "enjoyed longevity" up into her eighties when she died, which would have meant she was born in the rat year, at least, although there was nothing ratlike about her. And when my parents immigrated to America, they subtracted years from their age on all their papers in the immigrant tradition so that nothing official bears their true birth dates.

Perhaps it is not important.

My mother was the most beautiful woman alive in China. Everyone who knew her would tell you so.

She had round eyes, wide-set so that she could see both what was on the outside and inside of people when they spoke. She had a slender nose and a straight mouth, she did not smile much. Her face was as round as the moon, her figure slender and willowy. She was born into a wealthy family, a good family, an old respectable family from the north. They were tall pale people who could afford to educate their children—even a girl. Her father, my Wai-gong,[1] was the founder of the first Christian college in Nanjing, and a member of the local elite. Her brothers were tall boys, well educated, a little spoiled. They were sent by their father to study medicine in Bonn, Germany; they returned to Nanjing as surgeons. They liked to spend money. The eldest married a Shanghai starlet, a wanna-be movie star. In order to attract her, he sold his share of the family estate to my mother. Selling land to buy a fancy car! Land was the only thing that lasted in China, but there was no convincing him of the error of his ways. After the Communist Revolution, he had no money to bribe his way out of the country, nothing worth selling but a broken-down foreign car with parts impossible to find. The starlet's friends were gone, and they remained behind. During the Cultural Revolution, he was beaten for being a Western-educated doctor, and his wife committed suicide.

If during her years of exile in New York my mother knew what had happened to this favorite brother, the one with the tallest nose and the playful heart (even if he never smiled in photographs, preferring to look like a romantic, like Leslie Howard in *Gone with the Wind*), my mother never talked of such things. I found out about it much later, after she was dead. I had returned to China for the first time in thirty-five years and my one surviving uncle told me everything at the top of his lungs, how those who had been left behind had suffered and how some had died. We sat on small wooden stools in his cramped Beijing apartment, a fan whirring in the background stirring up dust, absolutely useless to cool the sweat pouring from our bodies.

But again I'm getting ahead of myself, digressing into another story altogether. A monkey trait. Excuse me.

The most important person in my mother's family, as she would have told you, was her mother, who was the most industrious, most kindhearted, most wronged woman in all of China, if not all the world. Her mother stood less than five feet tall, a result of having her feet bound when she was a child. At the age of three, the servants wrapped her feet in ten-foot-long strips of cotton, two to two-and-a-half inches wide, plain muslin—the dye from colored cloth could

---

[1] *Wai-gong* means "maternal grandfather" in Chinese, literally "outside male," to differentiate from the intimacy of *Ye-ye,* "your father's father."

seep into the festering wounds and cause infection. They left the big toe straight then bent the four smaller toes down into the pads of the feet and wrapped them tightly. The idea was they would gradually bend her foot in half, bringing the heel toward the toes, slowly breaking the bones over months, wrapping the foot tighter and tighter so that no blood could flow to the flesh, until her feet no longer grew, until the pain was as familiar as the nose on her face. In principle a girl would be able to walk again but in the tiny, mincing steps that men found attractive, and without crying out. Women who cried were so annoying after all. The process of foot-binding took years, all of childhood and adolescence sometimes, to perfect the "three-inch golden lotuses," as bound feet were euphemistically called. Such feet had to be washed daily once a woman was an adult because the rotting flesh stank. Rarely could bound feet be unbound if they had truly attained the most desired length—four and half inches or less, at best the toes would fall off and she'd be unable to walk, and at worst the gangrene would spread quickly through her circulatory system and the woman would die.

It's hardest in the beginning because children are by nature disobedient, noisy creatures who will cry when they hurt even if no one wants to hear them. And in the beginning, my mother's mother cried with lungs that exploded with power, like steam engines, as she shouted for all to hear as she lay on her pallet in the farthest corner of the family compound where she would be least disturbing to her father, the Old Master. So she lay on her pallet, on the cotton quilt, screaming, alone, except for a cat that was supposed to catch the mice who slipped along the floor carrying crumbs to their nests in the cushions of the chairs.

As my grandmother cried and shrieked, the old women who passed in the alley could not help but hear her sick-animal cry as they hobbled over the cobblestones to the vegetable market, woven baskets swinging on their arms. The servants gossiping in the kitchen tried to ignore the sound, stuffing cotton into their ears. The other children—the boys—were sent to school at the clan tutor's hall so that their miserable sister's screams did not disturb their studies, which included memorizing four books—the Confucian classics— over a period of five years. The shrieks continued nonstop for three months, unabated. No one could remember a child with such strength and willpower, especially a girl.

But finally, a missionary and his wife came to call on the Old Master and his wife. They were a curious couple brimming with book-learned Chinese, smelling of soap and hairy Americans' sweat, proclaiming the message of a foreign god who promised Eternal Life. The missionary's wife heard and could not forget the cries of the sick girl-child hidden in the far reaches of the compound. The wailing made her tea taste bitter. The screeching made her husband scowl. And the combined discomfort of the exotic foreigners made my grandmother's parents feel strange, almost embarrassed, which was not the way a Chinese family should feel in front of foreigners who were obviously not as wealthy and spent too much of their time with the poor.

The missionary's wife continued to call, bringing presents—English books and American biscuits in bright tins that kept things dry, crisp, and away from the mice, which were abundant this year and arrogant, no doubt due to the shantytowns and beggars filling up the alleyways. In the late 1860s the refugee situation was getting worse, as peasants tired of starving in the countryside flocked to the cities, almost a thousand each day. China was still in the hands of "foreigners," the non-Han Manchus who controlled the Forbidden City in Beijing. There was now a boy emperor sitting on the throne while his mother, the Empress Dowager Cixi, drained the imperial coffers. Twenty-some years after the end of the Opium War, England was selling thousands of tons of opium, addicts lined the alleys, and every important family had at least one son, uncle, or father who would have sold his ancestors' bones for another pipe.

So while China was in the hands of foreigners content to cut her like a melon, the missionary's wife would visit, and my grandmother would scream like a whistling bomb as the missionary's wife explained over tea and onion cakes about heaven and hell and how you could burn eternally among demons for torturing a child; my grandmother's mother developed such a headache. One day the headache would not go away. It pressed against her left eyeball like a knitting needle. It throbbed in her left temple like a drum. And the idea that this missionary's wife could get her child to stop screaming came to my grandmother's mother like a breath of the Holy Ghost, cooling her burning brow, soothing her roiling nerves. This missionary's wife had all the answers. Life would be much simpler to listen to her; my grandmother's mother would not have to follow traditions and raise her family right and honor her ancestors' wishes and who could know what those wishes were unless you paid hundreds of taels of copper coins to a worthless squint-eyed fortune-teller who might or might not know what he was talking about.

"Who will marry a girl with big feet except a peasant?" my grandmother's mother asked the missionary's wife. "I do not want my daughter working in a field, selling her children for food, dying an old woman when she's only thirty."

"A Christian man does not care if a girl has big or small feet. Only her soul matters."

My grandmother's mother waved her hand at the servant girl who was rubbing her temples. The girl stopped and moved away. My grandmother's mother sipped her tea noisily, the hot water burned her tongue. She swallowed quickly, her head throbbing like the heart of a bird. "But there are not very many Christian men in China."

"There will be," the missionary's wife said with utter certainty, her gloved hands folded in her lap, her thin lips set in a straight line.

And so after three and a half months, my grandmother's feet were unbound.

My grandmother sat on her bedroll, wiggling her toes, a smile on her face as she told my mother about the day they unwrapped her feet. The smell of pus and fresh blood rose like moths from the muslin, pushing into the nose and throat of the missionary's wife so that she turned as green as celadon and ran into the courtyard to vomit into a ceramic goldfish bowl. The servants stood on both sides, holding my grandmother's arms in case she would jerk away or scratch at their faces, trying to stop them. "But I held very still. I knew exactly what was happening even though I was a very little girl. It was the happiest day of my life." My grandmother smiled at the memory, her brown teeth glistening.

My mother wiggled her own toes, which were a little pinched, it's true, in her new fashionable high-heeled leather pumps but she didn't dream of complaining. "You've had a hard life, Mother."

At first my grandmother's toes had refused to uncrimp, they were as bent as claws after their months in bondage. The missionary woman directed that her feet should be bathed twice a day, powdered with alum, then allowed to dry in the air—they must not be allowed to fester. She read from her medical book, her hands shaking slightly, her voice high but firm. "Do not allow her to put her full weight on them. The legs must be massaged three times a day to restore blood flow. The dead skin must be peeled off with tweezers. I'll show you."

And the pale woman with the watery eyes leaned over my grandmother's feet with a miniature set of tongs and pulled at the loose strips of blackened flesh until they peeled away like the skin of a tangerine. Her new feet lay as pink as boiled shrimp, curled and moist on the cotton sheet. They were then rewrapped, but not so tightly, until gradually they did not need to be bound at all.

"You do not need to worry," said the missionary's wife, in her careful Chinese. "God is with us. You will be able to walk like a human being again."

But my grandmother was not worried. She lay back against the cotton quilt, staring into her mother's frowning face, her amah's rough hand against her feverish forehead, and she had a vision. A chorus of fat women with wings and enormous feet hovered above her head, laughing joyfully as they beckoned her to join them.

The American missionaries in Shandong province had plentiful supplies of Western medicine, which arrived in wooden crates from the port city of Qingdao (formerly Ts'ing-tao), with funding from some of the wealthiest American industrialists to Christianize China. Most important perhaps they had self-confidence, God, and a new concept, physical education, on their side to help my grandmother walk "like a human being again." And when she did walk on her damaged feet, it was like walking on broken glass, but they explained to her that with Jesus all things were possible. And when she learned to walk so fast that no one, not even the children her age who liked to tease about such things, noticed that she walked with a slight limp, my grandmother knew that it was true, with Jesus all things were possible. She need only wiggle her toes at night to prove it.

The missionaries taught my grandmother to read and write. They taught her geography, the fundamentals of math, the principles of music, and the basics of nursing. Like all good Chinese girls of her generation, she also learned embroidery, knitting, crocheting, cooking, how to raise silkworms then boil them alive in their cocoons to release the silk, how to spin it into thread, how to run a household, manage servants, bargain for a better price for almost anything, and how to be obedient. Because she was educated and Christian, she came to teach at the missionaries' school. Because she was educated and Christian, she had the usual difficulties finding a husband.

For a Chinese woman, Christianity offered much: an education, health, and a husband who could have only one wife, who was forbidden the vices of opium, drink, gambling, and the teahouses with the singing whores. For Chinese men, however, Christianity was a comedown.

But her family owned land at a time when an entire family of farmers might have no more than one *mu*, about a third of an acre, to farm and live off of, making them wealthier than ninety percent of China's population. Eventually, a matchmaker found a man willing to marry my grandmother. A teacher at another missionary's school.

His family was neither wealthy nor educated, which did not bode well according to the fortune-teller whom my grandmother's mother hired to examine the photograph of the tall, solemn-faced man who would become my grandfather.

But the missionary's wife said, "We must not judge a man at face value." Although in China there were fortune-tellers who were trained in the art of judging, based on the shape and contours of his face, not just the man but his entire destiny, my grandmother merely nodded as the woman explained everything. "A man is the sum of his actions, his faith, his heart. Not his wealth."

"I will follow God's will," said my grandmother, her eyes cast modestly downward, where she could admire her feet.

I don't know the contents of my grandmother's dowry, the acres, animals, and jade that accompanied her into her husband's family, but I do know that my grandfather became a wealthy man after he married my grandmother. And between her land and her family's connections, he finally had the means to obtain his ambitions, which were not inconsiderable.

"We've got to leave this village," he complained to his bride. Everyone here knew his wife's family, knew where his money came from, knew that he was the son of a poor man, done well by embracing the white foreign devil's God. He imagined the men he passed in the streets snickering at him in his brand-new clothes, the fur lining peeking from the edges of his cotton sleeves, like a scarecrow in imperial robes.

The sniveling intellectuals, the hunchbacked exam candidates, skinny and shivering in their students' blue robes, quoting classical poems he did not quite understand. The merchants' sons able to spend in one night gambling at the teahouse what he could not earn in a year of teaching. Even the missionary with his sharp nose and even sharper tongue, constantly correcting him when he spoke, constantly reminding him, "You have so much to be thankful for. Think of where you came from. Now you, too, are an educated man. Thanks be to God." He meant my grandfather should thank him.

But my grandfather did not want to think of where he had come from, only where he could go next. And so he moved my grandmother, far from his family and hers, to a southern city, Nanjing, the former capital of the Ming dynasty, a grand city where fortunes could be made and a man with ambition could get somewhere.

My grandmother's clan owned sizable tracts of land in Nanjing and it was my grandfather's brilliant idea that they give a plot to the missionaries to build Nanjing's first Christian college. It was about time the missionaries thought on a grander scale, he explained, time to move out of the backwaters, from the cold severe north to the bustling, hustling south. He would quite naturally sit on the college's board of regents to ensure that the Christian message of the institution not be compromised.

Alone, far from her family, from her classmates and students, my grandmother found the city of Nanjing a surprisingly cold place. She could not get used to the damp winters. Nanjing was south of the *Chang Jiang,* the "long river," as the Yangtze River was called by locals, but it was not the warm, southern city she had imagined. The wind was cold. Her bones never felt warm. There were no heated *kang* beds, with warm bricks beneath the clay bedframes, quilts piled on top, the way everyone slept in the north. Instead there were coal stoves that stank and whose fumes made her dizzy. The southerners believed that the inside temperature of a house should never be a season apart from the outside, or else the humors of your body would be thrown off balance. If it was winter on the street, it was winter inside as well. She tried to explain that in her hometown, in Shandong, where the snowflakes fell as thick as goosefeathers and covered the streets, the ground, and the roofs like a white river, they had heated their homes. It was not necessary at all to live in the same season inside as out. It was better to live in comfort. She tried to explain to them about Western medicine, as the missionaries had taught her, about germs and hygiene, but they scoffed at her mad fairy stories.

In the spring, the rains fell continuously, three weeks at a time with no sunshine. Her clothes were moist and sticky against her body. Even when the rain stopped, the air felt wet and hot.

Summer came and the rains stayed away. As did the wind.

"Nanjing is one of China's four furnaces," the natives explained, laughing as they sweat, drinking hot, boiled water to make themselves cool.

Years passed like this.

My grandmother felt weak. She had never felt weak in her entire life.

She gave birth to two sons. She was a rich, respected woman now, a college regent's wife, and there were servants to take care of the boys. She should have been happy or at least proud, but she felt instead almost feeble. She rarely saw her boys. Her husband had explained that she understood nothing about raising boys, and that they would be better off in the hands of experienced amahs, and then later with more experienced tutors. Although she had once been a teacher, her husband explained that because he now was a college regent, he knew many, many city-educated teachers, all of them far more qualified than she, better educated, more worldly, and she would merely be holding her sons back if she tried to teach them anything. Was that what she wanted?

Of course, that was not what she wanted.

Her sons grew up, tall, smart, and spoiled.

My grandmother gave birth to a girl.

It was the beginning of a new century. I'm not sure of the exact year, as I mentioned earlier. Perhaps the year of the horse, which would have meant the girl would be strong, with stubborn tendencies. Or perhaps the year of the snake, which meant the girl would be strong, with a secretive nature, a woman who could foresee history.

After my uncles were born, the house had been decorated with red paper cutouts, the characters for "double happiness," for "prosperity," for "fortune" and "long life" adorning all the windows for the world to see. Firecrackers were lit, exploding with the force of a thousand drums, the red paper wrappers fluttering into the sky like flames. Two servants swept the courtyard with bamboo brooms for two days afterward to clean away the mess.

When my mother was born, my grandfather was away at a meeting for the college, where men with less money listened attentively to his every word, while men with more education barely disguised their boredom. My grandmother instructed the maids to hang crosses in the windows, her way of thanking God. There were no firecrackers.

"Mei-en," my grandmother called my mother. Beautiful Blessing.

It was true that her sons were my grandmother's responsibility to her husband's family, she thought, to ensure that their surname would be carried on, that his ancestors would not be dishonored, even though as Christians this kind of thing was not supposed to be important anymore. But a daughter! Her husband did not care about a girl, and my grandmother could raise her as she pleased.

My grandmother's head began to swim with plans.

She would start a school for girls. Her husband didn't care, it was only a primary school and unimportant. But she knew what she wanted: modern. Western. (The two terms were nearly synonymous in the first part of the century.) She invited her friends, American missionaries from Shandong, to come and teach.

"I can't offer you very much," she wrote, "just land upon which to build a school. A new opportunity in this new city."

At this point in the early part of the twentieth century, it was not a good time to be a Christian missionary in Shandong. A movement of impoverished, displaced farmers and other unemployed and desperate men and women calling themselves "The Boxers United in Righteousness" had risen up in the poorest villages a few years earlier. The Boxers had killed missionaries as well as their Chinese converts, burning their churches and schools and hospitals. They felt the foreigners with their foreign god and foreign privileges were behind all the ills of China, polluting the empire, draining the power of the nation. They drank magic potions and boasted not even bullets could pierce their flesh. They grew in numbers as the poor finally found a way to vent their despair and anger—and to let their desperation be known.

The Boxers spread west and south toward the capital. The Empress Dowager Cixi on her throne in Beijing heard of their movement and gave them her blessing. The Boxers' reign of murderous terror came to a peak in 1900, and then in 1901 the Western nations intervened. Goaded on by Christian churches in their home countries, appalled at the massacre of the holy, France, Great Britain, Russia, Germany, the United States, and also Japan brought in 20,000 troops equipped with heavy artillery and handily squelched the so-called Boxer Uprising. Their magic potions had not proved effective after all. A disheartened empress dowager then was forced to erect a monument to the memory of the more than 200 Westerners killed, to punish cities where the Boxers had had strong support, and most importantly to pay an indemnity in gold equal to twice the Qing empire's annual income to the Western nations (the infamous "Boxer Indemnity"). Although the Boxers had been defeated by the time my grand-mother's letters reached her American friends, many had already begun to question their calling to do God's work in Shandong.

And now came this invitation from one of their most devoted converts!

Teachers, nurses, and their preacher husbands packed their trunks and headed south. Among them was a giggly, spirited young woman named Eleanor Goodkin, barely out of her teens, just ar-rived from the American heartland with her tall, somber husband, a newly ordained minister. Eleanor would become my mother's music teacher, her confidante, her closest friend. And even after Eleanor would finally leave China to return to the United States, some thirty-odd years and three miscarriages later, a heavy heart in a thin body, with her husband who'd had enough of the savage Chinese and their endless wars, my mother would continue to write her American friend every week, no matter where we were as we fled from the Japanese army. And even when we had no paper to spare for letters, my mother continued to write, composing the letters in her head, keeping them in her heart.

But now, when my mother was but a little girl with braided pig-tails on both sides of her head, running with big, natural feet through the courtyard of her mother's home, my grandmother's friends arriv-ing weekly, my grandmother could imagine only good things for her daughter's future, and she felt her energy and confidence return.

At first the school was small, but the idea of educating girls was catching on, and soon the dark classrooms with pitted chalkboards were full. Leading intellectuals began to write essays denouncing the old traditions that had made China so weak compared to the West. They denounced foot-binding, the illiteracy of women, the backwardness of Chinese society, which refused to study the West. Eventually there was a waiting list seventeen families long for my grandmother's school.

In late 1911, a band of revolutionaries led by warlord Yuan Shi-kai and the intellectual physician and "founder of modern China" Sun Yat-sen overthrew the Qing dynasty and in 1912 inaugurated a new government, the Republic of China, in Nanjing. And all the land that my grandmother's clan had owned plus the property they had bought since their move from Shandong rose astronomically in value. It was an unbelievable stroke of good fortune. Nanjing, this humid quaint city encircled by a wall with twelve gates pointing at the twelve cardinal points, had become the epicenter of modern China.

My grandfather enjoyed his new wealth and the prestige that came with it. Young women looked at him now with admiration, they made eyes at him that could almost make him forget his undistinguished origins. He made new friends, with fancy lineages and fancy clothing. They laughed at all his jokes.

My grandmother made plans.

A hospital. A secondary school. The best of everything for her students—and her daughter, of course—the best tutors, the best textbooks, music and physical education, the study of a foreign language—English, of course. Study of the Bible and the Chinese classics.

My grandmother moved like a windstorm, her small, round face glowing like the moon. There was so much work to be done, so much work, and she would do it! With God's grace, she would!

She raised silkworms, oversaw the operation of her Chinese Christian Hospital and Modern School for Girls, she faithfully attended services on Sunday as well as Bible study. She translated religious tracts as well as pamphlets on hygiene, child care, and women's health. She walked faster than any man.

Her daughter flourished in the company of doting foreign women, who were so pleased to see their hard work and sacrifice in this impoverished country paying off in this bright-eyed creature.

There was a stage and a piano to the side, where Eleanor waited almost in shadow, arms poised above the keys. She had recently bobbed her hair, which made her face look rounder, almost Chinese, and for the occasion she had pinned a yellow flower to her lace collar. My mother was ascending the stage, dressed like a schoolgirl in black cotton slippers, a flowered blouse and skirt that fell just below the knee. Her hair was pulled back into a single braid. She took her place at the end of the line of her classmates, boys and girls, dressed in their Sunday finest. The other students looked shabby and young next to her, like green radishes. Standing erect, her chin up, my mother could have been a movie star visiting from Shanghai, raising funds for the war effort. She could have been a famous singer as she tapped the microphone, checked the volume. She nodded at Eleanor, and the American tore into the music, perhaps something classical like Brahms, but most likely a hymn with a singsong two-four beat. The congregation sang along in both English and Mandarin; Eleanor's husband had translated the words so that each note could be represented by one Chinese character. My mother smiled and nodded in time to the hymn, but did not sing. She was not a singer.

Now the missionary walked to the corner of the stage. The light was harsh, the dark shadow of his nose fell like a bruise across his right cheek. His tongue darted out to lick his thin lips, and he had to clear his throat. "Brothers and Sisters, welcome to our seventeenth annual Nanjing Christians' Association Revival. I would first like to thank Mrs. Ethel Watson"—he nodded toward a shadow in the audience, there was faint applause—"whose selfless devotion and expert penmanship have produced tonight's lovely program." He did not acknowledge his wife, Eleanor, at the piano.

If my mother was bored or tired of waiting, she did not show it. Her face remained as calm and smooth as the surface of a lake on a still afternoon. She could feel all eyes on her tonight as she waited graciously in the spotlight, her black hair shining like the night sky, her eyes bright and round, her lips unsmiling, determined, while the missionary led the captive audience in prayer.

My grandmother was in the audience, beside her husband who was dozing. She poked him surreptitiously in the ribs. She reached into one of his long sleeves and plucked a hair from his forearm. He awoke with a start, slapping his coat as if he'd been bitten by a mosquito. My grandmother coughed quietly into a small, worn hand-embroidered handkerchief that my mother had made for her and that she refused to give up now although she could afford newer ones, pressed and starched, of the finest imported linen.

The missionary sensed he was losing his audience and the scratchy-rope feeling in his chest tightened. He felt mildly irritated at the Chinese girl standing center stage, although it was hardly her fault he was boring. "All right, then we shall begin. Mei-en"—calling upon my mother first—" 'Let them alone.' "

" 'Let them alone. They are blind leaders of the blind. And if the blind lead the blind, both will fall into a ditch.' Matthew, chapter fifteen, verse fourteen." My mother nodded modestly as the hall applauded.

The missionary called on her classmates, and most were able to finish the verses. He called on them, over and over, until finally only my mother was left on the stage.

Soon members of the audience were thumbing through their Bibles, calling out phrases. My mother smiled graciously and answered correctly, never dropping a word. The woman at the piano was crying, her heart full. My grandmother did not smile outwardly, that would be too proud, and sinful, but in her head she thought, My daughter, the Tsao family warrior.

The missionary's nose glistened with sweat. His cough fatigued him. "Heaven and earth."

" 'Heaven and earth will pass away. But my words will by no means pass away. But of that day and hour no one knows, not even the angels in heaven, nor the Son, but only the Father.' Mark, chapter thirteen, verse thirty-one."

"I'm sorry, Mei-en, but that is not correct."

My mother inhaled sharply. "Verse thirty-two."

"No," said the missionary, rather happily, "I was speaking from the Book of Matthew."

There was a gasp in the audience followed by a rustling of pages. And then the missionary glanced down at his Bible and saw that indeed he had been reading from the Book of Mark, but he had looked only at the first character, the word for "horse," pronounced "ma," used to represent both "Matthew" and "Mark" in Chinese. "Excuse me," he said, clearing another wretched ball of phlegm from his throat, but before he could continue there were shouts from the audience, a waving of hands, as everyone now had caught his error.

"Mark! Mark! Mark!

"Ma Ke!" a new Chinese convert shouted.

"Yes, I'm sorry. It *is* the Book of Mark."

My mother smiled graciously. "But you were right that I was wrong. It was not verse thirty-one. But both thirty-one and thirty-two."

Eleanor at the piano broke into a joyful rendition of Handel's *Messiah,* which normally she reserved for Christmas and Chinese New Year, for she could not contain her feelings now.

The applause sounded like thunder, as if the heavens had opened right at this moment, and no one could hear my grandmother coughing with a sound like a frightened goat even as she smiled until she cried. Men turned to my grandfather, smiling, to say his daughter was really a talent, a *tiancai,* who knew even more than her father, how proud he must be. He shook his head as if in modesty, saying, "No, she is spoiled. What good is all this for a girl?" and the others smiled and nodded, enjoying his good-humored joking, after all, nothing is more insufferable than an arrogant, boastful parent. What a good man is my grandfather, they thought. No one saw that he had stopped smiling.

After all that he had done here in Nanjing, a man who had made a college out of a soybean field, a man who had constructed a Christian empire, dammit, to be eclipsed by a sixteen-year-old girl was more than he could bear. My grandfather stood abruptly and walked out of the hall, forcing his wife to hurry after him.

Later my grandfather's resentment would grow in his heart like a cancer. He would dishonor his wife, drive his children away, surround himself with friends who liked only his money. He would earn my mother's wrath and perhaps even her hatred.

But for now, he seemed merely grumpy.

My mother should have been a man. Everyone thought so. She could have memorized the "Four Books": the *Analects* of Confucius, the writings of Mencius, *The Great Learning,* and the *Doctrine of the Mean.* She could have taken the national exam and become a high official—if only the examination system hadn't been abandoned after the emperor was overthrown and the republic established. But anyway, she was a girl and girls did not take government exams. So instead she had memorized the missionaries' Bible.

And because of my grandmother's private school, she had also learned geography, mathematics, the piano, and English.

Too bad she's not a son, some of the older women said among themselves. What a waste of all that education.

Others thought, What a daughter-in-law she would make!

There were suitors. Matchmakers offered the most eligible families, surnames with wealth, power, even some with character. But my mother and grandmother had other plans.

It was 1919. The first year that girls as well as boys were allowed to take the national examination to enter a national university. All over China anxious students went without sleep as they studied, their eyes burning, their shoulders aching, as they hunched over copybooks. Math, geography, Chinese classical literature, history, a foreign language. There is a famous book on the traditional Chinese education system. It's called *China's Examination Hell*.[2] In it, the Japanese author describes vividly how Chinese scholars of old were driven to hallucinate and even to speak to ghosts after studying too hard for the national exams. They needed to memorize the Four Books of the Confucian canon in their entirety so that they could finish a line from any of the classics if given the first three characters. They also needed to be able to write creatively, constructing well-argued and thoughtful essays on any number of possible topics, from the metaphysical (the meaning gleaned from the brevity of the butterfly's life) to the academic (the various interpretations of a single Chinese character throughout the classics). They practiced calligraphy so that they could write in all the invented styles known throughout antiquity. They also had to be able to develop their own style of calligraphy; a scholar should be an artist, too. By passing an exam, a man could obtain an official position in the bureaucracy. Within the space of one generation, he could change his family's fortunes, from impoverished peasants to a powerful bureaucrat's clan. Put into effect during the Han dynasty in the second century B.C., the exam system had provided upward mobility for centuries. Whereas in Europe at that time you had to inherit your power, in China even a man from humble origins could become part of the government so long as he was smart.

---

[2] Ichisada Miyazaki, *China's Examination Hell: The Civil Service Examination of Imperial China*, trans. Conrad Schirokauer (New York: Weatherhill, 1976).

Although the bureaucratic exam system was abolished in 1905, the idea that intellectuals should become China's leaders was firmly entrenched in people's minds.

And now all over China *girls* as well as boys were studying as though their lives depended on it because public universities were opening their doors to the novel and foreign concept of coeducation.

In 1920, out of a population of 450 million people, less than 40,000 students were enrolled in China's universities.

In 1920, my mother was one of eight women in all China who scored high enough on the exam to enter Nanjing's most prestigious school, National Central University.[3]

---

[3] In 1920 the school was known as National Southeastern University. Later the name was changed to National Central, which is the name that appeared on all my mother's official papers. We use the name National Central throughout for simplicity's sake.

4

THE GIRL FROM PURPLE MOUNTAIN

The Tsao family, circa late 1910s. Front row (left to right) Ruth's mother and father. Back row: Second brother Shou-li, Ruth, eldest brother Shou-tao.

~ *May-lee* ~

If I am to understand the woman she became, I must try to see the girl my grandmother once was.

There are only a few pictures from my grandmother's youth, from her days before she met my grandfather. One is a formal family portrait, a miniature print two-by-three inches. Her parents, already quite elderly, sit side by side on stools, while their children stand behind. They are all bundled against the Nanjing winter. My grandmother is dressed in a dark coat-dress embroidered with swirling ocean waves. Her eldest brother, his cheeks still chubby with youth, stands hunched with his hands in his pockets, chin tucked into the folds of his collar. Her second brother is dapper in his chic jacket patterned after the high-collared suits Sun Yat-sen always wore. (Later, they will be dubbed "Mao suits" by the Western press because the chairman will force everyone in China to wear them after the revolution.) I can't judge the age of my grandmother from the picture, she could be a teenager, she could be in her twenties.

In the next picture, a formal photograph, she is dressed soberly in missionary black, her hair drawn into a severe bun, a long simple chain with a pendant around her neck. My father thinks this picture must have been taken in honor of her high school graduation.

But the final blurry picture, a photocopy from a magazine, stands out. It is a publicity shot to show off the first class of women to enter National Central University, the Eight Female Geniuses.

My grandmother is standing with her seven female classmates and their gym instructor, who herself has recently returned from studying modern physical education in the United States of America. My grandmother is hot in the white cotton shirt with three-quarter-length sleeves, the heavy blue cotton bloomers that give the girls the figure of a duck. This is someone's idea of a sexy photo, all the young *nu tiancai,* the female geniuses, in their gym clothes. My grandmother's black cotton stockings are itchy, but she waits patiently, squinting into the sun, resisting the urge to bend over and scratch her calf as the young photographer fusses with his camera. He adjusts the flash. He looks through the viewfinder, shakes his head, then hefts the awkward wooden tripod over one shoulder and sets the camera up two feet to the right, shakes his head again and moves the tripod back. His face is as red as boiled crab. It's fall in Nanjing, but it's not getting any cooler as the noon sun beats on their heads. "Just hold still, hold it, hold it!" he cries as he dips back down behind the camera. In his haste he clinks his eyeglasses against the viewfinder and accidentally knocks out one of the lenses. The girls watch as it bounces once then rolls away into the grass. The photographer drops to his knees, one hand holding the metal eyeglass frame and its single lens to his face, the other hand frantically patting at the crabgrass.

In this era no one smiles for photographs. Not for family pictures or engagement shots, certainly not for official photographs that will appear in a magazine. But in this photograph of my grandmother and her classmates, they are all smiling with closed lips, biting the inside of their cheeks, trying to keep from laughing out loud. Perhaps the second after the photograph is taken, the flash still burning blue in their eyes, they will laugh, first one then all the rest at once. My grandmother clutches the hand of the girl standing next to her, who grabs her shoulder as they double over, gasping for breath.

It is hard to imagine my grandmother as a girl, but here she is, smiling out at me from the faded photograph as though she were about to burst.

With her round apple cheeks, her schoolgirl's stance, legs planted apart, slightly bowed but a solid stance nonetheless, I think now that my grandmother looks so very young. At the time the photograph was taken, it would still be nearly a dozen years before my father was born. She looks happy and innocent.

In later pictures, she will look tired and worried.

I like this photograph of the eight female geniuses very much.

My grandmother provided a note to accompany this photograph. In her precise calligraphy she explains that she was one of the first eight women admitted to National Central University in 1920. She singles out the woman in the middle as the physical education teacher.

I wish I knew her classmates' names, who were her friends, when the picture was taken and in what magazine it appeared, how she felt when it was published. But why would she have recorded any of this information? When she first made the photocopy for her scrapbook, she must have thought she would never forget.

Now I can barely imagine her, my frightening grandmother, this smiling girl.

What else do I know of her youth?

My grandfather liked to talk of Nai-nai's many suitors. One of them had been so distraught at my grandmother's refusal to marry him that he'd tried to hang himself. Ye-ye enjoyed this story. He liked to tell it at holidays when he and Nai-nai came to stay in our house in New Jersey. They'd come with about twenty different bags of things they thought they'd need. My grandmother thought regular luggage was a waste of good money so they brought their things in various plastic bags saved from trips to the grocery stores in Chinatown, big holiday shopping bags from department stores like Macy's, and old purses. Everything smelled faintly of dried fruits and medicinal teas—these necessities that couldn't be found in the desolate suburbs. I remember I'd come home from school and the house would smell both like candy and like medicine, and I'd know immediately that my grandparents had arrived.

Because Nai-nai's hips hurt, she would sit on the piano bench in the living room and supervise while my grandfather and uncle and father brought in her many bags and lined them up on the living room carpet. I remember once Ye-ye told the story of her rejected suitor as he brought in her bags. He embellished the dramatic ending, the suitor's friends rushing to tell my grandmother that he had tried to hang himself. Imitating my grandmother, Ye-ye stood perfectly erect and waved a hand airily, saying firmly, "He should use a stronger rope!" Then he laughed happily.

My grandmother crossed her arms on her lap and looked away, but she smiled then too.

My father always liked this story of my grandmother's suitor because it was a happy story, before the wars, with a triumphant ending— from the Chai point of view, at least. My father would embellish it, add details, turn it into a bedtime story for my brother and me, his way of talking about China without talking about the war. Later as I studied more about China in college and went to live in Nanjing, it was this story that I thought of first when I visited the grounds of my grandmother's university, walked the cobblestone streets outside its stone wall, hiked on Purple Mountain where she and her class-mates liked to visit on weekends. This story was my way of revisiting my grandmother's youth, with China on the brink of collapse but before everything went completely wrong.

Here is how I imagine my grandmother's suitor:

There was a boy, a student. Maybe he was a few years ahead of my grandmother in school. A young man. He was ready for the responsibility even if his round cheeks, his unruly black hair, made him look like a child at times, especially when he smiled and his cheeks dimpled. He was my grandmother's first serious suitor. Seri-ous because he was the first she took any notice of at all.

He was smart, of course, or she never would have given him a second glance. Perhaps he spoke in a rapid-fire staccato. He wanted to be a revolutionary, change society, save China, but at twenty-two had not yet come up with the perfect method. "It is up to our gen-eration, our responsibility." When he spoke at student rallies, in protest marches through the broad sycamore-lined avenues, he could move crowds to cheer and shout.

She agreed with everything he said.

But he was not a Christian.

"It's superstition. When we die, there is nothing more."

"But the West is very powerful. The English, the French, the Germans, the Americans, they all believe in God and their countries are all so much more advanced in science and technology than China."

"How do you know? Have you ever been there?"

He was the most infuriating, arrogant, pretentious *boy* she had ever met. And she told him so before leaving, turning on her heel and storming out the door of the classroom where they and their classmates had been making banners for a march, criticizing the slowness of the republic's efforts to reform education and welcoming a famous American philosophy professor on his tour throughout China.

After that, they argued frequently, during which the time passed quickly, and my grandmother would discover another hour had passed and her essay was not written, a book not read, and all she had to show for her efforts was a wasted conversation with *that boy* again!

He smiled when he saw her so that all his teeth showed, even the ones in the very back of his mouth.

She decided to ignore him.

My grandmother was strolling with her classmates through the pine trees at Purple Mountain, just east of the city limits. Purple Mountain holds Nanjing's most important treasures: a Ming dynasty emperor's tomb and the gallery of giant stone statues shaped like animals that lined the path to its entrance, the five-hundred-year-old Beamless Hall, and perhaps most important of all, the tall forests that provide shade and comfort in the deep heat of Nanjing's furnacelike summers.

It was unusually warm for April. No one could sleep. The city's residents had been turned to sleepwalkers, sweating in the thick humid air. The last rainstorm had done nothing to alleviate the suffering. Students, unable to concentrate, happy for an excuse to leave their books, were flocking to Purple Mountain, my grandmother and her friends and her suitor among them.

The boy, the young man, I mean, could not believe his luck at finding Mei-en alone in the pines. Her friends had sauntered off for a moment, perhaps they were visiting one of the quaint pagodas. My grandmother was looking for interesting rocks, a hobby of hers, like that of many Nanjing people. She bent to pick up a smooth stone, which was speckled with a vein of mica like a branch of plum blossoms, and when she looked up again, the young man was there, grinning. Startled, she dropped the stone and stood up quickly.

The boy hastily bent over and picked up the rock. He offered it to her, then trying to be both clever and tender, came up with a pun, linking the "Mei" of my grandmother's name meaning "beauty" and the "Mei" that meant "plum blossoms." Punning is a very important cultural activity among Chinese intellectuals. The characters of China's most beloved and most beautiful novel, *Dream of the Red Chamber*, pass many a languid afternoon thinking of clever poetic phrases, puns, and allusions.

Unfortunately for my grandmother's suitor, it was not a very good pun. Something like "Beauty is the plum of my eye." (It's even worse in Chinese than in English if you can imagine that.) He knew that it was terrible as soon as the words had left his mouth. My grandmother knew it too, but she was too polite to laugh.

Before either could speak again, their classmates arrived, laughing loudly enough for both of them.

"There you are, Mei-en! We thought we'd lost you!"

But while my grandmother tried to laugh gaily along with her friends, even tossing her head to show her lightheartedness, no sound came out of her mouth, and to her surprise, she blushed a deep pink instead.

She ran ahead of her classmates now so that they could not see her burning cheeks.

Because modern times required modern methods, the boy did not ask his parents to write Mei-en's to ask her hand in marriage. Instead he asked her himself. Because he was nervous, he asked her in a letter, replete with allusions to classical poems and antique literature. He wrote a hundred versions then sent the most florid.

At first my grandmother thought he was joking and laughed when she read the letter. When she realized he was serious, she replied quickly, in a letter of her own, stating diplomatically something to the effect: "We are too young to consider such grave matters now."

Embarrassed, she refused to talk of the matter again when they were together with friends and no longer conversed with the boy if she was alone.

The boy was debating what to do next when he heard the terrible news that Mei-en was leaving to study abroad—in Japan!

"It's all for the best," his friends said. They assumed that in Mei-en's absence, he would recover his dignity and sensibly fall in love with a different girl. They were wrong.

Before her trip to Japan, my grandmother could not adequately explain why she did not want to be married, even to herself. After all, marriage was considered the normal aspiration for a girl of her age. It was only after her weeks spent abroad, when she discovered the depth of her ambitions, that she found the confidence to refuse her suitor completely.

The Japanese Ministry of Education had offered a scholarship to the eight female geniuses to come to Japan to study, all expenses paid. Japan was the center for the Chinese overseas students in the early 1920s. Japan was modern and wealthy, relatively speaking, while China was poor, dominated by warlords who controlled regional armies, and divided by foreigners into zones of influence: the Germans controlled Shandong province, the French the southern provinces of Guizhou and Yunnan, Shanghai had been carved into concessions governed by foreign countries each with sovereignty to try any Chinese under their country's laws while no foreigner could be tried under China's. Japan was a modern Asian state, a model for idealistic students who wanted to reform their country. Everyone wanted to study in Japan. Japan was not yet the enemy.

(Long after her return home, my grandmother would continue to recount her adventures to her brothers, her husband, her sons, until they felt as if they, too, had shared in her journey, seen the possibility of China's potential with their own eyes.)

To her mother she reported that the Japanese treated her "like a Chinese princess." Everyone was so very polite. She gave two recitals and her picture appeared in the papers. The girls lived in a funny hotel, where they slept on the floor. The Japanese were not like the Chinese, she observed, as they slept on straw mats and their walls were made of paper and slid open and shut. It was as though she were lying in a jewelry box every night when she went to sleep. She hadn't found a church yet so she read the Bible and said her prayers in the hotel room on Sundays. She promised to find something nice for her mother, a tea set, something special. She reminded her mother to use her mentholatum rub every night and to take her cod liver oil.

To her brothers she wrote that yes, it's true what people say about the Japanese. The men and women bathed together in the same room! However, it's very strange, the men did not look at the women. She went with her host family to the public baths, when suddenly a group of men came in. It was very shocking, and she left very quickly. This was why she could never go into medicine even if her brothers should like her to follow in their footsteps, she explained. She was too modest for it.

To Eleanor, her beloved teacher, she felt she could truly express her heart. She wrote long, rambling, hopeful letters (as she would later tell her eldest son): "I feel I have lived my entire life like a frog in a well; I thought the sky was two feet across and now I see that the world is larger than I ever imagined. How shall I ever be contented back in my well? I am filled with unusual ideas and notions. I want to do so much, change so much. There is so much that I find wrong with China and I do so want to reform my motherland, until she shines as brightly as Nippon." She could not find the words to express exactly what she was feeling. The arrogance. The hope. The excitement. For she was suddenly aware of her own youth, that incomparable feeling that anything is possible and that she was capable of accomplishing all that she wished and hoped for.

"I truly think it is up to my generation to make a difference in the world. And we are capable. Though I do not yet know how."

She wrote in flawless English with a confident cursive. As she was very young still, she dotted her 'i's with tiny circles.

Finally, to the young man she sent a postcard illustrated with the most neutral image she could find, perhaps an inky rendition of a small animal, a bunny or a cat. On the back she wrote simply "Best wishes from Japan!" in English then signed her name formally in Chinese, Tsao Mei-en. When the young man received the card—actually three weeks after she had already returned to Nanjing, the overseas mail was so slow then—he was at first puzzled, then frustrated. He turned the card over and over, studying it in his sweaty hands until the cardboard began to wilt and separate at the edges. Best wishes. His best wish, that they should be married. It was an allusion. She didn't want her classmates to see. *Best* wishes. She had been thinking of what he most wished for, of course! And the cat.

He studied its expression, placid, round eyed, content. Fat. A cat. A kitten. An animal. And then he got it. A pet! A cat was a pet. This was no alley cat, no stray, but a well-cared-for, contented, beloved pet. He was her pet, of course. She had meant for him to understand. Mei-en never did anything without thinking twice. She was so clever. Of course, of course. She was calling him her pet. She was thinking of his most desired wish while in Japan.

But her answer?

But of course she could not say on the back of a postcard or something so impersonal as a letter. That would have to wait till they could talk in person. Intimately.

He pressed the postcard to his lips, until he realized he was smudging the writing. Then he tucked the card into his shirt and carried it with him everywhere, even to bed.

He was talking cheerfully with a friend as they wrote big character banners for a rally demanding education reform when he discovered she had returned. His friend said she had been back in Nanjing for several weeks, as her classmates had been by to discuss politics.

The young man tried not to let his disappointment show. He ran his hand through his hair so that it stood up on end. "You must be mistaken. Mei-en's still in Tokyo." He almost mentioned the postcard but caught his tongue in time.

No, another classmate chimed in. He'd seen her just last week with her American friend, the Christian woman.

He could not answer. His tongue had turned to sawdust. He was disappointed, confused, betrayed, dejected, angry. He jumped up and stepped away as if he would leave his ridiculous friends right there. They were shallow and immature, they would never make a difference in this country. He shouted over his shoulder, "What a waste of time! Who is going to read your banner?" But by the time he had crossed the campus, he had recovered his optimism. Of course Mei-en must have only just returned and it was only natural she spend time with her family and her family's friends. How unseemly it would be for her to rush home to a man! She was too demure, too modest, for such brazen acts.

But how he wished for such brazen acts as he lay awake on his bed, his hand over his chest, fingering the postcard through the worn cotton of his nightshirt.

When my grandmother saw him again, it was quite by accident.

She was walking arm in arm with a girlfriend when her classmate laughed shrilly into her ear and pinched her arm. "Look, it's that boy again. He looks like a lovesick water buffalo."

It was true.

He was coming toward her with the queasy expression exactly reminiscent of a lovesick ox. Even the nostrils of his flat nose were twitching.

Oh, dear God, she thought.

"Mei-en!" he shouted.

"Sssh!" she hissed, glancing around, a ridiculous thing to do as of course everyone on campus could see as he waved his arm above his head and ran toward her.

Her classmate hid her face in her sleeve as she laughed.

"It's not funny," my grandmother whispered angrily.

Someone approached, perhaps a teacher. My grandmother and her classmate flagged him down and accompanied him now. They were saved. The young man stopped running in mid-stride. His mouth fell open. He looked absolutely pathetic.

My grandmother pretended she had not seen him and instead focused all her attention on her professor's face, nodding seriously as if she were fascinated although she could not concentrate on a single word he said. But her classmate waved gaily over her shoulder as the two young women, one on either side of their classical Chinese literature instructor, walked away into the distance.

There was no hesitating. She had to write a letter at once.

Dear Friend.
    I cannot marry you. I am too young. I do not wish to be married now. I must continue with my studies.

She reread it and crossed out the "I am too young" and the "I do not wish" parts. No point in giving him conditions he could argue over. I can wait, he'd say. We can marry later. She knew him too well. She began again.

I cannot marry you. Believe that I have given your proposal much thought. You should find another girl.
    I have made my decision. It is final.

There. Clear. Concise. It seemed a little harsh, even brutal on a second reading, but she had no choice. Better to be honest than to mislead him with kind words and false hope.

He was the proverbial rejected suitor who won't take no for an answer. He tried befriending her brothers, my grandmother's classmates. He even attended a Sunday church service but was asked to leave by the pastor's wife when he got into an argument with the pastor: "It's wrong to tell the Chinese to wait for heaven. 'The meek shall inherit the earth.' The Chinese nation is meek already and we are being divided like a prize. The foreigners control Shanghai. The Japanese control Manchuria. The warlords and bandits control our cities. The Chinese must be strong and bold. Like tigers. We have been sheep for too long."

A crowd gathered from among the congregation. Some looked disturbed by the ruckus, they wore the wide-eyed expression of the perpetually confused. Others nodded in sympathy with the young man.

The pastor cleared his throat quickly and planted a sweaty, avuncular hand on the young man's thin shoulder. "Young man, it is easy to stir passion, much harder to suppress your emotions, to forgive, to find peace, and to spread the word of love."

"We don't need to suppress our emotions! We need to act upon them!"

"You are young and all young people think this way. But Jesus has promised all who follow Him eternal peace and eternal life."

"Life is not peaceful or eternal. Those are contradictions—"

The pastor's wife signaled with a nod of her head to a group of three Chinese men along the fringe of the crowd. They were burly fellows, one with a harelip, the others with less visible deformities. The kind pastor and his wife had saved these foundlings, given them clothing, enough food to stay alive, and work as servants in their household. They should be eternally grateful and they were. The men approached rapidly now, and the young man found himself surrounded. They picked him up easily beneath the shoulders and "escorted" him from the church grounds to an alley that smelled of chicken entrails and unwashed children. A curious dog approached, its ears flattened and its thin tail between its legs. One of the men, the one with the harelip, was startled. He was afraid of dogs. He let go of the young man to grab a piece of brick from the ground and threw it at the dog. The young man saw his opportunity and squirmed free of the others' grasp. He did not stop running until he had reached the great stone gate of the university.

He was exuberant as he relayed the incident to his friends. "I really got that preacher! He could say nothing! Nothing!"

"I thought the whole point was to win back Mei-en?"

What good were his friends if they only served to remind him of his failures?

It became clear after several months of my grandmother ignoring him completely that she might indeed have been somewhat serious when she said she did not want to see him. That she might actually not want to marry him after all.

He took to walking alone through the city. His friends found him increasingly didactic and bitter and he found them frivolous, too concerned with debating books and abstractions. At the south entrance of the city wall, he came across a public execution. The crowd was watching with blank faces as a thief was shot by men wearing the uniform of the new republic. They might also have been the soldiers of the warlord Sun Chuan-fang. They were most likely thugs, in any case. After the man was shot, a smaller circle broke from the crowd and pushed forward around the crumpled body, curious.

The young man turned away disappointed with himself and the world.

A man with soiled clothing, a gray cotton shirt and black pants, his legs wrapped in white strips of cloth in the manner of soldiers and rickshaw pullers, tugged at the young man's sleeve. He turned quickly and the older man stepped back, head bowed.

"Excuse me, kind sir, my children are starving. I have no money. My farm has been sold by the landlords—"

My farm has been flooded, overrun by bandits, by soldiers, by pestilence, by drought. There were hundreds of these beggars with the same story.

A tug on his other sleeve. A small girl with flushed cheeks and a blue mole between her watery eyes had grabbed his coin purse. He ran and caught her handily. She screeched like a monkey and tried to pull away: But the farmer was there, too. He grabbed her roughly by the arm and slapped her readily, first on one cheek then the other before the young man could stop him. She didn't cry but hung her head.

"I'm sorry, young gentleman. Forgive my daughter, she has no manners. Since we live on the streets, she has learned bad manners." The older man prostrated himself at the young man's feet, rubbing his face in the dusty road.

"Stop it. Stand up." The young man felt sick. He wanted to run away. His throat was constricting.

The little girl looked up at him through her filthy hair.

"Little girl, you've picked the wrong man to rob. I'm just a poor student." The young man opened his cloth purse and gave her the money for his supper. She grabbed the coins then took off running again, dashing between the legs of startled pedestrians.

"Thank you, thank you, kind sir. I am so ashamed—" Her father clutched at the young man's cloth shoes.

He walked away, then broke into a run, as fast as his feet would carry him, his long student's robe flapping behind him like a flag.

The next day at the gate of the campus the beggar and his daughter were waiting, squatting together on a square of cardboard. They recognized the young man immediately. The girl ran toward him first, grabbed hold of his robe. Her father hobbled over.

"Kind sir, kind sir, I'm so glad to find you. My daughter and I thank you for your generosity—"

"I'm just a student. Students have no money—" The young man dug into his pockets. There was little there besides lint.

"My daughter likes you very much, kind sir. She can cook, run errands, clean your room, do your laundry. Why don't you take her?"

The young man stared at the beggar. "How can you talk this way about your own daughter?"

"She's not very expensive. She's just a little girl, I know. But she is stronger than she looks—"

"You have no shame," he began, but then he saw that the older man was serious, he would sell his daughter. The young man wished he were dead. He wished he could leave this world right then and there because there was nothing, absolutely nothing he could do to change the sickness of the world.

The farmer named a sum. "You see, not very much. Not very much and it will feed her brothers and baby sisters at home for a long time. Please, kind sir . . ."

The young man had an idea. "I have no money right now." He pulled out his pockets to show them. "Nothing," he told the little girl who was reaching for his pockets just to be sure. "But wait here and I'll come back this afternoon."

He decided to borrow the money from his friends, telling them he needed to buy a new set of English-Chinese dictionaries from Shanghai. He'd pay them back, he promised cheerfully. He had no intention of paying them back, actually. He had no desire to live that long. But when his friends joked that he was going to run away to Shanghai with their money, forget about books, and they'd never see him again, he laughed, too. They were so pleased to see him laughing again, joking, that they pooled together their extra cash readily and handed it to him.

"I hope these are good books," one said. "This is my cigarette money for the month. How am I supposed to survive?"

"You could always sell yourself as a day laborer."

"What a strange sense of humor you have." They all laughed.

The man and his daughter were waiting by the gate. They looked as though they had never moved from their square of cardboard. The older man jumped up as soon as he spotted the young man, who gestured for him to stand back and follow him discreetly to an alley, away from the bustling university gate. The young man had no desire to conduct such sordid business in plain view.

The beggar accepted the money readily, and as soon as the coins were in his hand, he was gone. No more thanks, no good-byes to his daughter. He simply turned away and disappeared around the corner. His daughter did not appear to be particularly saddened by her father's departure. She stared at the young man with eyes narrowed as snot dripped from her left nostril toward her lips.

He handed her a handkerchief. She turned it over in her hands as if she expected to find coins or food hidden inside.

"Here, let me." He took the handkerchief back and moved to wipe her nose. The girl grabbed his hand between hers and bit down. "*Ai!*" He pulled back and the girl ducked as if she expected him to hit her. "Come on," he said, holding his right hand with his left. He turned and walked down the alley.

He was not sure the girl would follow, but she did. He continued walking down the tree-lined avenue that led to the Catholic cathedral and next to it the somber stone building where the sisters ran an orphanage. He walked up the four steps to the large wooden door and thumped on the door with the iron knocker.

A small round-faced nun in a gray habit opened the door a few inches. She saw that it was a young man, dressed like a student, and opened the door wide enough for her to look at him with both eyes.

"I have a child for you. An orphan." He turned around. The girl was still there, staring at her feet.

The nun looked at him without moving.

"I thought you could take her in." The student searched in his pockets but he'd given all of his money to the girl's father. "I'll bring you some money, of course. A donation. For her upkeep."

The nun opened the door wide enough for the child to enter.

"Go on," he said to her. "They'll help you here."

She hesitated then ran inside. The nun shut the door firmly in his face. He stood there alone on the steps for a moment, not sure if he should do something more. But the nun didn't come back, the door remained closed, and so finally he left.

The next problem was how to raise more money to give to the nuns. Charity was not cheap. He couldn't possibly ask his friends for more money. Finally he decided he would have to sell some of his things. He had a scroll his parents had given him when he passed the entrance exams to college—calligraphy of a poem by the famous Tang dynasty poet Li Po. Probably not worth much. He had the watch his father had given to him. It had been his grandfather's. But what was more important? Preserving the past or protecting the future? He would sell the watch.

When he returned to the orphanage a few days later, a different nun answered the door, older with three of her front teeth missing. He asked about the girl, but she seemed not to understand.

"She was about this high." He held out a hand. "She had a blue mole between her eyes."

"Oh, that one. She ran away."

"You didn't go after her!"

"We did. But she was with a man who claimed he was her father. What could we do?"

He gave the nun the money anyway.

Walking back to campus, he passed twenty-seven elderly women begging, thirteen cripples, two blind deaf-mutes, and scores of children black with dirt, smelling of dried excrement, and he had not a cent to give any of them.

It's a curse to be Chinese, he thought.

That night he wrote a long letter to my grandmother. He wrote simply, sincerely, directly from his heart. He wrote about his hopes for the future, his bouts of despair, and his anxiety for his country. He said he respected and loved her and the mere thought of her gave him strength when he felt most alone. At dawn he reread the letter and found it juvenile, foolish, and ineloquent. He then tore it to bits and set it on fire, borrowing the match from his roommate.

Perhaps if he had sent such a letter to my grandmother, things would have turned out differently between them. But then I would never have been born so I'm pleased he did not have the courage to expose his heart.

After my grandmother rejected his next and final marriage proposal, he jumped onto a chair in the middle of his room, tied a bedsheet to the beam and tried to hang himself. But the sheet tore and he succeeded only in breaking his arm when he fell heavily to the floor. Or so one of his friends recounted to my grandmother the next day.

"If we hadn't come in right then, he'd be dead by now." The friend shook his head, his eyes still round with excitement from the memory.

My grandmother did not appreciate emotional blackmail.

"If he were serious," she said, "he would have used a stronger rope."

But then she regretted saying it. "Tell him, tell him only the weak kill themselves. He will always be strong." And she refused to answer any of his letters or those of his friends from then on.

~ Winberg ~

I never met this young man, my mother's former suitor. I've never even seen a picture. She never discussed her feelings about him. She probably felt it was inappropriate conversation for a mother and her son. I have no idea what he looked like; I have my imagination, but little more than that to go on. But when my mother was an old woman, living in New York with my father, she received a letter one day from an "old friend" from Nanjing. He was now in exile too. He would like to see her. It was her former suitor.

I remember the startling way she laughed suddenly, as if she'd just remembered something gay and lighthearted.

He would be in New York for a few days, the letter said.

At first she thought she might visit him—with my father, of course. But then she couldn't decide what to wear. Then she couldn't decide what to say. And finally she decided not to see him. She did not answer his letter, pretending she had never received it rather than tell him that she would not see him.

She said she hadn't wanted to disappoint him. She'd changed so much. She wanted him to remember her as he'd last seen her, young and beautiful.

So I never got to meet this man nor see what he had become.

However, my mother had discussed this man, her suitor, with my father after they were married and living together in Chicago. She and my father were very much in love and they could discuss all manner of things about their lives while they lay together on their narrow bed in their drafty apartment, dreaming about the future. My father told my mother all about his past, his family's troubles, his big plans to reform his country once they returned to China, and my mother told him about her past, her family's troubles, her big plans to reform her country . . . and all about her former suitor.

Later, much later, my father would tell me about this man and his persistence, his hopeless, helpless love for my mother.

My father was not at all jealous. On the contrary, he was very proud.

5

SELECTING A HUSBAND

Charles's Northwest-
ern University Law
School graduation
photograph, 1932.

~ *May-lee* ~

During the era of the republic, the Chinese character for ocean, *yang*,
also came to mean "foreign," "Western," and "modern." Even today
Chinese–English dictionaries include these three definitions. The term
yang was at once standoffish—insisting upon the distance between
things Chinese and things foreign, literally *from overseas*—and com-
plimentary, an odd mix at first glance but quite symptomatic of the
era. *Foreign, Western, modern* people and ideas were firmly a part
of everyday life in most major urban areas in China, and most Chinese students and intellectuals were looking increasingly to the West,
as well as Japan, for ideas on how to modernize their country. At
the same time, foreigners were hardly a benign presence in China.
Companies exploited the cheap labor market, and China suffered
huge trade deficits with most of the Western countries. The great
port city of Shanghai, the so-called Jewel of the Orient, had been
carved into concessions in which the foreign powers administered
their own courts and controlled their own police forces. "No dogs
and no Chinese allowed!" a sign at one of the foreign clubs proclaimed infamously.

Furthermore, the Western powers periodically united militarily against China to force concessions from the government. During the Opium War in 1839–1842, the British navy attacked the southeast coast, forcing the Qing government to open up various port cities to British citizens for trade, including opium, and to cede Hong Kong to the British. The Treaty of Nanjing, which ended the war, ushered in an era of unequal treaties signed after military intervention, with China required to pay huge indemnities, give administrative control of key portions of various port cities as well as mining, railroad, and trade rights to foreign powers, and open the country to Christian missionaries. After the Sino-Japanese War of 1894–1895, China was forced to pay more than 200 million ounces of silver to Japan, open up four more treaty ports, and worst of all cede Taiwan and the Pescadores islands to the Japanese. As my father described earlier, eight foreign nations sent 20,000 troops to quash the Boxer Rebellion in 1900 and then imposed an indemnity greater than the Qing government's annual income. But the final straw, for Chinese intellectuals, would be the 1919 Treaty of Versailles, which put more Chinese territory under Japanese control.

Although the Qing dynasty had been overthrown in 1911, and the new Republic of China declared in Nanjing, in fact, China quickly dissolved into competing military factions headed by regional warlords. Nanjing did not remain the seat of the government for long. The government returned to Beijing within months and a period of civil warfare continued until 1928, when Chiang Kai-shek succeeded in convincing the warlords to swear allegiance to him, and the capital of the republic was once again firmly established in Nanjing. Because China was weak as a state, foreign powers and their industries could exploit the natural resources and labor of the people to their own advantage.

In an effort to improve relations with the West and to gain some respect as an ally, the Chinese government authorized some 100,000 men to go to Europe during World War I to help the Allies' war effort. Most were put to coolie labor—some 96,000 were employed in France in late 1918—to free up British and French young men to fight as soldiers. More than 500 of the Chinese workers died when their boat to Europe was sunk by a German submarine. Some 2,000 more died in Europe, due to harsh work conditions, exposure, and even bombs falling on their work camps.[1] But despite these sacrifices, this bid for more equal relations with the West did not succeed.

On April 30, 1919, in Versailles, U.S. President Woodrow Wilson, British Prime Minister David Lloyd George, and French Premier Georges Clemenceau agreed to allow Japan to take over all Germany's railway and mining rights in Shandong province as well as control of the port city of Qingdao as part of the Treaty of Versailles.

On May 4, in what would become one of the most famous protests in China's history that century, college students and other citizens took to the streets of Beijing to protest the treaty. As demonstrations spread across the country in what would be known as the May Fourth movement, a new era of intellectual fermentation began.

Chinese intellectuals were acutely aware of their country's weakened state and desperately wanted to *jiu guo*, or save the country, as the film, literature, and newspapers of the era put it. And for many Chinese, this meant studying everything that the world outside China had to offer in an effort to fix what had gone terribly wrong in their country.

The result was an era of great cultural change and exchange. Equal rights for women were championed and the universities became co-educational. Intellectuals began to address the issue of illiteracy in China, as an estimated 75 to 80 percent of the population could not read. The grammar of classical written Chinese was completely different from that of the oral language and required years of intense study to master. Now many intellectuals, including Dr. Hu Shih, who had studied at Columbia University under the pragmatist philosopher John Dewey (who would later visit China himself), created a new written grammar that more closely resembled the spoken vernacular. It was during this period that the Chinese Communist Party was founded in an effort to address the terrible working conditions of the urban labor force.

The May Fourth movement, despite its origins as a protest against Western imperialism, was not xenophobic. All across China, the leading universities invited prominent scholars and activists from around the world to come to China and share their views. Margaret Sanger, the American feminist renowned—perhaps notorious—for her efforts

---

[1] Jonathan Spence, *The Search for Modern China* (New York: Norton, 1990), p. 292.

to educate women on contraception, Albert Einstein, British philosopher Bertrand Russell, and the Indian poet and Nobel laureate Rabindranath Tagore, among many others, lectured in China in the early 1920s to enthusiastic crowds.[2]

At the same time American missionary groups, including the YMCA and YWCA, continued to organize Christian groups in both rural and urban areas, and many Chinese, eager to explore new ideas from abroad, converted from Buddhism or at least openly studied Christianity.

It was during this atmosphere of great social upheaval, of national crisis and intellectual fervor, that my grandparents came to be engaged.

And quite against all tradition, but completely in the spirit of the times, it was my grandmother who chose my grandfather as her husband.

~ *Winberg* ~

Graduation was strangely disappointing, my mother thought. It was (most likely) 1924, the year of the wood rat, a year for exploration, but everything seemed to be coming to a close for her instead.

The sky was grim, determined to rain, my mother's hair was damp and limp against her neck, strands falling from her once-tidy bun in wilted thatches.

My mother posed for her official portrait in her Western-style black gown and mortarboard. She could feel the sweat beading on her face.

Riding home between her parents on the rickshaw, their elbows pressing into her ribs, my mother was suddenly stricken by a feeling of suffocation. The air was liquid in her throat.

The whole of humanity was creaking by their pedicab (a rickshaw powered by a bicycle). Beggars camped along the side of the dirt streets, busy pedestrians sidestepped to avoid their reaching hands, the city was filling up with refugees from the countryside as famine and poverty and raids by rival warlords' armies forced people to

---

[2] Spence, p. 317.

leave their ancestral homes looking for work or charity in the city, finding neither. A rich man's black Rolls-Royce honked its way through an intersection, ignoring the traffic cop's whistle. The underpaid policeman could only shake his gloved fist. Servants carrying sedan chairs marched in unison; their legs, which were wrapped in white bandages to keep their veins from popping out, looked like the legs of centaurs. They were half-man half-horse creatures, strapped to bamboo posts. From their perches on the chairs on the shoulders of their servants, mandarins with black sunglasses and thin cigarettes attached to long silver holders faced the sky like blind men.

My mother covered her nose with her sleeve. The humidity, the heat, the smells of the street—animals, sweat, urine, and fried pork dumplings—were turning her stomach.

A peasant tried to coax his donkey from the intersection where it balked and brayed as street children tried to grab a handful of potatoes from his cart. He chased them away with a whip.

A contingent of the new republic's soldiers marched into view and the pedicab driver veered away quickly into an alley. He had learned it was always, always best to avoid men carrying guns no matter whose uniform they claimed to be wearing.

A gaggle of old women with tiny bird-claw feet hobbled with canes, baskets over their arms. The driver shouted at them to scatter and they did, but not without shouting back, and one woman raised her cane at him, shaking it at him in protest.

Finally they were home.

My grandfather wakened, straightened his long white beard, and disappeared without a word inside. My grandmother took my mother's arm. Her face looked as though she had a secret to tell. My mother followed her to her bedroom.

She had wrapped and hidden my mother's presents in silk scarves at the bottom of her dresser. For my mother's graduation, my grandmother gave her two apple-green jade bracelets that she had been saving for an important occasion, a gold brooch, a bolt of black silk brocade to make a professional-looking suit, a brown tea set decorated with pale yellow flowers from Yi-xing—the city in China most renowned for its pottery—and a very expensive pebble. "I've called it 'phoenix rising from an ocean wave.' I'll get a bowl of water and you'll see what I mean when its colors come out." My grandmother smiled happily, perched on the edge of her bed, next to her daughter.

It is true that Nanjing people like to collect rocks. It is our peculiarity, just as people from Sichuan like to eat hot peppers even for breakfast and the people of Harbin troop out of doors in the coldest part of winter to hold ice festivals where whole temples are carved from the frozen snow.

There was a small museum in the southern end of town devoted to the Nanjing obsession. Its cases were filled with nothing but small ceramic bowls half-filled with water, a tiny pebble inside each bowl. A small, hand-lettered placard of four or five characters described in poetic terms each rock's special qualities. Its scientific name, like quartz or zircon or granite laced with a vein of jade, was completely beside the point. No, here the rocks were "monkey peering over elephant's toe" or "frog liver" or "moon reflected in a pool." For Nanjing residents, there was nothing strange about finding poetry in stones.

The most prized collectors' rocks came from a park known as the Rain Flower Terrace, so named because the rainwater brought out all the colors in the pebbles there, making the ground appear as though it were covered with blossoms. Later the park would become a prison to young students suspected of being Communist sympathizers and they would all be shot. Much, much later it would become a museum and a shrine to these "student martyrs" and busloads of schoolchildren from all over Nanjing would be brought in every year to look at the grainy photographs of the long-dead students and survey moth-eaten remnants of the handkerchiefs and shirts they once wore. But at the time when my mother was a young woman, Rain Flower Terrace was still a pleasant place to visit and its pebbles a prized possession.

My mother turned the pebble over and over in her hand, admiring its smoothness.

"I am so proud of you," my grandmother said simply, holding her daughter's hand with both of hers. She patted the hand with her handkerchief as if it were a small pet.

My mother knew then she could not tell her mother how heavy her heart felt.

There would come a day when my mother would bury the teapot in the backyard of her home, sew the jewelry into the linings of my brothers' coats, and the pebble would be lost in the shuffle and explosions and bayonets of the Japanese army's invasion of Nanjing.

When she returned to the city after the war, she would be reminded of this day as she ordered men to dig up the entire backyard until she found the tea set. But even though she would search continuously in the wreckage of her home for her mother's phoenix pebble, convinced that she could find it, overlooked by the Japanese, in a corner perhaps, covered with dust, she would fail. And although she would have witnessed beheadings, murders, executions, children sold for food and as food, elderly parents abandoned on the side of a road, babies abandoned in a blanket in a ditch, nothing would make her cry the way she did now, inexplicably and for three days, when finally she had to admit that the stone was lost forever.

Now my mother's life as an adult began. She was no longer a schoolgirl. Her parents had said nothing yet of marriage, for which she was grateful, but she was not yet sure what to do with her new adult life. She was an educated woman, with a college degree, her specializations were English and music. Naturally, she became a teacher.

A merchant family named Chai had moved to Nanjing with two sons and two little girls. The oldest brother was a graduate of the American-funded Qinghua University in Beijing. The younger was still a student there. The girls enrolled at my mother's school, the prestigious Middle School Attached to National Central University. The girls were very friendly to my mother, they liked their pretty young English teacher very much.

At first it was exciting to be a teacher; my mother could put into practice all the knowledge she had gathered, the new modern pedagogical techniques. She used her English on a daily basis. She devised her own textbooks and lessons as she found the available books lacking.

The elder of the Chai girls, the one who would become known as Gu Mu to my daughter, distinguished herself by her diligence and talent, the second by her complete lack thereof.

The younger girl, Orchid, was not clever. Her family's money could not buy her brains, but my mother would persist. It was a challenge, a good challenge, to teach a difficult student. Anyone could teach a genius. It took special talent to teach a slow student—skill, motivation, and a thorough understanding of modern pedagogical methods.

The second girl knew her alphabet already, thank goodness, but her pronunciation was terrible. She spoke Mandarin with a thick Anhui accent, she spoke English with an even thicker one. My mother drilled her.

"This is a pen. A pen. This is a pencil."

"Sissa peen. Sissa peencee."

"No, no, no. This. This." She showed the girl how to pull her lips back as if to smile, to press her tongue against her teeth. My mother exaggerated the motion for the girl.

The girl laughed like a hyena.

The word "this" can be one of the most difficult words for a native speaker of Chinese. There is no *th* sound in Mandarin, nor a short *i,* nor do any words end in the *s* sound. My mother believed it was best to learn the most alien sounds first, or the speaker would always speak with a Chinese accent, would always have difficulty making herself understood.

"I know it's difficult," my mother said patiently, "but if you can master these sounds in English, you can master the entire language. Try again. 'This is a pen.' "

"Sesss." This time the girl spit a little on the *s* sound.

My mother decided to change tack. "Who is it? Is it a man? Is it a man?"

"Hu eez eet? Ee dza nan?"

Orchid was growing bored with her after-school English tutorial. She did not want to learn English. She wanted to gossip about her older brothers. She folded her tiny hands over her notebook and leaned across the slick wooden desk. "My older brother came home very late last night," she began in her mushy Mandarin. "He was very noisy. They thought I was asleep, but I wasn't. I can hear everything in my room. My father was very angry. He called my older brother a 'scoundrel'! What does that mean, 'scoundrel'?"

"You shouldn't eavesdrop. It's not proper for a girl your age."

The little girl laughed, her whole face lighting up. "I know. That's why I do it."

Months passed like this. Then a full year. And before my mother quite realized it, two years. She was teaching English, helping my grandmother who volunteered at the missionary-run hospital, attending church services and Bible study. My mother could no longer remember all the Bible verses. They had become muddled in her head. She didn't let on, but she was worried. What is happening to me?

My mind is drying up. She was about twenty-five and was worried that she was growing old. Her father said as much. "The old maid," he called her behind her back. Her mother was not worried. There's no point in rushing things, Mei-en should use her education. There is so much good to be done in the world, and it's harder to do once you're married and have small children to look after. She knew. But it was true, her daughter was twenty-five and it was perhaps time to start thinking of finding a suitor. But how to find a proper one? A man worthy of her daughter.

My mother felt old and tired and alone. Her classmates from National Central University had scattered. Several married right after graduation and disappeared to have children. Her closest classmate went to Shanghai to study medicine. She wrote occasionally still, but how busy they had all become. How separate.

She received a letter. The calligraphy was practically a blur. "Mei-en, the most exciting news! I'm going to America! I've been awarded a scholarship to graduate school. Can you believe it? I was always the slow one, I never could understand things as quickly as you. Who would have imagined I would have this honor? It's a dream—"

My mother could not finish the letter from her friend. The bitter knot in her heart had constricted too tightly. She lay down on top of the cotton quilt on her bed and cried until her eyes were swollen, her sinuses inflamed, and her head pounded with the force of a booming cannon.

The next day my mother went to see Eleanor, whom she found chasing a thin white chicken in the backyard of the church with the cook and the maid.

"Whatever are you doing?" my mother asked, laughing.

"Don't laugh. Help us!"

The women chased the thin bird round and round the mulberry tree to no avail. Finally Eleanor stopped, panting in the middle of the yard, her fists on her hips. Her face was as red as the autumn leaves on the tree. She closed her eyes and pressed her palms together. "Lord, I know it is wrong to ask frivolous things of you, but if it please you, please strike this chicken down dead this instant."

"If you want to kill it, keep chasing," my mother called. "It's bound to die of a heart attack sooner or later."

"You're not helping, Mei-en." Eleanor fanned herself with the bottom of her apron. *Ting ting ting!* she told the cook and the maid in Chinese. Stop, stop, stop. "It's ridiculous. I'm the one who's about to have a heart attack."

The chicken retreated to the back of the yard where it crouched beneath a bush, peering at the women warily with one red eye.

"I've been all over this city looking for one good chicken, they're all so damn skinny—excuse me, so dang skinny these days. And look, this is what I find. It's not just skinny, it's part greyhound."

"You should have called on our house, Eleanor. We've got chickens. My mother always raises a few. Big fat hens. Very tasty. And very well behaved. They just jump into your cooking pot."

"I'll send you on your way if you can't behave yourself, Miss Tsao," Eleanor laughed. Then her smile faded and her brow wrinkled. "My husband has invited the dean of Fudan University over for supper to meet the president of our Christian Women's College as well as a few members of the board. And he only just told me this morning." Eleanor shook her head so that her damp curls bounced. "I haven't had any time to prepare."

"Don't worry. The chicken will come out sometime."

They watched the chicken retreat farther into the bush.

"Leave it to your cook. Let's go for a walk," my mother suggested.

"Oh, no, no, no. That's just what it's waiting for. I left it to Xiao Mai in the first place and that's how the chicken got outside. Originally, we had it tied to a chair in the kitchen. There's nothing to be done now but pray."

My mother sighed. Sometimes Eleanor could be so difficult.

Eleanor signaled for her cook and maid to bow their heads with her. "Dear Lord, grant me patience. Help me to catch this chicken, this wonderful creature you have created and endowed with extraordinary speed—"

My mother turned and tiptoed into Eleanor's house, into the dark and smoky kitchen that smelled of ginger, mustard, and cough drops. A cat, startled by my mother's presence, arched its back then ran behind a ceramic container of flour. My mother searched and found the steamer full of freshly cooked white rice. She took a cupful and returned to the yard where Eleanor was still praying desperately.

The chicken, in the meantime, had emerged from the bush and was scratching for bugs in the dirt.

My mother walked slowly but casually to the middle of the yard and dumped the rice onto the grass. Then ignoring the chicken, she turned away and took a few steps back toward the house. She counted to five with her back still toward the chicken, then slowly turned her head.

The chicken was cautiously approaching the rice, its neck stretched toward the white mound as it took one careful step at a time.

Suddenly Eleanor's voice chimed, "Look! It's the chicken!"

"Sssh" my mother hissed. "Don't move!"

The chicken had now reached the pile of fresh rice and was eating greedily. In a flash my mother bent over and plucked the chicken from the ground. She pressed its wings close to its body as she held it under one arm. "Got it!" she cried triumphantly.

"There you see." Eleanor beamed. "A little prayer in a time of need always does the trick."

Now that dinner was safely in the hands of the cook, my mother persuaded her friend to go for a walk. They took a rickshaw to the northern part of town, to Xuanwu Lake, formerly an imperial garden now open to the public since the fall of the emperor. It was beautiful this time of year, mid-autumn. The willow trees arched from sky to earth, the sycamores seemed aflame in orange and red. Young couples rowed across the glossy surface of the lake, the young men behind the oars, the young ladies carefully shading their complexions with silk parasols. Families posed for pictures in front of boxy Brownie cameras. College students sat on brightly colored picnic blankets, munching on onion cakes and fluffy *baozi* meat-stuffed buns. But even here, where my mother had enjoyed so many a lighthearted picnic with her college friends, her spirits felt dull and damp.

"Is it sinful to feel jealous?" my mother asked suddenly.

Eleanor, who had been enjoying the breeze off the lake with her eyes closed and her face tilted toward the sky, now looked at my mother in surprise. "What on earth could you be jealous of?"

"Is it sinful to be unhappy?"

"You're not ill, are you?"

"I should be grateful, I suppose. I have a job. I'm a teacher. I've always wanted to be a teacher."

"You're a wonderful teacher, Mei-en. I've met with some of your students. They speak so highly—"

"But I imagined, I imagined it would be different. I feel old."

"Do you miss your music?"

"I don't know."

"You mustn't let your creativity—"

"It's just that I received a letter," my mother interrupted her now, blurting everything out at once. "From a classmate from high school. She was clever but not *so* clever. I remember she used to stutter and she could never pronounce certain words correctly. Her English wasn't good at all. She didn't like English. She said she hated it in fact. It's just not fair. And my parents say I should be content. I have my education. I have my degree. I have my good job. But she wasn't half as good a student as I was. Is it wrong to be conceited?"

"Mei-en, dear, what are you talking about?"

"She's going to America. She's going to study in an American university and see the world and I'm never going anywhere and my parents want me to be married and it's not fair!" My mother burst into ugly, wet sobs.

Eleanor put a worn hand on my mother's shoulder. "Married? Do they want to find a husband for you?"

"I want to go to America too!" my mother cried. There, she'd said it. Finally. Somehow my mother felt better now. She sniffed then blew her nose into her navy blue handkerchief.

"America? Well, why didn't you say so? I might be able to help you." Eleanor patted my mother's back now as if trying to put out a fire with her hands.

My mother blinked. Had she heard correctly?

"Mrs. Linton. Mrs. Adele Linton. That was her name, I think. Or was it Ada? Oh, goodness Lord, my mind is going. What was her name?" Eleanor saw my mother's puzzled face. "Here I go again, talking to myself. I have a friend. Her husband teaches at a college, a Christian college. Let me write to her and see what I can do. I'm sure there are many schools that would welcome a nice Chinese Christian girl as a foreign student."

My mother could not believe her ears. Suddenly the air seemed brighter, the sunlight reflecting off the lake more golden. She heard laughter on the wind. The world was not such a bad place after all, and my mother did not feel so old anymore at all.

It took a while. Mail was slow. Eleanor was very busy. Her husband's congregation was growing and that meant there was more work for Eleanor to attend to: finances and the books and housework and charity and managing the church staff in addition to teaching and Sunday school classes while her husband was writing his sermons, which were more and more important because so many people would hear them now. A year passed. A year and six months. Eight months. But Eleanor had not forgotten. And one day she did receive a letter from the United States in answer to her queries, and there were names of women and addresses on a sheet of flowered paper for my mother to write to. And she did.

For the first time since her graduation, since she became a teacher, since the beginning of her adult life, my mother felt hopeful again.

But then the middle school prepared to hold an assembly. Maybe it was Lantern Festival, maybe Chinese New Year. It was a big event at any rate. My mother's English classes would perform, singing an American song entirely in English. My mother did not yet realize how important this assembly would be. To her, it was just another chore on top of teaching her classes and correcting the homework and trying to find time to study herself, to improve her English, just in case, just on the chance, that one of her letters had reached a sympathetic ear.

But if my mother was too busy to think much about the assembly, the Chai girls were abuzz with excitement . . . and with a matchmaking plot. They invited their older brothers, Huan and Chu, visiting for the holidays. "You've just got to represent the family," the eldest girl beseeched them. She was thinking of her less educated parents and the spectacle they would make at their fancy school assembly.

"Besides, Father already says he doesn't want to go. Too boring," Orchid pointed out.

"You have to meet our teacher, Miss Tsao," said the eldest girl. "She's quite brilliant. A National Central University graduate. A very modern girl."

"And she's really good-looking!" Orchid added. "Prettier than a movie star!"

The younger brother, Chu, felt he could not let his sisters down and agreed to come. He convinced his older brother to come along too, as Chu was too shy to go alone.

The assembly was endless, punishing, as every class performed, and some performed twice. Skits, speeches, songs, dance routines. By the time my mother's students were to sing, the audience was talking loudly amongst themselves. Grandparents cracked seeds between their teeth and spit the shells onto the floor. A few men were actively snoring.

My mother scowled. She allowed her students to take their places on the stage, but she would not let them begin until the hall was silent. She stood on the stage, one hand raised, until slowly people began to wonder what was going on and then nudged their neighbors to be quiet. My mother glared into the audience at pockets of noisy resistance, until finally she had commandeered the silence she felt her students deserved. She turned toward the semicircle of girls dressed in neat white blouses and navy skirts, and with a nod to the pianist, signaled her students to begin.

They sang slightly off-key and almost no one in the audience could understand the English lyrics, but they clapped readily (perhaps gratefully) when the singing stopped and my mother turned again toward the audience, bowing modestly. My mother had always known how to command attention.

My mother did not actually meet the Chai brothers after the assembly. She was too busy greeting parents, accepting their compliments on her students' performance. But she caught a glimpse of them both when the Chai girls pointed out their brothers. Huan, looking slick and as devilish as Clark Gable with his black mustache and pomaded hair, was talking loudly with some men by the door, a cigarette smoking like a just-fired gun in his hand. The younger brother, Chu, was round-faced, bookish, very young looking. He was sitting quietly, listening patiently as his youngest sister, Orchid, gossiped about her classmates and modeled her new dress happily.

This one glance at the two men from a distance was all my mother would have to go on later when the time came to make a decision and choose her husband.

The formal letter asking for my mother's hand came a few months later. The parents of Chai Huan asked the parents of Tsao Mei-en for her hand in marriage for their eldest son. They had naturally enclosed a photograph.

My mother resisted the idea immediately. Her father was angered, called her spoiled. "Do you want to be an old maid?" Even her mother thought it might not be a bad match. They were a respectable family. They knew Mei-en from her teaching, they obviously respected and admired her learning.

"He was smoking, Mother. He's not a good man. He drinks and dances. His youngest sister told me."

My grandmother nodded solemnly. These were serious offenses. The missionaries had explained all about how smoking and drinking and dancing lined the path that led straight to hell. But before my mother could feel relieved, my grandmother asked, "What about the younger brother, then? He is supposed to be the steady one." She had conducted her own investigations. Now she explained why the Chai family might not be so bad to marry into after all, a good family with extremely well educated sons. Then she pointed to the jade bracelet around Mei-en's wrist. "A good marriage is like a beautiful bracelet. The circle must be a little tight when you first put it on or it will come off too easily. The jade itself is cold, a little unpleasant against your skin until it has time to warm up. But we all like to wear them. A woman from a good family would feel naked without her bracelets."

My mother stared at her hands. So a woman from a good family was naked without a husband? She pretended she did not quite understand.

Sighing, my grandmother patted my mother's arm. "Of course. I would never force my beloved daughter to marry anyone against her will. But remember, even the most beautiful bracelet looks strange and sad when it's worn by an old woman."

"I need time to think. I don't want to rush into anything so important." My grandmother smiled. "Nobody is in a rush. Why not think about it for a week and then we'll give the Chai family your answer."

My mother tried to remember everything she had heard about the Chai brothers, especially the younger one.

Chai Chu had a kind face, it was true. And he was supposed to be the more diligent of the two brothers. He had received a Boxer Indemnity Scholarship, set up by the Americans to educate young Chinese in American universities with the money they'd extorted from the Qing government after the Boxer Uprising. Those students who had passed a national exam could study in America for five years, room and board and tuition paid for by the U.S. government. "My brother Chu is a genius," his youngest sister, Orchid, had complained, wrinkling her nose. "All he likes to do is study, study, study."

My mother sighed. She should be married, she supposed. It was expected. And what had she managed to accomplish on her own? She hadn't heard from any of the American universities she'd applied to. She should be practical. Her parents were right. It was foolish of her to waste her time on dreams.

She told her mother she would consider the Chai family proposal, but not with the older brother, Huan. She couldn't be married just to anyone. She would consider Chu.

A letter of inquiry was sent back to the Chai family. What about the younger brother?

My paternal grandfather was incensed. The elder brother must marry first! There could be no talk of the younger marrying! It went against the natural order of things.

But Huan did not particularly wish to be married, and he was in fact quite relieved to discover my mother had rejected him. Tsao Mei-en was certainly beautiful, he thought, but those Christian women were a problem. And besides, she was overly educated.

A letter was then sent to his younger brother, who by now was in the United States, finishing his senior year of college at Stanford University. As he sat on the edge of his bed, his cup of hot tea growing cold on his desk, he ignored his curious roommate and read the letter, over and over. It included my mother's picture. He was sure there was a mistake.

A letter was sent to my mother's parents stating that the younger brother would certainly be interested in marriage to their daughter.

My mother felt panic swell within her. From her stomach to her throat. She could not swallow. Her feet went cold.

"Wait, I have some conditions. I will not be sold like a cart of potatoes."

Her father thought she was being impudent.

Her mother felt it was only right.

First, Mei-en said, she wanted a sign of Chai Chu's seriousness. Certainly many men might say they wanted to marry, but he was out of the country, how could she know what he felt? She demanded an engagement ring of jade, the deepest green, like a forest at midnight, set in gold.

My father's family sold forty *mu* of their land and bought her the ring.

Second, my mother said, she needed to get to know her fiancé.

These were modern times, not the feudal past; there should only be love marriages, no more arranged marriages. In order that they should get to know each other, he must write to her one letter every single day from now on until their marriage. If after two years, they found they were compatible in views and thoughts, they could be married. But if she discovered that they were not compatible, the marriage would be called off.

My father found these conditions sensible and fair. He wrote her a letter immediately, accepting her conditions and expressing his relief and happiness that his fiancée was so modern in her thinking, so logical, sensible, and clever as to think of this method to get to know each other, considering they were separated by seven thousand miles, not to mention the ocean.

My mother began to feel worried. She felt herself at a crossroads.

"I won't live forever on this earth, Mei-en," my grandmother said. "It will be good for you to start a family of your own."

"Don't talk like that, Mother. It's morbid."

Mei-en thought of a third condition. She wrote that because she was Christian and believed in the saving grace of Jesus Christ, the Lord, and his Heavenly Father, she could not imagine marrying a man who did not likewise accept Jesus Christ as his Savior. She could not think of marrying Chai Chu if he did not convert to Christianity.

This was news to my father. He'd been raised a good Buddhist, and he kept a small shrine to his deceased grandparents in his dorm room at Stanford. Every morning he burned incense before their pictures, bowed three times, then prayed to Guan Yin, the Goddess of Mercy, for her aid and wisdom in navigating through this day. If he converted, he could not burn incense for his ancestors and he would not be able to maintain a shrine for his own parents when they were dead. He could not be a filial son. He almost refused.

But he looked at the framed picture of my mother that he'd set on the nightstand by his bed. He looked at it every night before he went to bed and every morning when he got up. Sometimes he looked at the picture for long, happy interludes in the middle of the afternoon, and even in the middle of the night—with the aid of a match so as not to disturb his roommate—when he himself had difficulty sleeping.

"I will study Christianity and then give you my answer," he wrote sincerely in his daily letter to my mother.

He went to the library and, with the aid of the reference librarian, checked out many heavy, leather-bound books on Christian thought. He sought out the Stanford chaplain, who was more than happy to pass many an entire afternoon in discussion with this earnest Chinese boy seeking to understand Christ.

The silver-haired chaplain put a heavy hand on my father's shoulder. "Charles," he said, for this was the American name my father had chosen for himself. "You are about to embark on a journey. A journey of faith. And once you have reached the journey's end, you will be a changed man."

My father thought the idea rather frightening.

He attended Sunday services in the chapel, and if he could not quite understand the chaplain's sermons, which were long-winded and filled with quotes from the King James version of the Bible, he studied the pictures in the stained-glass windows: a man with his heart exposed, flames emerging from his chest, a bird floating above his head. Sad-eyed Apostles, their eyes rimmed in coal and lead, glowering at the congregation. Behind the altar, the almost naked Christ writhed in nearly life-size agony, his feet and hands nailed to a wooden cross.

It was hard to understand, this religion where a father God would allow an angry mob to kill his only son.

But Christian heaven seemed a lot like the Western Paradise where good Buddhist souls went if they honored their ancestors and their parents and followed the eightfold path of righteousness, which was not all that dissimilar to the Ten Commandments. And he especially liked the precept "Do unto others as you would have them do unto you," so similar to the sage Confucius's commandment "The gentleman does not do unto others that which he would not have them do to himself." The Goddess of Mercy—a kind bodhisattva who intervened on behalf of the miserable humans as they struggled here on earth—was similar to both the mother of Christ and the Holy Spirit.

Perhaps it was not such a strange religion.

My father had taken the liberty to request another small picture of his fiancée, and when it arrived, he carried it in the breastpocket of his suit jacket to classes and in his wallet when he went to work at night on weekends as a busboy at a local restaurant, a good job for foreign students. And after he was fired from his good job for foreign students because he did not understand that the tips left on the tables were for the waitresses and not for him, only my mother's picture could comfort him as he sat on the concrete steps outside the kitchen, glumly waiting for his ride back to the dorms, feeling completely and utterly humiliated.

Yes, he decided, he could convert for Mei-en.

By the time his letter announcing his new religion reached Nanjing, my mother had been accepted into graduate school on a scholarship at Wittenberg College in Ohio.

Now I don't need to be married, she thought.

"You can be married in America," her mother said, smoothing Mei-en's cheek with her veiny hand. "A modern woman. Just as you always wanted."

Delighted that his fiancée, whom he had never actually met, would now be in the same country, my father decided to attend Northwestern University Law School. As a Boxer Indemnity Scholarship recipient, he could have gone to any university in America—Harvard, Yale, any of the Ivy League, or remained at sunny Stanford where he was well liked by his professors. But Chicago would bring him closest to my mother.

"I will drive every weekend to see you," he wrote to her happily, although not only did he not own a car, he also did not know how to drive.

Everything was as my mother had wished and yet nothing was as she had imagined. She thought of the ancient curse "May you get all that you desire."

A knot grew in her throat until she felt she was choking.

My mother ran all the way from her parents' home to the stone chapel with the listing sycamore in the front lawn and the busy mulberry peeking over the stone wall surrounding the pastor's home next door. Her hair had fallen out of her bun and sweat roiled off her forehead in waves. No one was in the church, so she fled outside again and ran next door. She pounded on the door of the Goodkin residence until the maid answered in alarm, and my mother rushed past her into the parlor where Eleanor was at the piano poised to tear into a secret Beethoven symphony while her husband was out with converts trying to force Christian pamphlets into the hands of pedestrians.

"You must help me, Eleanor," my mother cried, not knowing exactly what she wanted her friend to do. She stood in the middle of the dark carpet, panting, all eyes focused on her flushed face. A clock on the mantelpiece ticked like a metronome. "You must help me choose an American name!"

6

AMERICAN ROMANCE

Ruth and Charles's engagement picture, 1929.

~ *May-lee* ~

In America, my grandparents went by the names Charles Chai and Ruth Tsao.

When they met for the first time in San Francisco, my grandmother explained to my grandfather how she had spent hours and hours poring over the Bible, trying on different names, researching different meanings, but it was her mother who in the end had suggested Ruth. Her mother had especially liked the verse proclaiming Ruth "better to you than seven sons." (Ruth 4:15)

My grandmother explained that she herself felt Ruth was a particularly auspicious name for embarking on a trip. Ruth the Moabite woman had chosen to follow the ways of the land of Judah rather than her own people. "Your people shall be my people, And your God, my God." (Ruth 1:16b) Ruth therefore was a virtuous woman with an open mind.

When pressed, my grandfather admitted that he had chosen the name Charles for himself because it began with a *ch*.

~

After a brief visit in San Francisco, my grandfather and another Chinese student who owned a car escorted my grandmother across the country to her college in Ohio.

This first journey across America from California—known throughout China as Gold Mountain—to the American midwest with its huge expanses of fields, corn and wheat and oats, no rice at all, must have been exciting to my grandmother for any number of reasons. She was seeing an exotic new country, there was the novelty of taking a road trip *in a car,* not to mention getting acquainted with her fiancé. But neither she nor my grandfather ever talked about this trip. Perhaps my grandparents' memories were too private to share with children and grandchildren.

However, many, many years later, after the family had immigrated to America in the 1950s, after all the wars, my father with his first car would re-create his parents' first roadtrip, driving my grandparents and his brothers across the United States. My father had just won $13,000 as a contestant on the television game show *Name That Tune* and he was in the mood to celebrate. So he took a break from graduate school and invited his brothers, also college students by this time, and his parents to tour the country.

In the pictures they took, they seemed to have hit every major theme park and tourist site between Niagara Falls and San Francisco. My middle uncle wears a headdress and shakes hands with an American Indian dressed like an extra from a John Wayne film. My youngest uncle poses in profile before Mount Rushmore. My grandparents sit on merry-go-rounds at Freedomland Amusement Park with their sun umbrellas shading their faces to keep them from getting tans. There are many commemorative photographs taken before kitschy "Indian villages" and Old West corrals with men dressed like cowboys but also pictures of a more personal nature, such as my grandparents standing before the entrance to their honeymoon apartment in Chicago, one of Ye-ye's law school classrooms, Nai-nai's beloved Wittenberg College campus.

My father labeled this section of his photo album: "Land of the Free!"

These pictures tell the kind of happy story with a happy ending that my family liked to share, the story of having survived as opposed to the tales of what they endured.

~

Looking at my grandparents' engagement photograph, taken in a fancy Chicago studio, I can barely recognize my grandparents in the faces of the bright-eyed couple staring back at me. The woman is beautiful, breathtaking. Her hair permed into deep black waves, she wears a flowered print dress, an orchid corsage pinned to her shoulder. She stares directly into the camera, unsmiling in the Chinese tradition, but serene. My grandfather is dapper in a slate-gray suit, his patterned tie chosen to match the pattern of my grandmother's dress. His black hair is parted in the middle, slicked to the sides; his thick black owl-eye glasses are the most prominent feature of his face. Against tradition, he smiles faintly, unable to contain his pleasure upon meeting his fiancée and discovering that she is every bit as lovely as her photograph.

This is not how I remember her, my grandmother. Yet even as an elderly woman with false teeth and an itchy wig on her head, my grandmother still carried herself like a beautiful woman, head high, back straight, someone who was used to being watched. But the beauty was hidden now behind the survivor's face.

By all accounts, the years of her courtship in America were the happiest of my grandmother's life. Now graduated from Stanford, my grandfather was studying law at Northwestern University. Every weekend he brought my grandmother a special Chinese feast that he cooked himself, taking the train from Chicago to deliver it. My grandmother waited for him at the train station in Springfield, Ohio, with a friend or two from her sorority, as she felt it would be inappropriate to meet him alone. Sometimes my grandfather also was accompanied by his cousin K. K. Chai, who was studying at nearby Antioch College in Yellow Springs. Eventually, as a result of these visits, K. K. himself would fall in love with one of my grandmother's classmates, a Japanese foreign student who went by the name of Mary Shinowara. These weekend outings were carefree, joyous times spent strolling through the pretty Ohio countryside, picnicking beside a lake, laughing and enjoying each other's company.

In all the photos from her Wittenberg days, my grandmother is smiling, she is dressed in frilly frocks with high-heeled shoes, hair curled, bejeweled. She will never look like this again, and not simply because she will grow older.

Later K. K. and Mary would also marry in America and, like my grandparents, eventually they would return to China. When they all met up again in Chongqing, the wartime capital of China, after the fall of Nanjing to the Japanese army, their college days would seem an almost unbelievable dream.

"She used to be such a sweet girl," K. K. would say, his face a bitter gourd of worry now, a Chinese man married to a Japanese woman, married to the enemy.

It didn't matter that Mary Shinowara Chai had devoted herself to fighting the Japanese, with more vehemence than even Generalissimo Chiang Kai-shek, who would rather fight the Chinese Communists. She taped Japanese-language propaganda broadcasts weekly, denouncing the Japanese emperor, Japanese imperialism in China, Japanese war crimes.

Her voice had become a river of rebuke, each syllable sharpened into knifepoints, hurtling across the airwaves.

She was famous in the war effort. But to many people, too many people, she was still Japanese, the enemy.

"I should never have married her, I suppose." K. K. rubbed his hand through what was left of his hair. "We should never have come back. What was I thinking?"

My grandparents could find no words strong enough to console him. Instead, they reminded him of their happy days in Ohio, until they could laugh together again, reminiscing at this fantasy of a past they once shared.

But when my grandmother was a student at Wittenberg, living in a dormitory named Ferncliff, the future promised to be only as exciting and triumphant as she imagined.

Ruth Tsao was a popular girl, a good student, charming and gay, full of wit and promise. She did not feel like a foreigner, a stranger in an exotic land. She had many American friends, and when she stood with them in pictures, she smiled now too, just like an American. After she received her M. A. in education in 1929, she decided to stay on an additional year, at the encouragement of her music professor, to continue advanced work on the piano.

She wrote long letters every week to her mother, to her brothers, to her missionary tutors. There was so much to describe. So much happiness to share. She described her dorm room in all its intimate details, the plaster molding along the ceiling, shaped in voluptuous curlicues and trailing vines, which she liked to watch at night when she left her curtains open so that the moonlight crept across the ceiling and the moldings seemed to sway and breathe with the blue light. She liked the happy zing! and ping! sounds from the radiator, which flooded her room with summer warmth, even when thick, downy snow lay across the lawn like the fur of a white rabbit. The smell of the fresh paint in the hallways. The laughter tinkling from the washroom. The solid silence of her own room when she shut the door behind her and sat at the oak desk, leather-bound books and clean white sheets of paper set before her purposefully.

Later she would name her firstborn son, my father, after her alma mater, the name Wittenberg shortened to a more wieldy, more Chinese two syllables: Winberg.

Much later she would select a mausoleum named Ferncliff.

Two years after my grandmother's arrival in America, my grandparents were married at the Fourth Lutheran Church on May 24, 1930. It was the first time a Chinese couple was married in Springfield, Ohio, and cause for much excitement. The mayor declared a holiday, the president of Wittenberg himself walked my grandmother down the aisle, as her own parents could not be there. The church was quaint and lovely, all polished golden wood pews and stained-glass windows. It was packed to capacity.

In the photograph that later appeared in the town newspaper, my grandmother wears a white dress—quite daring for a Chinese woman, red was the traditional color of a bride's dress. Her cloudlike veil floats around her onto the ground for six yards but her dress is short, just below the knee, flapper-style. Everyone who sees this photograph admits she is stunning. Once again, my grandfather could not believe his good fortune. In his rented tuxedo, he looks dignified and pleased. You can't even tell in the photographs that the shoes pinched his feet terribly and gave him an ingrown toenail on his right big toe.

Nine thousand miles away, my great-grandmother framed the copy of the wedding photograph, a few months late due to the slowness of the mail, and displayed it to all her friends. I don't know how my great-grandfather felt about his daughter's American-style wedding. He'd recently bought a new maid, a young girl—younger than his daughter—and she was occupying all his time now that all the children were out of the house and out of the way and there was only his old, sick wife left to keep him company.

My great-grandmother continued to work in the missionary-run hospital as long as she was able, and then even she was forced to admit she was too sick to help at all. Her strong, feet-saving lungs were now phlegm-filled, pus-filled, leaking blood. She coughed frequently, sometimes all night long, relatives would later report, a severe illness. The dampness of her room where she slept alone, far from her husband's so that she could not hear him with his new girl, did not help.

When she died finally, hanging on for two years but dying anyway just before her daughter was to return from America after being away for four years, her husband did not waste any time before marrying the young girl who had been his maid.

Nobody wrote to tell my grandmother.

And when my grandmother finally did arrive in Nanjing, she found her mother fresh in her grave and her father remarried to a girl nearly half her own age.

Her sadness was surpassed only by her rage.

But for now, in America, in college, Ruth Tsao was happy. As happy as she had ever imagined she could be. Perhaps happier even than that. Ruth Tsao had married out of love. She had an American master's degree. She was full of hope and expectations, for herself and her husband. She told the yearbook committee at Wittenberg that she planned to become dean of a women's college in Nanjing. Her husband would be a lawyer. They were a modern couple living in a modern age.

The American papers reported some Japanese aggression in Manchuria, the Chinese papers provided more in-depth coverage, but this was hardly news. The Japanese had been encroaching into China since the Sino-Japanese War of 1895. They had factories in every major port city, controlled railways in northeast China, had sent farmers to colonize parts of Manchuria. There were protests against the Japanese as well as other foreign imperialists in every city; my grandmother's desire to make her country stronger had motivated her to study abroad like so many students of her generation. But Ruth was not aware that all-out war with Japan loomed on the horizon.

The papers also reported the rise of a dictator named Adolf Hitler, but their tone was always derisive, making it easy to dismiss this fringe element who could not possibly be a serious threat to the thinking man's world. Her brothers had gone to university in Bonn to study medicine, after all, and they had reported to her that Germany was a modern country with advanced medical instruction and techniques, with liberal faculty and a lively intellectual community.

America was suffering from the first year of the Great Depression, but America was such a grand country, with friendly people and wealth to spare. Ruth Tsao saw America's wealth in its new concrete buildings with central heating and indoor plumbing, the public parks with their expensive fountains and even more precious green lawns, the shiny automobiles that outnumbered bicycles and pedestrians on any street, the poetry of Whitman, the songs that praised "amber waves of grain." America the Beautiful. America the Bountiful. Rich enough to give scholarships to students from all the way around the globe in China. America's problems seemed minute and faint, like the distant rumble of thunder on a summer's day, the flash of lightning on the horizon. Far away, and out of mind.

In the year of my grandparents' wedding, they were filled with a buoyant, American optimism.

After her marriage and graduation, my grandmother left her beloved Wittenberg, and her equally beloved Ferncliff, and moved to Chicago to live with my grandfather while he finished his J.D. degree.

Chicago, 1930. The center of jazz and hog futures, big-city politics and small-town manners, the hometown of Al Capone and Boss Daley, of Chinatown and tongs, of blizzards that raged white and howling for days and summers that reminded her of Nanjing.

Americans lined up for bread. Children begged in the streets. Gangsters shot each other in restaurants, before nightclubs, behind closed doors of factories, from the windows of fast-moving cars.

Charles and Ruth now lived in a tiny one-bedroom apartment on 226 Superior Street in a modest neighborhood near the Law School of Northwestern University. Charles conducted his research in Chinatown, determined to complete a pioneering study of overseas Chinese judicial practices: what had remained the same as in China, what had been adapted to life in America. A difficult task as Charles spoke no Cantonese, the language of the southern Chinese who lived there.

He enlisted a classmate to translate, but the two of them stood out, skinny students from north China, butting into other people's business. They were outsiders, elite scholarship students who didn't have to earn their living in restaurants and at day labor jobs. Soon the gang bosses had their very rough-looking henchmen follow Charles and his classmate wherever they went on their interviews. Just because someone was Chinese didn't mean he automatically was accepted in Chinatown.

To earn extra money for living expenses, Charles took to selling Chinese knickknacks sent by his mother-in-law. He dressed in his blue silk scholar's robe—to look more authentically exotic—and marched through the most expensive neighborhoods, calling out "Chinese antiques! Oriental embroideries! Emperor's treasures!" until someone opened a door and beckoned him to come inside to show off his wares.

Then he explained that this delicate cloisonné vase, this lovely silk embroidery, this ancient scroll, were in fact family heirlooms, treasured for six generations, but now to pay for his studies, he was forced to part with them. Of course, these souvenirs were most likely whatever his clever mother-in-law had picked up in the Confucius Temple antiques market the week before she mailed them, but his customers were buying more than vases, they were getting a good story to boot.

Usually after completing a transaction—so happy, happy, happy!—Charles would then hurry straight back to his apartment. He could have made more money, of course, if he'd kept at his rounds instead of returning after his first success, but Charles was never much of a salesman.

And this was the funny part, he'd admit to Ruth later, because he was originally destined to be a salesman. A soybean-oil shop clerk. He'd never told his wife these stories before, about his humble origins, not after all the glorious things that the matchmaker and his sisters had said, but now that they were safely married, he felt free to tell her about his past.

In fact, he'd grown up in a merchant family who'd seen better times in past generations and as of late were struggling merely to maintain their lifestyle. His father had sacrificed greatly to educate his firstborn son, Charles's elder brother, Huan, sending him to study at a university. Although Charles had received a middle-school education, he was then supposed to stay at home and run the family business. It was Huan who had helped Charles secretly escape the family home in Anhui province, inviting him to visit him in Shanghai under false pretenses so that he could take the national entrance exam. Neither son mentioned that Charles had taken the exam until—surprise, surprise!—Charles was awarded the top prize of all. An American Boxer Indemnity Fund Scholarship. This comprised a six-year scholarship to Beijing to study in the American-run preparatory school Qinghua College and then a scholarship to study anywhere in America through a Ph.D.

For his deceit, Huan earned his father's wrath. But Charles in an effort to make peace had assured his father that he would still take care of the family. However, he explained, because China's future depended on its people receiving a modern education, he had no choice but to seek a Western education. Thus, his father had relented and granted his younger son permission to continue his studies.

Finally Charles even admitted that his father had sold the family's last forty *mu* of land to buy Ruth's dark green jade and gold engagement ring.

Ruth did not react angrily to his confessions. If anything, she was even more pleased that her husband was so hardworking, so honest, so extremely intelligent. A man whose successes were due to his ability, not to his connections.

Charles and Ruth never fought in Chicago. In their memories, even at the end of their lives, they recalled only happy times, only fun adventures in the Windy City. And by the second year of their marriage, my father was conceived.

By the time I knew my grandmother, however, some forty years and several wars later, her optimism had waned considerably.

Nai-nai liked to talk about her secret worries with my mother in the kitchen of our house in New Jersey. While Ye-ye and my father and uncles shouted together about politics and business, Nai-nai slipped away to tell my mother about her hard life, about the nature of people, about the difficult relationships between men and women, about everything important. My mother, American with Irish-Catholic, German, French, and English roots, understood all about family and hardship. She was the eldest of eight children, and when she was seventeen, her parents had wanted her to marry a farmer, but instead she'd shocked them by choosing to work her way through college then pursue a career as a journalist and artist. By the time she was in her thirties, they'd given up all hope of her marrying, and then she'd surprised them again by choosing to marry this professor from China, Winberg Chai.

Two headstrong women, Nai-nai and my mother got along famously.

My parents were married on St. Patrick's Day in 1966, the year after the landmark Civil Rights Act struck down the old antimiscegenation laws. That summer Ye-ye and Nai-nai paid for my parents' honeymoon to Niagara Falls because Nai-nai's favorite soaps had taught her that Americans regarded this as a highly romantic location. Ye-ye, Nai-nai, and my father's two younger brothers also accompanied my parents on this "honeymoon." As a child I remember watching the Super-eight films of my parents dancing in evening wear on a ship, my grandparents smiling and clapping in the background. None of us thought this arrangement at all strange.

As my grandmother talked to my mother in our kitchen, free to discuss matters of the heart without the men present, I sat on the floor by the door, pretending to play with my Barbies, pretending I was too bored to listen to every word they said.

"All those old women, they always say, 'Charles, Charles! Ooo, Charles!' " Nai-nai waved her hands about her face as if to ward off flies. "They are after him. I know it." She clicked her tongue against her dentures.

My mother laughed, but Nai-nai was serious.

"My father married the moment she was dead. He couldn't wait," Nai-nai said, scowling. She stared at the ceiling fiercely now, as if she could see all the way to heaven, directly into her wronged mother's face. She nodded. "He will marry again the moment I am dead!"

"Don't worry. Ye-ye loves you very much," my mother assured her.

But Nai-nai shook her head at her daughter-in-law's naïveté. "Those women in the senior center, I know what they are after!"

"Those women" were my grandmother's best friends, her confidantes, the heart of her life outside the family. For ten years, my grandparents had regularly attended a Jewish senior citizens' center in Manhattan, just a few blocks from their apartment on West Seventy-first Street. It had been the epicenter of their social life since my grandfather's retirement. Here they found friends to commiserate the sorrows of old age, my grandfather's second heart attack, my grandmother's cataracts, the outlandish price of tea. Their Chinese friends were dead or moved back to Taiwan or to the suburbs to be with their children, which was practically the same as dead in my grandmother's eyes.

Ye-ye and Nai-nai had an open invitation to live with us, of course. But Nai-nai refused to leave the City, always with a capital *c,* because on the East Coast there was only one real city—New York. Everywhere else including our house in New Jersey was Countryside, was Boondocks, was Nowhere.

My grandparents came to the senior center by accident. They had been looking for a church to join; Nai-nai's missionary education made her heart long for the happy Bible socials of her youth. But the Christian churches located within walking distance from their apartment had proven disappointingly cold. In their eyes, my grandparents were Chinese first, Christian second, which is to say they were exotic creatures, like a pair of winged deer who'd happened into the chapel on the way to the circus. One minister even suggested that they try a church in Chinatown, unaware that the Cantonese services would be unintelligible to my Mandarin-speaking grandparents.

Then one auspicious weekend, they discovered the senior center next to the Jewish temple, filled with people just like them, people who had survived hardships, even wars, people who liked Chinese food. Soon Ye-ye and Nai-nai became the senior center's first Chinese, and first non-Jewish, members.

But there was the widow factor at the center, the ever-increasing ratio of available women to fading men. I'd seen them, these blue-haired hussies spilling onto the sidewalk around my grandmother. They were slick all right. They smiled, they held her arm, they told me I was so tall. They cooed, "What a pretty granddaughter!" They told me how much they enjoyed my grandparents' stories. Nai-nai smiled when she was at the center, she put in her teeth just for these outings. She cooed back to the chirping widows, "See you later, see you!"

But when she was safely in our house, talking with my mother, her eyes narrowed when she thought of *those women.*

"He is waiting for me to die," she said firmly.

As a child, I could not imagine how my grandmother could feel this way. But then again, I knew nothing.

7

A BIRTH IN SHANGHAI

Winberg, 1932.

~ Winberg ~

I have a happy story to tell. It involves, quite naturally, my birth.

In 1932 the world was as startlingly ripe and pink for the taking as a freshly peeled litchi fruit. My father had completed his Doctor of Jurisprudence and had been offered a teaching position at Northwestern University Law School. He was very excited by the possibility.

But my mother explained that it was impossible to stay in America because she was pregnant with their first son. She wanted her son to be born in China, she said. They should go back.

My father was disappointed, of course. Perhaps they could stay in Chicago just one more year, they could save some money, and he would have a year of teaching experience—in an American university!—under his belt.

But my mother knew how one year could become two, and two three. Already four years had passed since she last saw her mother. Her mother's health was fragile. She'd made up her mind, she said.

My parents left America.

~

Ruth stood on the deck, the salt air like feathers against her cheeks. Sunlight glinted off the waves in sparks of gold. As they passed the island of Formosa, a school of dolphins paralleled the steamer, bobbing in the waves.

Inside her belly, I kicked like a swordfish. In the privacy of her cabin, she lifted the skirt of her *qipao* above her belly and watched her taut skin bubble and pulse. It was unbelievable to her that there was another human being inside her, growing, kicking, thinking. One day, this creature would come out and be a separate being. Would cry and laugh. Talk one day. Walk and run. She was drowsy, the rocking of the ship, the warmth of the close, stuffy cabin, conspired to put her to sleep. But Ruth shook her head, pinched the skin of her inner arm. She wanted to watch me kicking from inside, pushing her skin out like the bubbles in a boiling stew. Soon, soon, she thought. Just wait, she whispered, smiling. Secretly, she was happy I was so bold, so impatient to be born.

Charles ranged from a little nauseated to retchingly seasick. My father had not slept in two weeks. The rocking of the boat made him dream of earthquakes, of the trembling El train, of careening taxicabs. Even when his stomach was nearly still and he was almost able to sleep, the images of trouble seeped into his dreams. His wife in danger. Sometimes she was still pregnant, in this new silhouette of hers like a penguin that's swallowed a beach ball, this vulnerable waddling shape. He saw her as if from a distance. And suddenly there was DANGER, never specific, never anything he could spot outright or pinpoint, just a feeling of extreme anxiety, as he saw his wife from a distance growing smaller as she teetered unsteadily along a road or a hall or a sidewalk and he ran toward her but with each step fell farther behind.

He woke up in a sweat, his nightshirt wet against his back. He blinked in the darkness.

His wife lay placidly on her side, her breathing surprisingly shallow and quick now that she was expecting, like an animal.

Greenish light from the moonlight reflecting off the sea seeped into the room through the tiny round window, fell onto their narrow bed in a puddle.

He was aware of the sea beneath the boat extending for miles and miles, teeming with scaly fish with teeth and dead eyes, whales and sharks and unimaginable monsterlike creatures, all swimming just beneath the ship in the black ocean.

He did not sleep again that night until once again the sun had risen abruptly above the horizon and morning flooded across the world with the suddenness of a gunshot.

The world had taken a sea-green cast, from the too bright cloudless sky to the seething never-still waves.

Charles looked at his reflection in the washroom mirror, and the man that looked back at him from the depths of the shiny glass had a sea-green cast to his skin. Shaving, he cut himself in three places, his hand shook with the ship. He stuck little toilet-paper kisses on the wounds.

"You look like a rabbit with mange," Ruth laughed, seeing him.

Every day was like this, a rocking, unstable, ever wakeful feeling of anxiety and nausea until finally seagulls like snowflakes whirled into the sky and Charles knew he was home.

He listened to the birds cawing into the wind and he thought even they sounded different from the birds in America, as if they too spoke Chinese.

The Bund of Shanghai. The busiest port of all China. Perhaps of all Asia. The jewel of the Orient. Skyscrapers stretched from asphalt to sky, solemnly facing the sea. Huge cargo ships with masts like forests towered over tiny Chinese junks, the lone sailors riding in the bow like cowboys on their trusty mounts, rope coiled like lassos over their forearms.

All my father's metaphors were mixed as he watched Shanghai Harbor from the deck, standing beside his wife. Coming back to China, he suddenly felt very American. He discovered he could not remember how to say "obstetrician" in Chinese.

My mother, on the other hand, felt no such displacement. She was coming home. She was ready to begin her real life.

I was ready too. I wouldn't wait till she was home with her mother, my grandmother, in Nanjing. No, we were in China, where she wanted me to be born, even though it meant I would never be president of the United States. I had kept my end of the bargain. No tricky shipboard delivery.

We were on land now, and I wanted to test my legs.

~

The way the story has always been told, I was nearly born on the dock just as my parents descended from the ocean liner.

A cousin was waiting on the dock, as well as the new husband of my father's youngest sister, Orchid, and a couple of this man's servants. My father's family had moved to Shanghai during his sojourn in America. My father's sisters had both married well—the elder to an engineer, the younger to this slick-looking businessman, wiping the sweat off his round pumpkin face with a silk handkerchief.

The cousin shouted with delight when he spotted my father, much changed, looking mature and distinguished in an American suit, round black-rimmed glasses, his hair slicked back over his large ears. My much-pregnant mother held my father's arm as they descended the gangplank together.

Now the reunited family, cousins and in-laws, were shaking hands and exchanging bows and pleasantries as they waited among the jostling crowds for my parents' steamer trunks of treasures from America—books and picture albums, clothes and trinkets, and special gifts for the family, including a carved-oak walking stick for Ruth's father and a lovely blue-flowered ladies' scarf for her mother that she'd picked out especially from the famous Chicago department store Marshall Field's. The wind carried the pungent smells of China—garlic and incense, salt water and rotting fish, strong perfumes and a delicate fruit like peaches on the wind—surrounding them in an embrace, when Ruth bent over suddenly.

Charles thought that she had lost something and crouched to help her search the ground, when he discovered her face twisted into a knot of distress, her mouth gaping open in a jagged O.

"What's the matter?" Charles grabbed his wife's shoulders.

But his cousin had grasped the situation immediately. He thumped Charles on the back as panic seized his throat, causing his voice to emerge in a squeak: "It's the baby!"

"No, no, no!" shouted Charles, as if he could persuade me to wait. "Not yet!"

In a frenzy the men began to shout at all once. They bumped into passers-by, they stepped in front of taxis and rickshaws and buses. At one point, they all ran down the street in opposite directions, trying to hall a cab, abandoning Ruth to the sidewalk. She leaned against a rail on the boardwalk and panted her way through another contraction.

Finally it was decided that Charles's brother-in-law would wait for the steamer trunks with his servants while Charles and his cousin accompanied Ruth to the hospital.

"Don't worry, don't worry." Charles's brother-in-law smiled broadly, clapping him on the shoulder. "We have plenty of space in our home for your trunks. You're going to be a papa now. You have other things to think about."

He dispatched one of his servants to flag down a taxi, which he did handily, much to the relief of Ruth.

As Ruth's aunt was now the head of the obstetrics ward of Bethany Hospital, Ruth naturally directed her panicked husband and his wild-eyed cousin to take her there. But both men babbled at the same time to the taxicab driver, confusing him sufficiently so that he took a wrong turn and got stuck in traffic behind a rickshaw and a limousine and a farmer's cart piled high with dead pigs while a contingent of turbaned Sikhs marched through an intersection. Both Charles and his cousin were shouting together, telling the driver to honk, back up, turn around, rush ahead, drive onto the sidewalk, and stay put all at once.

The driver swore rudely—in Shanghai dialect so that his customers would never know just how rudely—and turned down a winding alley clogged with shacks and small stands selling tofu and hot peppers. The cab reemerged on a thoroughfare and managed to get to Bethany before Ruth's water broke.

"Aaaiiieee!" Ruth screamed, and for a second, both Charles and his cousin were stunned into complete silence.

In a panic, Charles's cousin jumped out of the taxi and with a tremendous burst of adrenaline slammed the door shut behind him with such force that the window glass shattered immediately into six hundred pieces.

With this, the driver had had all that he could take. It wasn't his cab after all. The owner would have his hide. He'd be beaten to death. And even if he wasn't beaten to death, there would be no point in being alive because he'd never earn enough to pay for this window. "Twenty-five dollars!" he shouted. "You owe me twenty-five dollars!" He blocked the back door so that Charles and Ruth could not get out.

"You thief, you bandit!" the cousin shouted. "Whoever heard of paying twenty-five dollars for a cab ride!"

"You pay me for my window!" the driver shouted as he leaned against the door while Charles tried to force it open from the inside.

"Help, help!" Ruth cried.

The cousin tried to pull the driver away. "Move! Can't you see she's going to have a baby! Move, you stupid egg, you turtle's egg!"

The taxi driver swore now so terribly in Shanghai dialect that two women passing by on the sidewalk on their way to factory jobs nearly fainted from shock.

"How am I going to pay for this? You're the idiot!"

"Crook! It's a cheap window. That's why it broke!"

"This is a quality cab. Don't you know anything! You don't know anything about cars!"

The cousin and the driver had completely forgotten about Ruth by now. The contractions were painful, and coming closer.

"I'll pay, I'll pay," Ruth panted at the man, and counted out twenty-five dollars from her purse while Charles's cousin watched her.

She would never forgive him for this unchivalrous act. She would retell this story at every family gathering from Thanksgiving to Easter until the year of her death when she grew silent and didn't try to argue about the past anymore. How when she was in labor, practically ready to give birth on a curb, her husband's cousin made *her* pay for a taxicab window that *he* had broken. The injustice!

Charles and his cousin helped Ruth out of the cab and the cabbie drove off still shouting out his window at the cousin, who was also still shouting back at him. Charles, too, was shouting like a madman. He was shouting, "Help! Doctor! Emergency, emergency!" He was loud, and nurses came running from the hospital to see what was the matter.

They brought a wheelchair and helped Ruth to sit down and then wheeled her inside. Ruth had grown calm although the pain was more intense—perhaps *because* the pain was more intense.

Relieved that Ruth was now in the hands of experts, Charles and his cousin could safely go to the waiting room, where the cousin took off his shoes and jacket and stretched out on a chair in the corner and took a nap. Charles paced, sat, paced, walked into the hall and paced until he was escorted back into the waiting room by a young orderly who explained that the other patients, seeing him pace, were beginning to feel anxious.

Charles then tried to pray but that only made him feel desperate. He wished his cousin would wake up so that he could talk to him, but his cousin snored, openmouthed, head tipped back toward the ceiling. Charles could only wait.

While he was waiting, he sweated and sweated until his undershirt, cotton shirt, and good American jacket were completely sopping wet and he had lost six and a half pounds.

He thought, quite incorrectly, that he could not possibly ever feel more anxious than he did that day.

And finally, the moment we'd all been waiting for. I was born.

My mother later told me that my birth was the happiest moment of her life, that I was the most beautiful, most perfect, and most intelligent baby she had ever seen, and that I was plainly destined for greatness.

My father said that when he was finally allowed to see me, his firstborn son, he was quite disappointed because I did not resemble a baby so much as a boiled shrimp—red, wrinkled, and writhing.

I naturally prefer my mother's version.

"What shall we name him, the little darling," my father cooed, watching the baby sleeping in his wife's arms, tired from his journey into this world.

My mother did not hesitate. "I've already decided. Winberg."

"What?"

"After Wittenberg. My alma mater."

Later, friends would joke that I was lucky my mother never attended the Massachusetts Institute of Technology. But for now, my father merely nodded, too tired from all his sweaty waiting to argue with my mother. Besides, he figured that she was exhausted and would change her mind.

Of course, he was wrong.

My father chose the two characters that would most auspiciously represent my name in Chinese and that were the closest phonetic match. The first character 文 means "civic, cultivation, the best." The second 伯 means "primacy in the hierarchy of family relations." Together they mean "first and best."

I have always liked my name very much.

8

THE STEPMOTHER

Winberg and Amah, 1932.

~ *May-lee* ~

By the fall of 1932, much had changed in China since my grandparents were last home, Charles in 1927, Ruth in 1928. The government had finally united under the leadership of Generalissimo Chiang Kai-shek, ending the "era of the warlords." After Dr. Sun Yat-sen's death from cancer in 1925, Chiang had organized a so-called National Revolutionary Army in Canton and launched a Northern Expedition to unite the country. In four years, Chiang achieved what everyone thought was impossible: he had convinced China's warlords to swear allegiance to the new republic under his leadership. He had achieved this unity through a combination of battles and backroom manipulations, offering key posts to loyalists, pitting enemies against each other, orchestrating a few necessary assassinations until only he was left with enough power—that is, military allegiances and foreign ties, including foreign funds and arms—to lead the nation. Now alongside their regional banners, all the warlords' armies flew the flag of the republic: a white sun, symbolizing the spirit of unending progress, in a blue sky on a crimson field. Blue for democracy, white for socialism, and crimson for nationalism, representing the official doctrine of Chiang's Nationalist party, the Kuomintang (KMT).

In 1928, Chiang moved the capital of the Republic of China back to its founding city, Nanjing, and Beijing, whose name meant "northern capital," was officially demoted, even its name changed to Beiping, meaning "northern peace." Now Chiang poured money into sprucing up his capital. The white sun flag flew proudly from the budding skyscrapers, six and seven stories high. He spent a million U.S. dollars to build a marble mausoleum on Purple Mountain in honor of the republic's founding father, Dr. Sun Yat-sen.

To the delight of the missionaries, in 1927 Chiang married an American-educated, Christian convert, Soong Mei-ling, whose family was one of the richest and and most powerful in China. Her eldest sister was infamous for her financial cunning, her middle sister was Dr. Sun Yat-sen's widow. By 1932, her brother, the Harvard-educated financier T. V. Soong, was named China's premier; her brother-in-law H. H. Kung, a descendant of Confucius, served as Minister of Industry and Commerce.

In 1930, Chiang held a very public baptism and became a Methodist. America's newspapers took note. Henry Luce, publisher of *Time* and *Life* magazines, was especially pleased. Luce had been born in China where his parents were missionaries. He liked the idea of China under the hands of American-educated Christian converts so much, he would famously refuse to allow his reporters to cast any aspersions on "elegant" Madame Chiang and the "Ningpo Napoleon," Chiang Kai-shek. Luce put Chiang on the cover of *Time* for the first time in 1931, along with Soong Mei-ling, above the rubric "President of China & Wife."

My grandparents must have carried these optimistic images in their heads when they hurried home to China to welcome the birth of their first son, but in reality, China was still reeling from a series of military defeats to the Japanese and was moving closer to war. In September of 1931 in what would be known as the Mukden Incident, Japanese troops set off explosives on the rail lines outside the Manchurian city of Mukden. After a series of skirmishes with Chinese troops stationed nearby, the Japanese launched a full-scale attack and took over the city. Despite a call for an investigation into Japan's actions by the League of Nations, by the end of the year Japanese troops controlled all of Manchuria. In March of 1932, the Japanese put the former last emperor of the Qing dynasty, Pu Yi, on a puppet throne in Manchuria, which they now called "Manchukuo," meaning "land of the Manchus." Japanese troops were again involved in skirmishes from Shanghai to Heilongjiang province as anti-Japanese riots and protests broke out up and down the eastern seaboard. But despite the obvious distress of his citizens at these developments, Chiang Kai-shek did not send his troops to Manchuria but rather to attack parts of China where the rival Communist party had been successful in establishing bases of support.

By October of 1932, all the forces that would destroy the dream of reforming China as a republic—the coming war with Japan and the civil war between the Nationalists and Communists—were already present when my grandparents arrived in China. Yet my grandparents were optimistic about their country's future and their own. They had read the glowing reports in America's premier newspapers and magazines of China's reconstruction. They, too, believed what their hearts wanted most in the world to be true: that Chiang Kai-shek had united the nation and that the republic was on the road to reform. They had nothing but big plans and high hopes.

Their optimism endured until shortly after my father's birth, when my grandfather returned to Nanjing and discovered that nothing would turn out as he had hoped.

~ *Winberg* ~

While my mother waited with me in her aunt's hospital in Shanghai, my father returned to Nanjing with his new leather suitcase packed with his good gray suit; his silver-framed engagement photograph; a tiny black-and-white snapshot of Ruth holding a large round bundle that did not quite reveal my face but which my father knew was there, in a shadow, peeking from a fold; his foreign diplomas; gifts for his in-laws; a letter of recommendation from the preeminent American jurist Professor Andrew A. Bruce; and a copy of the March 1932 issue of the prestigious *Journal of Criminal Law and Criminology,* which included his article—in English—"Administration of Law Among the Chinese in Chicago," the publication of which was a very significant achievement for an overseas Chinese student in America.

He had returned to the hustle-bustle capital of New China, construction of towering six-story buildings at every intersection, the flags of the republic flying proudly from silver poles, bespectacled students still protesting in the streets, waving white banners: "Resist Japanese Aggression!" and "Down with Foreign Imperialism!" Everything had changed and everything had stayed the same.

The October weather was extraordinary, Nanjing at its best. Air as crisp as the yellow, hand-sized leaves of the French sycamores lining the broad avenues. Sunlight warm and comforting, falling like a blanket from the sky, which was plump with clouds as white as snow geese. It was without a doubt the most exquisite time of the year, the most wonderful month in my father's life.

My father had returned to China after five years in America with a fat baby son, a beautiful modern wife, and a suitcase full of accolades. He, the soybean-oil merchant's son. The second son who was destined to be a clerk. The skinny boy with the flat nose and the big ears and the voice like an elephant's trumpet.

Every taunt directed his way by a jealous classmate. Every slight ever made by an overly arrogant professor. Every self-doubt he might have ever entertained. Gone. Rolled off his psyche like raindrops from a duck's back.

My father would have burst into song if he could have carried a tune. He would have danced down the street if he hadn't converted to his wife's strict religion and discovered that dancing was now against his religion. But it didn't matter. In his heart, he sang with the voice of a thousand dragons, resounding and powerful enough to shake the earth. In his mind's eye, he danced with a top hat and cane, like the hero of every Hollywood musical he'd ever seen.

He beamed, his head swimming with big plans and big emotions, as he sat on the hard seat of the pedicab en route from the Nanjing train station to his wife's family compound. As his own family had all moved to Shanghai and the house they rented had long since been vacated, my father would stay with his in-laws, whom he had never met. But if he had any worries whatsoever about this arrangement, if he had any presentiments of the disaster upon disaster to come, my father was able to chase them away in a second, dismissing them as fatigue from his train journey and nothing more.

His complete lack of premonition would become legendary in our family. But for the moment, my father's sanguine nature was still a blessing.

My father rode through the streets of Nanjing, his suitcase of good fortune balanced on his knees, the crisp autumn breeze a caress against his smooth cheeks, and he thought: I can do anything!

He arrived at his wife's family's house, located behind a stone wall, the imposing gate locked. He banged the brass knocker against the wooden door. Finally a servant answered. The man's eyes bugged out of his thin face when he saw my father standing there in his rumpled Western suit and large suitcase.

"Oh, you're so early!" He bowed to my father and took the suitcase. "Follow me."

Then the man took off in a near run into the interior of the Tsao family compound. It was a traditional-style house, single story, the rooms arranged in a square around a tiled courtyard. There was a garden of large, craggy limestone rocks and bamboo in the center of the courtyard and a large ceramic fishbowl decorated with a pattern of chrysanthemums in pinks and golds. My father stopped to peer into the rim. Three large-eyed goldfish skirted around the bottom like fireflies. A fourth lay on its side on the surface of the water.

"One of your fish is dead," my father called to the servant, who was rapidly scurrying down the corridor with my father's bag.

"It is all right, young sir." The man nodded. "Do not trouble yourself."

"But it will make the others sick."

The man looked uncomfortable. "Yes. Don't worry. I will take care of it."

"I don't mind. We can do it now."

The man did not move. He stood rooted in the open corridor, under the wooden roof of the veranda, holding my father's suitcase in one hand. He stared at his black cotton shoes as if he had not heard. "We're almost at your room."

"It won't take a moment. Do you have a net?" My father thought, Perhaps this servant is not used to taking care of animals. Perhaps he thinks it is beneath him? But my father would show him that kindness to animals is not beneath anyone. My father searched among the vertical rocks of the garden, among the bricks stacked in corners, among some garden tools propped against a wooden beam, for a fishnet. He found one and handily removed the dead goldfish. "There," he said, smiling down at the three fish who were now bobbing to the top, their round mouths breaking the surface, expecting to be fed. "They'll be much happier now. Do you have their food?"

The man was still staring at his shoes. "Please, young sir. We should go to your room."

My father looked at him, surprised. He still held the net, dripping, the dead fish wrapped in the corner like a small butterfly, just a tiny patch of color.

Suddenly the servant dropped my father's suitcase to the floor, ran over to him, grabbed the net, shook the dead fish back into the ceramic bowl, then tucked the net under his arm and ran back to the corridor. Picking up my father's suitcase, he rushed away without waiting to see if my father was following.

"Wait! Why did you do that?"

But the man was running now. He turned, entering a doorway, and disappeared from sight.

My father was obliged to hurry after him.

He followed the man into a darkened room, the shutters drawn. The man opened them now. A flood of sunlight revealed a rectangular office equipped with an ornate rolltop oak desk with an inkstone, new ink stick, set of calligraphy brushes, as well as Western-style steel-tipped pens and a vial of ink. There were two red lacquer chairs with new embroidered cushions. A bookshelf, empty. A bamboo wastebasket, empty. A polished brass coat tree, which appeared to be brand-new and seemed so out of place, so foreign here in China, that my father stared at it as if he had never seen one before.

The servant followed my father's gaze and smiled now for the first time since my father had entered the house. His front teeth had been replaced with silver caps, which caught the sunlight and glittered as though he had a mouth full of sparks. "Yes. Granny[1] ordered that

---

[1] The term in Chinese, *nai-nai,* literally means "grandmother," but here it is used as a term of respect for the elderly wife of the head of the household. The Tsao family servants came from the countryside and did not use more sophisticated terms like *fu-ren,* or "mistress of the house." Chinese people often call each other by kinship terms even if they are not related to each other.

for you when she heard you would be coming back. Just like in America, right?"

"Why, yes."

The man shook his head happily, his eyes watering. "Granny always knew what was right." He gestured to the desk, the chairs now. "The Old Master hopes you will find this suitable for your office."

"Yes, of course. But—"

But the man was already rushing out the door, the suitcase tucked under his arm, his footsteps already fading, like the faint rustle of mice.

My father hesitated a moment, looking for clues in this room. He could not understand this strange greeting.

Then he hurried into the corridor only to find it deserted. The servant, and his suitcase, gone.

The long corridor was now empty. The doors all closed. He was completely alone. My father wandered down the empty veranda. It was cool and damp in the interior of the courtyard, nothing remained here of the warm October day he had left outside the gate. He paused, listening. The bamboo creaked with ominous sounds like a secret language. He could hear the distant street, a car honking, a rickshaw's squeaky wheels, faint like a memory.

Where was everyone? Why was no one here to welcome him? Perhaps the telegram he'd sent had been improperly relayed? That must have been it.

Suddenly a door opened behind him, with a *crrrroak* like a bullfrog. The servant popped his head out and gestured for my father to follow him inside.

It was the bedroom of a young girl.

"You will be staying in Miss Mei-en's room, of course." Small cloisonné bud vases were lined up neatly on a rolltop desk. A pair of embroidered slippers waited beside the bed, the colorful quilts and pink crocheted bedspread rolled into a bundle at the head. Pictures of the Holy Family adorned the walls along with a calendar bearing a watercolor of three Tang dynasty court ladies playing musical instruments. The year read "1928."

"Granny wanted everything as Miss Mei-en had left them. She missed her very much."

My father was so touched seeing his wife's girlhood room that he was overcome with emotion. For a moment he could not speak.

Another *crrrroak*. The servant was halfway out the door when my father stopped him.

"Wait. I have to ask you something."

The man looked worried, as if he had just been caught stealing. But he stood still, his hands together, his head bent. "Of course, young sir. What is it you need? Shall I find the cook to make you a snack—"

"Why did you throw that dead fish back in the bowl? That's very dirty."

"Yes, sir. I'm sorry, young sir. Of course, you're right, sir. But we must leave the fish."

My father sighed. Was he talking to an imbecile or an eccentric? "What for?"

"It's a lesson."

"You must explain what you mean. I—I order you."

The man looked up, seeming almost relieved. "In that case, I must tell you. The Old Master has ordered that we leave the goldfish in the jar until Little Granny finds it and removes it herself. He says this is the only way she will learn to care for her fish, she is the one who bought them at the market, and she should not bring animals into the house if she doesn't want to look after them. The Old Master has never liked animals—"

"Wait a minute. What do you mean by 'Little Granny'?"

"I mean, of course, I mean, the Old Master's . . . You know, the head of the household, Madame Tsao."

"My mother-in-law."

"No. I mean Little Granny."

My father was growing angry with this game. He was certain now that this man was testing him. Playing him for the fool, the outsider. My father would not be humiliated like this. "I order you to stop babbling. Do you think I'm an idiot?" he shouted. His voice rebounded off a far wall of the courtyard, returning as if to mock him: *Idiot!* "Speak clearly! Who is this 'Little Granny'?"

The man hunched his shoulders and glanced around him. When he answered, his voice was so low, nearly a whisper, my father had to lean forward to hear him, "Why, it's Ah Ling, of course. You know, Ah Ling?"

"How could I possibly know who Ah Ling is?"

"You really haven't heard, then?"

"I will have you fired if you don't answer me!"

"In that case, young sir, I have no choice but to answer." The man sighed wearily, as if he were being asked to give up one of his fingers for a medicinal soup. But before he could continue, there was a soft knock on the door. An old woman's face peered in the crack.

Seeing my father, her cheeks pulled back into a smile. "It's you! Not five minutes ago, the telegram arrived saying you're coming. The Old Master's just sent a group to meet you at the train station and you're already here, isn't that funny?"

The servants exchanged glances.

"If you need anything, anything at all, something to eat, another blanket, just ask," she chattered nervously. She had a wide, kind face, and almost no teeth. She wore a turban over her head and a plain gray cotton dress. Often servants of well-to-do households dressed well themselves but my father had noticed that the servants here wore plain clothing. Not shabby but unadorned. He wondered if this was some kind of Christian habit. It gave them all the somber formality of a mourning party. "You needn't worry about a thing. An important scholar like yourself. And Miss Mei-en's husband. There's no need to worry about anything."

"Why should I worry?"

"No reason, no reason. Don't mind me, I'm nobody," she said.

While my father was distracted by the old woman, the servant seized the opportunity to slip out the door and disappear.

"I should pay my respects to my in-laws."

"Yes, yes, yes. Of course. But perhaps you would like to rest first? After your long journey?"

"Won't my in-laws find that rude?"

"I shouldn't think so. Not them." The old woman walked over to Mei-en's desk and slowly brushed her hand across the polished surface of the wood. Her hand had left a shimmery path in the dust like the track of a giant snail. "Miss Mei-en will be returning soon, I hope? And the baby?"

"My wife and son will rest in Shanghai with her aunt until I find— until I am settled in my new position. There's no need for them to be burdened with the move. I want to get everything ready and in place, before they move here. My wife had to endure much hardship, traveling all the way from America while expecting."

"Such a considerate husband. Just what the family needs." The woman smiled politely, her mouth closed around her toothless gums this time. She bowed, turning to go. "We're all looking forward to Miss Mei-en's return. She's been away so long," she sighed. Then she stopped at the door, suddenly turning back to my father. "I'll bring you some hot tea. You should rest before you meet your in-laws." The door creaked shut behind her.

My father changed now out of his sweaty, confining Western clothes and back into a more forgiving *changshan* long shirt of light gray silk that fell to mid-calf and loose cotton trousers. He took off his glasses and rubbed the bridge of his nose. The journey from Shanghai had tired him more than he'd at first realized. He couldn't think straight. Why was everyone acting so odd? he wondered. Perhaps they thought him unworthy of their beloved Mei-en? And what had the man meant by "Little Granny"?

My father's heart jerked suddenly, his mouth fell open. Could his father-in-law have taken a second wife? But then he shook his head at his own paranoia. Christians were allowed only one wife. He was being foolish.

Charles washed his face in the porcelain basin by the bed, the cool water refreshing him, helping to calm his nerves. With customary optimism, he convinced himself his nerves were frayed from the anticipation of meeting his in-laws, when he heard a rustling in the corridor outside his door, whispers, and the *patpatpat* of slippered feet. A knock.

"Yes?"

A young teenaged boy now poked his head in the door. He had wide-set black eyes that looked perpetually startled, thick brows like two moths stuck to his wide forehead, and bristly black hair that stood straight up on end like a paintbrush. The overall effect of his features was the appearance of someone who'd just survived a great trauma. "You-you-you're to meet the Old Master n-n-now," he stuttered.

"Very good." My father dried his face on the rough cotton towel hanging on the nightstand. "Let me get their presents." He dug into his suitcase, sifting through his packets of important papers, clean underwear, socks. The gifts had to be in there somewhere.

"Is it true?" the boy asked. "You-you-you're really from A-A-America?"

"I was a student in America."

"It must be very gr-gr-grand. Why else would Miss Mei-en st-stay away while Granny was so-so-so sick. You m-missed the w-wedding banquet, you know."

Suddenly the door creaked open and a voice whispered from the hall: "Sssh! Stupid egg!"

The boy hung his head.

"Wedding? Her second brother's, you mean? Yes, it's too bad, but Mei-en will be back soon." My father patted the boy on his spiky hair. "I've found what I've been looking for. Shall we go?"

Outside the veranda was deserted again, whoever had been eavesdropping on their conversation gone.

The boy led my father through the maze of corridors and rooms leading to inner rooms leading to more corridors. More servants appeared, dressed more formally. They bowed their heads as my father approached but looked up quickly once he'd passed, eager to see what this new "American" son-in-law was like. Finally my father was led—like a new exotic pet, he thought—through a double door made of lacquer, pine, and bronze fittings into a formal sitting room, which was unpleasantly chilly and damp.

My father blinked, trying to adjust to the dim lighting. An old man who must be his father-in-law sat in a straight-backed chair. He nodded at my father. The old man's health appeared to be fragile, his face was gaunt, jagged cheekbones protruding like rocks beneath his deep-set eyes, a thin white beard tumbling from chin to chest like an errant collar. There was no sign of his wife, Mei-en's mother. A servant girl—very well dressed, very young, but not particularly pretty—waited upon the old man attentively, handing him a handkerchief, taking his teacup, massaging his arms with her fists. He reached over and patted her arm. The girl giggled.

My father cleared his throat but then did not know what to say. Fortunately his father-in-law spoke first.

"Your new mother-in-law and I are very pleased to make your acquaintance," he said.

My father looked puzzled.

The maid nodded her head. "I am very pleased to make your acquaintance." She repeated the old man's words exactly, even imitating his northern accent.

"My *new* mother-in-law?"

"Yes. Your new mother-in-law is very pleased that her new son has come to live in our humble house," the old man said. "She looks forward to meeting her most treasured first grandson."

The maid took a deep breath. "I am very pleased that my new son-in-law—"

"Your new *son*," the old man corrected her sternly.

"I mean, that my new son has come . . ." She couldn't remember the rest. "Has come," she finished abruptly. Then she blurted out, "I really, really want to see the baby! I love babies!

My father understood now that this girl was not the maid. The strange behavior of the servants, the somber house that seemed to be in mourning, this was the secret no one wanted to tell him. His wife's beloved mother had died and her father remarried! All this must have occurred sometime between his mother-in-law's last letter to them in Chicago just a few months ago and their arrival in Shanghai. She had never let on that she was so ill—perhaps she had not wanted her daughter to worry. Certainly his mother-in-law had never mentioned Ah Ling.

My father swallowed. He did not know what he should do so he relied instead on formalities and tradition. "I am very honored to make your acquaintance finally." My father shifted his weight from one foot to the other. "My wife has always spoken so highly of her family."

There was an extremely awkward pause.

Sweating, my father busied himself presenting the meager gifts he had managed to fit into his suitcase. He had none of the more expensive presents his wife had chosen—the silver watch for her father, the leather-bound atlas, the elegant walking stick—which she had wanted to hand out herself. But now his meager offerings seemed like a deliberate slight. Well, there was nothing else to do. He wiped his forehead and offered his in-laws the following gifts:

An American Bible, illustrated with both color plates and black-and-white etchings. A framed picture of the Holy Family. (In China they were always drawn with black hair and Chinese features, but in this picture Mary, Joseph, and the Baby Jesus were all rosy-cheeked and blond ringlets. His wife had thought her mother would find the difference in perspective interesting.) A pair of warm leather gloves for both father and mother. And a pair of galoshes. His wife had often spoken about how her mother liked to walk everywhere. And very fast. She had carefully chosen these boots, searching in many department stores for the perfect size, finally buying a child's pair, because although her mother's feet had always been considered large in China, they were still smaller than most Americans' feet.

Now he was giving them to his wife's stepmother. He was certain his wife would not approve, but what else could he do? A son-in-law staying at his in-laws' house must offer gifts.

Visibly irritated, Ah Ling glared at the galoshes, lying like two very large slugs at her feet.

"Oh, look at the technology," his father-in-law exclaimed, intrigued. "Rubber shoes."

"They keep your feet dry during the rains," my father explained. "You can slip them right over your shoes."

"Your mother-in-law is very pleased with these advanced gifts from America," his father-in-law prompted.

"Yes," she sighed finally.

"Forgive me. These are nothing. I am so sorry that I have such terrible things to offer you," my father said politely, bowing as one should when offering presents. "The rest of the things are in storage with my family in Shanghai. We hadn't time to ship them here directly on account of the baby."

"Oh!" Ah Ling's eyes lighted up. "There's more!"

My father could not imagine how he would tell his wife about her mother. About her father. About this new . . . *situation*.

But unbeknownst to my father, he had already been saved from this burden by Ruth's aunt in Shanghai, who explained everything to her now that the baby was safely delivered. How her mother had been seriously ill for two years before finally in the last months she had been bedridden, relegated to a room by herself in the recesses of the family home, how her father had found this young uneducated girl to be his "personal maid" and how he had married her immediately upon her mother's death, not bothering with any traditional period of mourning. "It was scandalous, of course," her aunt said, shaking her head. "We wrote letters criticizing him, but there was nothing we could do to stop him."

My mother would cry until her heart was torn to pieces, until her aunt feared for her health, until she felt that she could not possibly continue living. She would lie in her bed in the hospital, where she was allowed to stay, thanks to her aunt, for three months after my birth. She would listen to the chatter of the nurses in the hall, the cries of the babies down the hall, the love songs on the radio that my aunt placed in her room hoping to cheer up her pale niece. She would wonder how was it possible that life continued just as it always had, as if nothing terrible had happened, as if the world were the same place it had been when her mother was alive, as if she were not dying from a broken heart.

She would watch me, her selfish baby. I would force her to listen to my cries, change my diapers, learn to bathe me. I would demand her attention even though her mother was dead and betrayed and she no longer wanted to live.

Until one day, she woke up, the sunlight from the open window pushing through a crack in the somber green draperies, striking her in the face, sounds from the street far below rising with the wind, an indistinguishable blur of voices and horns and cars and carts, all this human activity, going on as if she didn't exist. And Ruth knew with certainty that the moment she died, the world would continue to go about its business exactly as it had when she was alive, exactly as if she had never lived at all.

She sat up, pulled her white cotton nightgown down over her weak legs, and forced herself out of bed. The floor tiles were cold against her feet, like teeth snapping at her toes. She searched for her slippers with one foot, reached for her robe with one hand.

Now she was ready to get up. She stood a little unsteadily at first, a little dizzy. She had been lying in bed too long. Her mother had always warned her about sloth: laziness went against God's wishes. What her mother hadn't warned her was that laziness made the body weak, just when she most needed to be strong.

Ruth shuffled across the room to the washbasin, filled with fresh, clear water. The water felt like snow against her face. Its iciness made her feel a little stronger. She plunged her face into the basin and then stood up straight again with her perfect missionary-taught posture, facing the narrow rectangular mirror on the wall. She saw the blurry face of a young woman, dripping wet, half drowned.

My mother shook her head. No, not half drowned at all. Wide awake, alert. And very much alive.

From this day forward she would not cry. She would rise early.

She would exercise slowly, walking around the ward, regaining her strength and her composure. She would eat well. She would hire a good wet nurse, an honest-looking northern woman. She would listen attentively as the nurses explained about babies and modern child-rearing techniques.

She was growing stronger every day and I was growing fatter.

She no longer prayed for death. She prayed for strength.

Ruth Mei-en Tsao Chai had decided to avenge her mother's ignoble death.

9

THE SOUND OF MUSIC

Ruth and Winberg at
the Tsao family guest-
house, Nanjing, 1933.

~ *Winberg* ~

November settled over Nanjing like a hangover. The sky, heavy with
swollen clouds, threatened sleet. The humidity pressed into my father's bones, everything ached. He had moved out of the Tsao family
compound, at his wife's insistence, and while anxiously looking for
work, now lived in the tiny guesthouse that her mother used to rent
out. What he discovered was that no one would hire him. No law
firm. No university.

All my father's ties in China were to professors from Qinghua
College in Beijing, all his credentials were from a foreign country.
No one knew him in Nanjing. And a good connection, good *guanxi,*
was worth more than a dozen stellar letters of recommendation, better than a hundred American diplomas.

Finally he registered with the Nationalist Government as a private
attorney. He was given the proper certificate bearing the balding and
uniformed likeness of founding President Dr. Sun Yat-sen and a half-
dozen official red seals. He hung a large shingle announcing "Dr.
Chai Chu, American-trained Professional Attorney at Law" outside
the guesthouse and waited for a client.

He waited. And waited.

My father was ridiculously unsuccessful as a lawyer. He lost his only case.

His father-in-law finally sent a client his way, an easy case, open-and-shut, involving a property rights dispute. My grandfather was trying to make amends, trying to ease the tension. He knew it wouldn't be easy when his daughter returned. She wouldn't understand how he felt about her new stepmother.

So now he sent this client to my father, who in return sent his thanks in a formal letter, promising victory and offering assurances for faith well placed.

My father was excited to argue his first case in China, to put into practice at last the modern jurisprudence techniques that he had studied so well in America. Dr. Hu Shih, described by *Time* magazine in a September 1929 interview with the famous scholar as "China's greatest living sage," had said that China's lack of a professional, equitable, and blind legal system was the single greatest hindrance to the nation's modernization. China's chaotic, haphazard applications of its civil codes, now being revised every two or three years, its arbitrary judges, its graft-taking bribe-giving lawyers, its decidedly unsystematic system of courts that varied from city to city, province to province, warlord to warlord, was the single greatest excuse offered by the foreign powers for seizing quarters of cities and administering them under their own laws, trying Chinese under foreign laws in their own country while refusing to allow any of the foreign nations' citizens to be tried by China's laws.

"What laws?" the world outside China seemed to scoff.

Well, Charles decided he would show them. He would show them that it was possible to be an honorable lawyer in China. My father would win his case by studying the legal code of the new republic, by insisting upon the application of its laws. He would argue and win a case—all without resorting to bribes, to red envelopes passed to judges and police and sometimes even opposing attorneys, to cultivating connections, pulling strings, and wooing influential patrons who could put pressure on a judge to rule in favor of your client.

Charles studied his client's ridiculously clear-cut case of property claims. He studied every angle, documents, receipts, and business records for the sale and purchase of land and capital. He interviewed business associates, even family members party to the deal, witnesses to the signing of the documents. He studied the new civil code thoroughly. He knew the legal precedents, rooted out any possible loophole and plugged it, documented everything. He wrote footnotes to his footnotes.

His client was astounded by Charles's diligence.

"I don't have enough money for all your work." He twisted in his chair in Charles's office nervously. "It's just a small matter. Please do not trouble yourself in this way."

"No case is a small matter when it is precedent-setting. We are not just fighting for your property—"

"Oh?"

"We are fighting for all of China!" Charles concluded readily.

The morning of the court session, Charles took the stand before the judge armed with a small mountain of paperwork. Later both the judge and the opposing attorney would admit that they were both shocked and terribly impressed by Charles's diligence, his intellect and his honesty.

Not that any of that made a difference. He hadn't paid out a single red envelope in bribe money. He hadn't pulled any strings. He hadn't issued any threats—veiled or otherwise. Charles lost his first and only case spectacularly.

(My father never spoke to me of this defeat or his disappointment. I know about it only because of my mother, who told me everything, years later, when I was a teenager and we were leaving China for good, waiting for our visa to go to Taiwan after the Communist victory. She wanted me to understand their hard life. She wanted me to understand what had gone wrong in China.)

November waned into an unusually cold December.

Charles's books had still not arrived. Nor his clothing. Nor any of his wife's American purchases. He wrote to his sister in Shanghai, asking her to please hurry and ship his things, he was working now and needed them.

The reply came just a few days before his wife was scheduled to return with their son to Nanjing. Orchid's calligraphy began neatly, crisply, but soon dissolved into a turgid ripple of brushstrokes, as the news grew worse and worse.

"I am so sorry. Believe me, I will have these scoundrels brought to justice. I will spare no effort in tracking down these bandits. To think I should have trusted them, let them into my house! What if they had killed us in our sleep? I tremble at night just thinking of it. We are so trusting, we Anhui people. I am not used to the wickedness of the city."

His youngest sister made less sense than usual. My father scanned ahead, trying to read her terrible handwriting.

"They have stolen everything. I am so sorry, my brother. I feel completely responsible. I wish I could have seen into their black hearts when I hired them. The new servants stole all your lovely things from America! My husband and I went to the cinema, and when we returned, the new servants were gone, and all your boxes with them . . ."

My father's stomach dropped to his knees and stayed there.

With winter like a shroud across the sky, my mother arrived in Nanjing in mourning for her mother, with me and a wet nurse in tow. She found that her husband was still unemployed. All of her American things had been stolen from her in-laws in Shanghai, so she had nothing with which to set up a new household, nothing of value left from her sojourn abroad. But if she worried about these things, she didn't voice her concerns. Instead she focused on one thing only, her first meeting with her father.

"He will explain this to me," she told Charles as she sat on their bed, watching him as he rocked the baby in his arms. "He will tell me how this happened."

Leaving the baby with Charles, Ruth went with her brothers, who had returned as surgeons from their studies abroad. She was dressed in a neat silk *qipao,* one of the loose comfortable dresses her mother had sent to her in Chicago when she had written that she was pregnant and her clothes were growing tight. Ruth's brothers were nervous about the meeting. They had counseled their sister to perhaps wait a little longer yet, she was still weak from giving birth.

"Nonsense," she told them. "I'm strong as an ox."

Their father greeted them in the formal hall, Ah Ling at his side.

The meeting ended minutes later. Rather than being apologetic, Ruth's father insisted that his daughter, newly returned from America, should first of all offer her greetings to his new wife. An act of respect and filial piety. My mother refused, turned on her heel and stormed out of the room.

My mother did not visit her father again, but he sent her messages via the servants. He insisted that she pay respects to Ah Ling as his wife. He did not want his wife to be treated as a second wife, a mere concubine. He offered a number of honorific terms in Chinese for his daughter to use, including *Xin Po-po,* which meant "new maternal grandmother." He felt this was a modern term for a modern situation, and appropriate now that Ruth had a son, but Ruth was deeply offended. *Po-po* was the term I would have used to address her mother had she not died. No one else deserved this title. What did it matter if her father had added a "new" to the front of it, as though people could be replaced like worn-out shoes!

She refused to use any of these terms of address and urged her brothers to follow suit.

Her father threatened to disinherit them all.

My mother tried to visit with old friends, where she shed diamond tears, explaining her father's marriage, to that maid, the girl younger than herself, how they'd carried on while her mother lay ill, defenseless, abandoned. They nodded, sympathetic, but there were so many problems now, the price of everything had gone up to here and who knew what the country was coming to and at least her father had *married* the girl.

Even Eleanor was distant. Rumors held that she'd suffered another miscarriage while my mother was away. In her forties now (at least) and childless, she looked at me jealously, a fat healthy baby with strong lungs. "The Lord has blessed you, Mei-en." She meant, The Lord has cursed me, why?

The skin around Eleanor's lips was cracked with fine wrinkles, her forehead creased with worries. "I count my blessings every day. I must remember to be thankful. Are not even the lilies of the field cloaked, yet they toil not?" By which she meant, You have everything I've ever wanted and you're still not satisfied?

Eleanor had grown so old, a fallen leaf waiting to blow away. My mother felt a tightness in her chest, like fear. She could not bear to look into her old friend's eyes when they spoke.

~

The new year arrived. Banners welcoming 1933 waved gaily from every storefront. Strings of firecrackers exploded before every doorway.

Lying awake at night in the cold bedroom next to my father, who slept fitfully, tossing about and kicking at the quilts, my mother felt her confidence retract into a tiny silver ball in her heart.

She had never anticipated that four years would be so long. She'd returned to her city to find her homeland a strange, incomprehensible place.

Her mother had walked this earth like an angel of mercy, giving her money, her land, her time, her life for the poor, for her hospital, for her schools, and now that she was gone, the world suffered from amnesia.

My mother could not sleep at all.

But when the sun rose in the morning, casting a cold blue light through the window, my mother knew that she was beyond despair. Instead her anger grew, a fire deep inside, crackling just beneath her skin.

My mother put on a smiling face and with her handsome, American-educated husband she embarked on a tour to commemorate her return to Nanjing. The prodigy, one of the Eight Female Geniuses herself, Ruth Mei-en Tsao Chai, took her son, bundled in thick knitted blankets and even thicker knitted jumpsuits, to visit church after church, congregation by congregation. I was more prize pumpkin than baby, immobile in cap and woolens and quilts, but my mother wanted me to appear protected, well cared for, a treasure. She wanted us to appear prosperous and important. She wanted to build a reputation.

Predictably at each church, the women cooed and the men offered their blessings, led prayers to God.

At her mother's own congregation, Ruth stopped to thank the minister and God. She brought a handkerchief to her eyes. "If only my mother could have lived to see my son. We rushed home. Charles was offered a very good job at Northwestern University, but I made him decline. I wanted to come home."

The missionaries nodded sympathetically. "It was not God's will."

"My homecoming is bittersweet," she said, ignoring her cue to stiffen her lip. "My father married to that young girl. It's disgraceful."

The men nodded now, wearily, and the women looked a little uncomfortable. Brother Tsao had suffered much, they knew, with a sick wife all these years. He had not meant to hurt his daughter. He'd given so much to their churches; he was a pillar in the Chinese Christian community when so much else was sand, they thought.

A pillar and a bankbook, my mother thought. They obviously knew who still controlled the family fortune.

She understood at once, everything. How this situation had come to pass. How no one had written to her. How no one had wanted to cross her father. Of course they wouldn't speak out against him now when they should have spoken earlier, before her mother had died, after all she had done for them.

The minister cleared his throat. An ugly sound. "The Lord calls on us to forgive as He has forgiven us our sins." He meant, It is time for you to come to your senses and stop carrying on so.

This time my mother came prepared. She had conducted her own investigations, bribed her father's servants, enlisted spies. As a result, she'd discovered that his new wife was also a Christian convert, a Seventh-Day Adventist, and that her father had joined Ah Ling's church.

By 1933, the missionaries in Nanjing were numerous, and the Catholics and Protestants and Adventists and others competed jealously for Chinese souls. It was a bitter rivalry. Protestant converts were warned: join the wrong side and all chances of salvation were dashed. Catholics and Seventh-Day Adventists went directly to hell, the same as heathens.

"Of course, as a Christian, I tried to mend our differences," my mother said, choosing her words carefully. "Bend our swords into plowshares. But . . ." She dabbed her eyes with a handkerchief. "But I dare not call my father a Christian anymore. He's been converted by that woman." She paused dramatically, sensing the building tension. "My father has become a Seventh-Day Adventist!"

"Oh, my!" The minister's wife fanned herself with a napkin.

The minister jumped to his feet. "But that's a cult!"

My mother shook her head melodramatically. "I only hope my

mother does not know what has befallen her husband on earth. Even in heaven, it would pain her soul." She turned her watery eyes to the missionary and his wife. "Pray for my family. Pray for us, please."

The minister and his wife joined hands with her right there in their parlor and offered a prayer to Jesus to bring his lost lamb back to the flock. They offered promises and condolences as they saw my mother out to her waiting sedan chair.

"Thank you," she said, waving to them. "God bless you."

Riding home, my mother felt her energy return.

Every week now my mother paid the minister of her mother's erstwhile congregation to desecrate her father's name in public—although this was not how it was phrased. Rather, she referred to it as making an offering to the minister in return for "prayers for the needy," for those souls who were in danger of going to Hell. She wrote the list of names of her father's friends, her enemies, carefully in good calligraphy so that there would be no mistakes. "Please pray for my father especially," she urged, "so that he will be forgiven for betraying my mother when she was ill and for converting to that cult. Please pray that he will come back to the true path of our Lord." She pressed the money into the minister's hand personally. "For the church," she said if he should put up the pretense that he did not want to take her money.

My grandfather's name was now mentioned in churches across Nanjing as a fallen man, needy of saving, or at the very least disdain. He was shunned by the best families. He was subject to lectures by pastors younger than himself by a generation. He was falling like a comet, his burning tail between his legs. His Christian empire crumbling like wet cardboard.

But he was stubborn, too; perhaps this was the only trait he shared with his daughter. He wouldn't give up so easily. Upping the ante, he made plans with the aid of his brother to sell all his former wife's belongings and properties, thus disposing of his children's inheritance from their mother.

My mother's brothers came to visit their sister, bearing pastry and baby toys. Then hesitantly, cautiously, they suggested that perhaps it was not too much to ask, accepting their father's new wife. After all, their money was running out and none of their careers was established yet.

They are spoiled boys, my mother thought, appraising her brothers clearly. They'd never had to fight for anything before, they didn't know how.

"My husband's a lawyer. American-trained. I'll take Father to court. We're in the right. Father will see," she said with utmost certainty. "We'll win."

Her brothers nodded politely, noncommittally. They were both familiar with her husband's success rate in court.

Although they were fighting with my grandfather, my parents were still living in the Tsao family guest house as my father still did not have a job. It seems a strange relationship by American standards, all these sworn enemies living together, but it's an arrangement that has persisted for centuries in China, families who don't get along but still live together. Perhaps they all hoped some compromise would materialize, saving them. However, this new turn of events made my mother realize that she would have to leave, and that meant it was time to find work for my father. She'd heard that her former professor from National Central University was an important official in the Legislative Yuan, and it was high time to pay him a visit, show off her son. Time to work the connections and get her husband a job.

They were rushed on this damp winter morning, my father combing water through his unruly hair, my mother trying to complete her toilet so that she did not look so harried, so tired, so unsuccessful. It was a new season, time for new tactics.

They were quite an entourage for a chilly day, my mother in her best fur coat, my father in his thick scholar's robe, their baby dressed in seven layers of hand-knit clothing and bright quilts. Arriving at her professor's home, they were escorted to a lovely room with an upholstered sofa and polished end tables, steaming cups of tea, plates of *guazi* watermelon seeds. My mother regaled her professor and his wife with tales of life in America and their adventure home on the ocean liner, the theft of all their American things—including gifts for her professor, she noted sadly. She did not mention at this juncture the family problems. She did, however, add that her husband had had difficulty finding work. People are so prejudiced, so backward, a foreign degree, foreign references, they don't understand what a scholar, what a treasure he is for China, she sighed.

Her professor agreed and, on the spot, offered my father a position as a law specialist in his department, to work on drafting the new Chinese Constitution.

This was the way things were done in China.

The family dispute continued through the rainy spring and steamy summer before finally coming to a head nearly eight months after it had begun.

August 18, 1933, my mother filed a legal notice drafted by my father in the most important and widely read newspaper in the capital, the *Central Daily News*. It was a large notice, on the front page, her name and the names of her brothers in boldface twice, at the beginning and the end. Expensive, but worth it. There for everyone to see.

> Tsao Shou-tao, Tsao Shou-li, and Tsao Mei-en announce:
> Regarding the Nanjing properties—Envisioning Virtue Hall and Establishing Righteousness Hall—the majority belonged to our late mother, Ms. Shao, as the fruit of her lifelong labor and management. Now certain parties, including our uncle and father, have secretly occupied and divided these properties without considering our late mother Ms. Shao's portion in their divisional procedures. These actions are all unacceptable. Now, according to Shou-tao and the other aforementioned parties, we propose a redivision of these properties that would be acceptable. Therefore, we declare that any transfer or sale of said properties before resolution of this matter will be null and void.

It was a bold move. The laws protecting property were new, the civil law code was revised every few years, and a woman's claim to property was a dicey affair. But my father, a specialist in the Legislative Yuan with a powerful patron behind him, was now in a favorable position to argue a novel case. And my mother's decision to go public early proved successful.

No one wanted to be embroiled in a messy lawsuit. No one dared try to buy my grandmother's properties now. My mother's inheritance was safe.

~

My grandfather could feel the condescension when he walked into rooms with rich men and rich sons, they looked at him, smiling and nodding, laughing behind their long beards, laughing into their sleeves. It was as if he'd made nothing of his life, the college, the Big Plans. All his friends found excuses not to come to visit, they sent him cards for his health, explaining they would have invited him to such and such party, meeting, gathering, but of course they were concerned for his health and didn't want to tire him. Of course. There was laughter hidden in their brushstrokes that only his sharp eyes could see.

Everything had gone to rot because of his spoiled daughter.

My grandfather was an old man when his world crumbled. He was suffering from a variety of ailments. I can almost sympathize. He never loved his first wife in most likelihood. Everything was arranged by their families. But he'd let her do as she pleased, run her schools and her hospital. He'd let her raise their daughter the way she wanted. He'd done his duty, hadn't he? It wasn't his fault his wife had become too sick to look after him anymore. He could have kept the second girl as a concubine, as a maid. Who would have objected? Who would have cared? But he'd done the modern thing. He'd married her. He'd even converted to her religion. A good husband twice. And he'd been a good father, hadn't he? He'd educated his children, they were all important people now, surgeons and foreign-degree holders. He should be enjoying his longevity. He'd done everything right. Wasn't he an honorable man? Hadn't he founded the first Christian college of Nanjing? Whose land was it sitting on after all? Yet no one smiled at him, no one important came to call.

And what of Ah Ling, the wicked stepmother? In another story, the kind with fairy godmothers and glass slippers, she might have been the heroine.

She was a maid with no education and the master had married her. *Her* of all people! A real-life Cinderella. Her fairy-tale life should have had a happy ending. But the prince was old, no longer handsome, suffering from a variety of ailments. His children were grown, older than she, and they hated her. Now less than a year into the marriage, Cinderella had discovered that the prince's money wasn't his and that the evil stepchildren wanted to take her fairy-tale life away, and turn her into nothing but the second wife of an old, unimportant invalid with no face. It was the way her mother had always said her life would turn out when her parents first decided to sell her as a maid.

There's a lot to pity when I look back on this couple, my grandfather and his second wife. They were caught between eras. Had they lived a generation earlier, everything would have turned out differently for them. No one would have batted an eyelash at their relationship. A generation later, under the Communists, and his second wife's class background would have been a plus. But it's hard to know how to live when the world is changing so rapidly that no traditions have been invented yet to justify your life. In another time, theirs might have been a happy story, a love story even.

Unfortunately, tragically besotted with his new love, my grandfather had forgotten that his children had loved their mother, even if he had not, and that they could not replace her in their own hearts so easily.

My grandfather agreed finally to give my mother and her brothers their inheritance as promised by their mother, his first wife. All of it. In cash and land deeds. She had won. But only if his daughter agreed that she would stop harassing him. She didn't have to call his new wife "New Mother" or "New Grandmother" or any of that. She need never visit his house again. He just wanted to be left in peace. If she agreed, he would give her—and her brothers—everything she wanted.

But what Ruth wanted was her mother back, and that of course was impossible.

She took her inheritance.

~ *May-lee* ~

One Saturday when I was a little girl, my father took the whole family to Radio City Music Hall to see the world-famous Rockettes and a movie on the big screen, *The Sound of Music*. My brother and I hummed happily along as Julie Andrews, the singing nun, frolicked with all those children through the orchards, melting the icy heart of Captain Christopher Plummer. There on the giant screen love conquered all, more powerful than even the Nazis. Life *was* better in the movies, especially when the film was in color and a musical.

But my grandparents were grumbling; their heads bent together, they clicked their dentures, a sign of distress. Nai-nai wiped her eyes with an embroidered handkerchief. Ye-ye sighed loudly as he patted her shoulder.

"What a terrible movie," they said afterward.

Because once again, the heartless world watched as a much older man married the maid, not much older than his children. His intended fiancée—the baroness, a mature woman of education and culture—was left faceless, eyes glistening with tears, abandoned on a balcony while the dishonorable captain lusted after, of all things, a nun.

A terrible man.

Nai-nai would never understand how anyone could enjoy watching such a thing. My grandparents shook their heads all the way to Ninety-third Street where we were meeting my uncles for dinner at Happy Family.

"Nobody likes an older woman," she said, pursing her lips. Then she cried all the way across town in the backseat of our Buick.

10

DREAM HOUSE

Ruth and Winberg in front of the house she built from her inheritance, around 1934.

~ May-lee ~

With her inheritance, my grandmother set about building a house. Not just any house, but the perfect home, the foundation for the rest of her life. Modern. Western. Two stories in brick, durable, with indoor plumbing and running water and heat in every room. In fact, the house resembled her college dormitory, Ferncliff. Most importantly, it was nothing like her family's compound, no single-story rooms clustered around an open courtyard, cold and damp. The past is past, she seemed to be declaring. A new house for a new life.

Four years later during the Japanese occupation of Nanjing, Japanese officers were stationed in her dream house. They didn't bother with maintenance, the plumbing and the heating were ruined, holes in the roof, the garden turned to dirt, rooms trashed. However, the house was still standing when the family made it back to their city after the war, which is better than can be said for most homes after the occupation. Unfortunately, just before my grandmother returned in 1945, her eldest brother rented her house to a White Russian, who turned it into a brothel. My grandmother would stare in dismay as young women, and some not-so-young women, leaned from the windows, smoking, while the Russian waved his copy of the lease at my grandfather, refusing to vacate. It took my grandfather's entire class of law students, carrying placards that read "Down with Foreign Imperialism" and "Victory for China," to rush in the front doors and physically carry out the girls and their pimp before my father's family could live in their house again, eight years after they'd fled Nanjing. After my grandmother had the worst damage repaired, everyone admitted that it was still quite a nice house. It was to my father's disappointment that she rented it for more than a billion (highly inflated) Chinese dollars[1] to the Americans now flooding the city as advisors to the new Chinese republic, and he never lived in it again.

All my childhood, I'd heard of this miracle house, the best house in the world, my grandmother's modern, American-style brick dream house.

A generation later in 1985, my father and I returned to Nanjing and found my grandmother's house, still standing, though the neighborhood was a bit rundown, tin-roofed shanties and squatters' shacks lining the twisting alley that led to the front gate. I was expecting the palace of my father's memories, but instead we found a long narrow brick house, now sooty-gray and dilapidated, with two brick columns that must have been imposing once but that now seemed merely in need of supports.

My father shouted now into the air, in Chinese and English, at the top of his lungs, "You've ruined everything! Everything is dirt! Everything is poor! The country is poor! You've ruined China! The Communists have ruined everything!" He shouted over and over, until his head turned an unhealthy crimson and his entire body was covered with sweat.

Because his mother's dream house, his childhood home, had been found and was nothing like he remembered.

---

[1] With the Chinese yuan devaluating daily, this amount could be the equivalent of either a few hundred dollars to a few thousand U.S. dollars today.

~ *Winberg* ~

The house I remember was as grand as the life of the family that once inhabited it. In 1933, when I was one, my father was drafting the new civil code for the republic, trying to remake the Chinese legal system with which he had become so disastrously acquainted. My mother was the principal of an elementary school. For a moment, my parents believed their troubles were behind them. They thought they could concentrate on the great task of saving China, of reforming their country, all these ideals they still cherished.

Then the in-laws came.

Charles's father and youngest sister, Orchid, arrived, ready to move into Charles's brand-new two-story house, so big, plenty of room for everybody all together, the way family was meant to be. They brought luggage, their own servants, and attitude. They installed themselves in the guest bedrooms, they filtered into every room. They bossed everyone around until even the servants complained to Ruth.

Ruth returned home one evening to discover her sister-in-law in her bedroom, sorting through her clothes.

"What are you doing?"

The young woman ignored her as she lifted a jade bracelet up to the light, checking for imperfections.

Ruth strode up behind her and grabbed her by the arm. "That's mine." She tried to snatch it out of her sister-in-law's hand. Orchid shrugged and let it slip to the floor with a clatter.

"Stop that!" Ruth knelt to recover her bracelet.

Her sister-in-law turned quickly and walked into the hall.

Quickly Ruth inspected her dresser to see if anything was missing. Her new green silk cheongsam was gone, two embroidered sweaters, the black jacket with silk chrysanthemums woven into the fabric. One pair of shoes was not on the shelf where she thought she'd left them. Ruth ran to the hall.

"Where are my shoes?"

Her father-in-law hobbled out of his room now. "What's all this shouting? I'm trying to take my nap! Some people go to America and come back, forget who they are, think they're all Americans now!"

"Orchid, where are you?" She turned to the old man. "Is your daughter in there?"

He retreated back into his room, slamming the door behind him.

Ruth pounded on the wood. "Orchid, are you in there? Come out this instant!"

Somewhere she thought she heard laughter. Ruth ran downstairs now in search of the maid. Why had she let that woman into her room?

"Xiao Li, where are you?"

But her maid was nowhere to be found. The Chais' maid from Shanghai was standing in the kitchen door, watching her with narrowed eyes.

"Where is Xiao Li?"

The girl made no effort to respond.

"If you are going to stay in my house, you will answer when spoken to. Have you seen Xiao Li?"

This time the girl said something, but in Shanghai dialect, completely unintelligible to Ruth.

Ruth returned to her room and inspected her dresser more carefully. A necklace missing, the one with the pendant shaped like a vase. And a white silk scarf. She inspected Charles's dresser next. Everything seemed to be in order there. A door in the hall opened, followed by the click-click-click of heels.

"Orchid!" Ruth ran out only to catch a glimpse of her sister-in-law sneaking down the hall toward her room. Ruth chased after her, but Orchid slipped inside and slammed the door shut quickly. Grabbing the knob, Ruth pushed against the door forcefully, but her sister-in-law had wedged herself and possibly a piece of furniture against it on the other side. "Open up! This is my house! What do you think you're doing!" But the door remained shut.

"When your son comes home, tell him I want to speak to him immediately," Ruth shouted down the hall to her father-in-law as she returned to her room. She slammed the door behind her. The pictures on the wall shook like so many knees knocking.

She heard a door open and her father-in-law shouted now, "A daughter-in-law should know her place!" The door slammed shut with a firecracker bang.

Another door opened. "When my brother comes home," a shrill voice yapped, "tell him I want to see him immediately." Slam.

Ruth considered shouting back at them, but sat instead on the edge of the bed. It had been a long day. She'd had to discipline several students who'd gotten into a fight. The parents complained. One man threatened to take the case to higher authorities. She threatened to expel his son, a bad influence on the other children.

"He must have picked it up at your school," the man had said, incredibly.

"This is the final warning." Ruth had remained calm. "One more incident and I will expel him. Now you may take him home."

The man had had nothing more to say, but the look he had given her promised trouble to come. No wonder his child was so ill-mannered, a father like that.

Ruth lay back against the soft covers. Somewhere below her, the baby was crying. She could hear his wails through the floor, a faint echolike sound of pure misery. I feel exactly the same way, she thought, hugging her arms around herself. She tried to burrow deeper into the sheets. Then suddenly she sat up. The quilt! That little thief had taken the quilt off her bed!

Charles returned by rickshaw to find the house in a state of war.

Ruth refused to come out of her bedroom until Charles had "talked" to his family. The shouting echoed down the hall. Charles stumbled back to the bedroom, hoarse and sweating.

"My father says I'm unfilial. I tried to explain we're not a traditional household—"

"Did he tell you his daughter stole from my room?"

"Orchid doesn't mean to cause trouble. She's just very old-fashioned. She thinks everybody's things are all family property. I explained to her we're a modern couple." Charles slumped against his wife, his skin damp, his body limp and humid. "I argued with my father. He said I was stabbing him. Each word was a knifepoint in his chest."

The scoundrel knew how to work his son over, she saw that immediately. But what she said was, "Thank you for defending me," and she leaned her head against her husband's shoulder and wrapped her arm around his back as if it were she who needed propping up.

"I tried to explain, but it's hard for him. He's used to the old ways."

Ruth nodded, squeezed her husband's arm. "You're a kind son. They take advantage of your kindness."

"No, I'm not. I've made him feel unwelcome in my own home.

He says I'm his only son." Charles sighed. "He refuses to talk to Huan. After Huan helped me to take the college entrance exam against his wishes, my father said he could never trust him again. It's all my fault."

"It's his fault for turning against his own son."

"He *is* my father. I promised him that I would look after him. You must find some way to make a compromise."

Ruth felt her throat tighten, but there was nothing more she could ask of her husband, could she? "So long as they respect the rules of our household, they may stay. They cannot treat any of us like pack animals, not my servants, not me."

"I've already explained." Charles's shoulders shook slightly.

"Then everything should be fine." Ruth was not used to lying, but she knew the truth was more than Charles could handle at this moment.

The truce was like a mine, like a live hot wire lying hidden in the house, ready to be tripped when least expected. The explosion came on a Saturday afternoon when Charles was attending a meeting at the yuan. Ruth was home with her in-laws, who still made no mention of any imminent departure.

Orchid was dressing for a party. Her husband's business associates were throwing a banquet at the most famous—and notorious—restaurant in Nanjing. Her husband was coming in from Shanghai just for this occasion. Of course, Ruth was not invited, not that she cared. She did not want to know anything more about her sister-in-law's marriage to *that gangster* than what she had already had to hear. Her sister-in-law liked to complain, but today Orchid talked incessantly about the banquet, the life she and her businessman husband led in Shanghai. "It's so quiet here in Nanjing. I'm not used to the provinces anymore. I've grown so used to the city. I feel like a native now."

"You should go back then," Ruth said as sweetly as possible. "Don't let us keep you from your husband."

Orchid ignored her and Ruth locked herself in the study to go over school financing papers.

Orchid spent the entire afternoon preparing her toilet for the party, feeling sorry for herself, monopolizing the bathroom and the servants. She couldn't believe the rudeness she'd encountered! Hadn't she played the matchmaker between Ruth and her brother? Yet they treated her like a stranger.

Nothing had turned out as Orchid had imagined when she was a schoolgirl reading romantic novels instead of studying for her classes. She'd married well—a rich businessman—and moved to Shanghai, the Paris of the East. Not bad for a small-town girl. She should have been enjoying herself. But her husband never had time for her, preferring his business friends' company to hers. (At least she hoped it was *their* company that he preferred!)

She'd come up with this idea to visit her brother, bringing their father, who was grumpy and hard to please. Let her brother deal with his moods for a change. How happy she imagined Charles and Ruth would be to see her again! She'd impress them both with her sophisticated, city ways. But her brother was busy, working all the time. Her sister-in-law even worse. When Orchid had tried on her sister-in-law's pretty clothes, pretending she was a professional working woman too, that selfish Ruth only complained. Secretly, Orchid suspected that her sister-in-law was still angry because her servants had stolen Ruth's American things. It wasn't Orchid's fault. How could she have known that she'd hired thieves? In fact, she'd brought to Nanjing one of the only things that the thieves had missed—a little blue scarf. She'd imagined Ruth would be grateful, but now Orchid realized her sister-in-law would never appreciate anything she did and decided to keep the scarf herself.

Orchid was ready at last at dusk.

Ruth didn't want to see her off, but she needed to check on the baby and left her study just as her sister-in-law was making her way down the staircase, bedecked like an ostrich trying to pass for a peacock. Then suddenly Ruth gasped. Her sister-in-law was wearing a diaphanous blue neck scarf with beaded flowers identical to the one Ruth had bought in Chicago for her mother. Ruth ran toward her and, before her sister-in-law could squirm away, she grabbed hold of the scarf. Incredibly, the signature Marshall Field's label was still attached.

"You liar!" Ruth hissed, twisting the scarf in her hands. Orchid grabbed at her throat. "You thief!" Ruth shouted. "You stole all our things from America! It was you all along!"

"You can't talk to me like that!" Orchid tried to pull the scarf off her neck, it was choking her now. She shoved at her sister-in-law with one hand, tugged at the scarf with the other. "You've forgotten how to be a wife, that's your problem. *I'm* always very obedient around my husband's family. My brother should divorce you—Ow!"

Ruth pulled her sister-in-law down the hallway now. She wanted witnesses. "Come here, everyone! Quick, quick! Thief! Thief!"

Her father-in-law, the cook, the nanny, the Shanghai servants all gathered from the four corners of the house. Everyone was mute, unable to fathom at first what they were seeing, these two women grappling down the hall.

"Let go of my daughter!" Charles's father rushed down the staircase, waving his cane.

The cook quickly grabbed a broom from the kitchen and now brandished it behind Ruth protectively.

"I'll call the police on you! Whoever heard of a daughter-in-law abusing her husband's family! I'll have you thrown in jail!" The old man teetered down the stairs.

Ruth gave her sister-in-law a final pinch and then let go. She pushed her hair back into its bun. It was too unbecoming to fight like this.

Her in-laws were both chattering, "like thieving monkeys," as my mother would later describe them whenever she spoke of this event.

"Bring me my son at once." Ruth nodded at the amah. "You're going to help me pack."

By the time Charles returned home, exhausted from a day of bureaucratic disputes, the house was as silent as a bird cage set before a sleeping cat. Two suitcases stood conspicuously alone in the hallway. He had just enough time to remove his hat and set it atop the coat tree when his father and sister swept down the stairs.

"*Aiya!* My chest, my heart!" His father clutched at his robe. "She's a demon. She's trying to kill me."

His sister pushed past their father. "I demand that you divorce her!" Her face was awash with tears, white makeup ran down her cheeks. She seemed to be dressed in feathers and sequins.

Charles took a step back. He wanted to run right out the door again. "What—"

His sister bounded down the stairs and grabbed hold of his arm. "Just because she went to America, she thinks she's better than everyone else. Just because she went to university."

"She's gone too far," his father croaked. He panted on the landing. "I won't put up with it a day longer."

Suddenly a door swung open with a bang. Ruth marched out of the sitting room, carrying the baby swathed in layers of blankets. "I'm leaving you," she told Charles. "You can stay with your family, but I'm going."

The amah appeared wearing a coat and a face like a hangman. She tried to pick up the suitcases. Ruth stopped her and handed her the baby.

One of the servants came to say the rickshaw had arrived.

"Good." She nodded at the luggage. "Please put these in for me."

Without looking at Charles, he rushed over to grab the bags then ran out the front door again.

"Good-bye," Ruth said to her husband. Then she turned to her father-in-law coolly. "I give your son back to you." She held the baby now protectively. "But I'm taking mine."

Then she was gone.

The silence that followed was like the terrible quiet after a bomb, before the cries of the injured and the wailing of the sirens. Charles sat numbly in the corner of the sitting room. The last rays of light from the setting sun slipped in between the curtains, falling in a puddle on the carpet at his feet.

"I always told you, a wife like that is trouble," said Charles's father finally.

Orchid waved her hands as if to clear smoke. "What kind of woman drags a baby after her at this hour? After what she did to her father, what family has she got left to go to? She's crazy. Who would have guessed? I never should have introduced—"

"A woman must follow the three obediences. A daughter obeys her father; a wife, her husband; a mother, her son. It has always been this way, since the age of the great sage Confucius—"

"You're leaving. Today." Charles marveled at the ease with which the words slid from his mouth. "You're going back to Shanghai."

His father and his sister stared at him in silence, uncomprehending. Then his father laughed gruffly. "You can't talk to your father this way."

"I'll miss my dinner party because of that woman. Look at me. I can't go anywhere now." His sister pulled at her dress.

"You have to leave tonight. I'll go with you to the train station. I'll see you off safely. I'll send a telegram to Elder Sister. Her husband can pick you up."

"What are you going on about?"

"Father, I'm sending you away."

Now the fight erupted in earnest. Many unpleasant things were said, or rather, shouted. Charles told his family that they were unreasonable, they were bullies, they were ruining his marriage. He told them he was sorry but that it was not working out with all of them together. China must modernize. They could not cling to the old traditions. His responsibility was to his own wife and child. His wife could not be treated like a daughter-in-law. There was no arguing with him. His mind was made up. They had to go. Now.

Charles was called an ingrate, unfilial, irresponsible, irrational. He was called a liar, a man who reneged on his promises, a coward. He was accused of being unloving, unforgiving, mean-spirited, and greedy.

His father proved he was not as feeble as he'd claimed, he could shout with his son, match him decibel for decibel:

"It's because we're poor. She thinks she can look down on us. She thinks she can boss us around. The daughter-in-law ordering her father-in-law around like a servant. Don't forget I sold my last *mu* of land for you. I have nothing because of you. I have nothing and you're putting me out of your house!

"Remember, it was you who promised to look after me. After your brother left home, it was you who said you would always be my son.

"You're ashamed of me. You went to America all those years, now you come back and treat me like a stranger. You're the one who's changed. Now you have cast your father out of your house.

"My only crime is that I believed you. I believed you'd always be my son."

Before he climbed into the rickshaw, refusing his son's company to the train station, Charles's father said they would never meet again in this life. And in the next, Charles would be sorry.

Charles thought his father was exaggerating as usual. He'd done what had to be done, said what had to be said, but he thought they'd be able to reconcile later. He imagined a more pleasant reunion—on neutral territory, where his home would not be turned into a battleground and his wife played as a pawn. Perhaps in Shanghai. Perhaps when the battles with Japan and the Communists and the warlords were over.

But he was wrong. His father would die before the war was over. Charles would, in fact, never see him again. He would never even visit his grave. And my father would feel both guilt and sorrow about this fight for the rest of his life even if it had saved his marriage.

But for now, Charles had to find my mother and me. The problem was he had no idea where to look.

At first no one would tell him anything. Not the missionaries who never liked him much anyway, and now that he was the husband who'd driven their protégée into hiding, they liked him even less. Not the servants who had all adopted expressions as neutral as soldiers. He was afraid to ask his wife's colleagues or her brothers. What would they think of him?

When the night passed and the next day, and he had still no better idea where his wife had gone, he began to worry in earnest.

The city was a maze of narrow cobblestone alleys, traditional compounds behind high walls, kerosene street lamps still in the process of being replaced by electric lights. If Shanghai was famous for its foreign concessions, its capitalists and gangsters, Nanjing was still very much a traditional Chinese city, where my mother's Western-style house was considered daring. University professors and Western missionaries were more numerous than businesspeople. It was a city that could close itself like a porcupine against outsiders.

My father felt like an outsider now.

Charles sat alone in his wife's dream house. For once the baby's crying did not wake him up in the middle of the night, he could have slept easily now except he couldn't sleep at all. He was alone. His bed was cold and empty. He missed the way his wife used to brush out her long hair at night then braid it in a single plait before going to bed. Sometimes while she slept, he'd stroke the end.

He paced through the silent hallways, in and out of his deserted bedroom, the baby's empty nursery.

Then he noticed the first clue. An address written on a slip of paper. By the time he arrived at what turned out to be her cousin's house, his wife had already moved on, but her cousin suggested that she was perhaps visiting a classmate. He knew then that his wife wanted to be found. A test for him. He liked tests, he'd always been a good test-taker.

He returned home to find that someone was communicating with the servants. Someone had brought baby toys and the carriage to his wife, because he found these things missing from the nursery. Finally, the cook admitted when confronted that he'd received a message to deliver them to an address not far from Ruth's cousin's house.

His wife continued to drop clues, and finally after a few days, Charles found her. He then explained that he had kicked his family out of their home, that he would never choose them over her, she was his life, would she come back, please?

And she did.

I have always been inordinately proud that when my mother left my father, she took me with her. Later, I bragged about this incessantly to my little brothers, how our mother chose *me* over our father.

She would leave my father once more, near the end of the war, when we'd survived everything and we were living in Shanghai, once again with my father's sister Orchid, and the fighting began again. This time, she'd take me *and* my brothers with her back to Nanjing despite the rumors that the Communists were poised to take the city. But I'd tell my brothers that this situation was different. She expected our father in Shanghai to agree to her demands, whereas that first time, when I was a baby and their marriage was still young, she'd had no idea really how he'd react. There was more risk when she gave my father back to his father and took only me as her compensation.

I don't know if my brothers believed me, but I know that this memory always made me feel special.

The aftershocks of this family schism persisted. Every night for the rest of my childhood when my mother tucked me into bed, she peered into my face and instead of seeing only her perfect first-and-best son, she now found traces of her in-laws in my features. I had the flat nose of my father's family, not the superior northern bridge. And in an effort to remedy my "southern nose," she'd pinch my bridge tightly between viselike fingers, pulling sharply on my baby flesh, trying to force my nose to grow. I whimpered and cried but she refused to yield. If I tried to turn onto my belly, feigning stomachaches and leg cramps, she would nonchalantly flip me onto my back like a turtle and hold my head in place so that she could pull on my nose. Later when I was older, she would encourage me to pull on my nose myself, which I did, because at least when I did it, the pain was less intense. Some nights she clipped a clothespin to my bridge, and though it burned and gave me headaches, she would not let me pull it off. But despite my mother's best efforts, the bridge of my nose remained low. Much to her disappointment, I did not inherit the Tsao family cartilage. Her first-and-best son was destined to look like a "flat-faced Chai."

II

SKIRMISHES

Photo commissioned by Ruth to advertise her new school. The banner on top reads: Nanjing Private Hou Sheng Kindergarten, Student Outdoor Activity Class, September 1936.

~ *Winberg* ~

By the time I was three years old, we were living the Chinese dream, or at least our version thereof. My father took pictures of us every few weeks. I am riding a wooden wheelbarrow. I am astride a wooden hobby horse. A fat-cheeked toddler in my mother's arms, I look directly into the camera lens, unafraid, proud, as if I could see directly into the future and my proper place in it.

Next door to our house, my mother decided, like her mother before her, to build a private school, which when completed would represent everything she had learned about a Modern Education thus far. The school was coeducational. The teachers, both male and female, would eventually teach math, English as well as Chinese, music, science, religion, and, of course, physical education. Traditionally, Chinese students sat all day memorizing characters, but my mother liked the American notion of building mind and body. She drew the designs of the playground herself based on the ones she'd seen in America because none of the Chinese carpenters knew what she was talking about. A tire on a swing, a jungle gym. Grass to run on. A school for children in all their aspects. She publicized her school with commissioned black-and-white photographs—I was always positioned directly in the center—and soon she had many students.

I was growing rapidly. Already too big for hand-knitted knickers and button-up blouses, I'm photographed wearing a double-breasted coat with a bomber cap, complete with goggles. I had a red wooden scooter, a wheelbarrow, a hobby horse, a biplane, a set of brightly colored building blocks, and trunks of other toys that I left strewn about for the servants to pick up. I had a younger brother now, born in the year of the pig, who was prone to fevers and who cried all the time. My father had a large guard dog that barked all the time and that I watched from a distance, a little warily, until my father showed me the complicated system of secret hand signals he'd devised to teach the dog when to bark and when to sit and when to charge.

I boasted to the servants that I knew how to control my father's dog and scared them with my daring as I darted on my scooter closer and closer to the sleeping animal. When I was just close enough, I rapped the dog on the nose with my shoe and the dog rose with a start, shaking himself and barking even before he was fully awake. The servants shrieked, too afraid to run toward the dog, urging me to come back inside where it was safe from the great beast, but I rode around the dog while it barked happily for the attention, wagging its tail, leaping on its chain.

My father's dog had golden fur that came off in my hands like pollen when I touched its muscular flanks. The dog smelled like the earth and rain and had a pungent odor all of its own that in my scrubbed world of the nursery and daily baths and doting servants I came to admire very much for its masculine exoticism, its hint of the large, uncontrolled world outside the hothouse my mother was building for me.

In summer at night when it was steamy still—whether there was sun or not made no difference, it was muggy the way only Nanjing can be, with a humidity that settled below the skin—I lay awake all night listening to my father's dog pant and shake its large body as it paced restlessly in our courtyard, occasionally barking fiercely, frightening off any thieves who might be tempted to try to scale the stone wall surrounding our house. The world was full of thieves, my parents told me, all of whom lay waiting just outside our wall, which was covered with shards of broken glass along the top, embedded in the mortar.

During the day, I admired the way the sunlight fell through the glass shards, casting across the lawn rainbow prisms that I cupped in my hands like exotic butterflies. At night, however, I would lie awake imagining thieves with black masks and long narrow swords. They appeared to me at night the way they appeared in the stories that Amah would tell me when my mother was out of the house. I saw thieves crawling over the wall, spilling into the courtyard like ink. Even as the glass cut their skin, thieves did not feel pain because they practiced a special kind of *qi gong* a martial art that enabled them to endure all manner of pain and cuts and bleeding without noticing them.

My amah had explained all this. Thieves who broke into rich people's houses and slit the sleeping people's throats, even the poor servants, and stole everything inside, including sleeping babies, whom they took away to their mountain hideaways and forced them to act as their servants until they were old enough to become thieves too. Sometimes, if they were very wicked thieves, they took the sleeping children deep into the mountains and sacrificed their victims to strange gods in bloody rituals that involved making meat pies out of little boys.

I woke up screaming with nightmares, but when my mother rushed in to see what was the matter, I could not explain to her what was troubling me. She told my amah to make sure I drank warm milk before I went to sleep and not to eat any fruit. She had read that fruit eaten before bed could cause stomachaches that led to nightmares. Amah nodded but was certain that evil spirits were trying to steal me away and only my loud cries could keep them out. While my mother was at work during the day, Amah burned incense in my nursery in the four cardinal points and placed mirrors in hidden corners, so that the demons trying to enter my room would see their own ugly faces and be frightened away.

In the meantime, Amah told me more and more stories about evil spirits that could seep under doors or hide in the wind and slip through windows and steal baby boys away to be their sons in the underworld where they learned to eat human flesh like all the other demons.

Still, I liked my amah very much.

~

By spring festival, when the year of the rat (1936) arrived to the beating of drums, to parades and firecrackers that shook the streets, I refused to sleep through the night, and Amah was allowed to sleep in my nursery all night again, rather than in the servants' quarters off the kitchen.

I was given red envelopes full of money from all my relatives and pastries shaped like fish and turtles. I wore a puppet shaped like a flying baby around my neck, filled with all kinds of candy—including snow-white taffy, sweetened watermelon seeds, plum pits that were both sour and sweet, and candied ginger that was so hot it burned my tongue and made my nose run although I could not stop from eating another golden piece.

My father brought home boxes of firecrackers from the big world outside our wall, and we set them off together, until my eardrums were pounding and the ground was red with spent paper wrappers. My father's dog howled for days, its ears aching from all the fireworks.

Then one day the dog was poisoned. In the morning after my parents left for work, the dog began to vomit, then cough. Pink foam turned to frothy blood as it bubbled from its mouth. By afternoon it was dead, all its limbs extended as if it'd been stricken in mid-leap. When my father returned home, he was so distraught to find his dog stretched across the lawn as though it'd been nailed to the ground that he carried it to the rickshaw himself and took his dead dog to see a doctor.

My amah burned incense in the backyard. She was certain that demons had invaded the dog through one of his ears, which had had an infection and which he had scratched at constantly the last week. She bowed in four directions, joss sticks smoking between her palms, as she prayed with her eyes closed. I watched from the doorway, my wooden sword in one hand, my toy rifle in the other, prepared for action.

My father returned to say the dog had been murdered, its intestines a sieve. Ground glass had probably been put in raw meat and given to him to eat, thrown over the wall, a common way to kill people's dogs apparently. My mother was worried and ordered one of the servants to stay awake at night in case thieves should try to break in, but my father thought it was the neighbor, who complained about the barking. If it was thieves, they should have timed it so he died at night; now we were alerted, he said.

Not all thieves are clever, my mother countered. Some are merely violent thugs.

For weeks we were all worried about thieves and it was hard for me to sleep. I lay awake, listening to Amah's snores, wondering when the masked thieves would arrive with their swords and where I should hide. I thought, first, under the bed, but I was certain poisonous spiders lived there and I did not want to be bitten. Then I thought I would hide in my parents' room. I knew the exact place, in the great armoire where my mother kept her cheongsams, but if I were a thief, that was exactly the first place I would look for things to steal, a lovely large cabinet like that, and so I decided this was not such a good hiding place after all.

Perhaps the warm bed in my parents' room. Maybe thieves would not see me between my parents. The wind tapped at the window with ghostly fingers while oblivious Amah snored heavily. With my blankets drawn up over my head, I listened to the bamboo creak of my mother rocking with my baby brother in my parents' room. I was jealous of the attention lavished on my brother, who did nothing after all but cry all day and all night from his fevers.

Finally I crept from my bed and ran straight to my parents' room. My father snored to wake the dead, but before I could slip beneath the soft quilts, my mother spotted me crouching by the nightstand.

"You should be asleep."

I explained that I was here to alert them that thieves were hiding on the roof, ghosts were tapping at my window, and the Devil lived under my bed with the spiders.

"Come here, Winberg." My mother beckoned me to her side, her voice a low and sleepy purr. "I'll teach you a prayer to keep you safe. Whenever you feel afraid, say, 'Now I lay me down to sleep, I pray the Lord my soul to keep. If I should die before I wake, I pray the Lord my soul to take.' "

Obligingly, I repeated the words, and although this was the most terrifying prayer I had ever heard, I didn't want to anger my mother. I held on to her hand and said instead, "Yes, Mama. Thank you."

"Go back to bed now. We mustn't wake your brother." She kissed my head.

I shuffled to the doorway slowly. I almost wished that the thieves would come tonight and kidnap me and take me back to their bandit lair in the mountains, then my mother would miss me. She'd regret she didn't let me sleep in her room. She'd regret she worried more about the useless, noisy baby instead of me.

As I lingered at the door, my mother suddenly called out, "Winberg, come back."

Joyfully, I scurried back to her. She bent over me and tugged sharply on my nose. I tried to squirm away, but her grip was firm. "Winberg, if you can't sleep, remember to pull on your nose."

"I think I can sleep now," I said and ran quickly back to my nursery.

In bed, I vowed bitterly that I would not sleep a wink, not the whole night long, I'd make myself sick and then everyone would be sorry, but I fell asleep almost immediately. When I woke the next morning, I was overcome with disappointment, sure that the thieves had come and gone while I slept and I'd missed everything.

By the time I was four years old, I'd grown used to my little brother, Di-di, who now followed me around the courtyard on his own wooden scooter while I slashed at invisible armies with a wooden sword. I was a general, my brother my lieutenant: I made him eat the leftovers from my bowl so that I didn't have to eat sour-tasting things that I didn't like; I made him pick up my toys; I blamed him for everything that broke. I liked having a little brother very much.

My parents were irritable all the time, however. My mother was expecting another baby, a little brother or sister, although she said it was not a good time because of something called "skirmishes." Apparently, the Japanese had brought these "skirmishes" to China and now they were multiplying, just like the rabbits that ate our garden all night long when nobody saw them. These skirmishes were a menace to the fabric of our society, my parents and their friends said. I imagined a flock of skirmishes like locusts eating everything in sight. I batted at them with my sword and taught my brother to shout *"Bandiaozi!"* (Scoundrels!) as we smacked the skirmishes down. The skirmishes were why it was not a good time to have another baby, my mother sighed.

I didn't understand why my parents couldn't order the baby to come another time, another year. My brother and I were fine as it was. I explained this view to my parents, but they only seemed more irritated.

My father had many friends visiting the house now. The men argued in the parlor, shouting about the Japanese and warlords, Chiang Kai-shek and the Communists, battles and concessions, air strikes and skirmishes, and the price of gasoline. I listened in a corner, fascinated by the excited way the men shouted and waved their arms and turned red in the face and uttered important-sounding phrases such as "The future of our nation depends upon . . ." and "The fate of the Chinese republic rests with . . ." and "The duty of the intelligentsia toward our society requires that . . ."

My father gave me a watch to play with so that I would be quiet while he talked with his friends about Important Things. It was a lovely silver pocket watch, the face inscribed with curlicue numbers, two delicate hands like compass needles ticking off the minutes magically, always the same steady rate whether I shook it, put it in my mouth, or sat on it. While my father was busy debating China's fate with his friends, I took apart his watch so that I could see the cogs and gears turning, exposed like the beating heart of a chicken, which I'd also seen when I watched the cook make supper. I spread the gears across the floor. But when suddenly the men rose to their feet and bowed their good-byes, I scrambled to put the watch back together again, only to discover that I had no idea where the pieces went anymore, and no matter how I arranged them, the watch no longer ticked at all.

My father did not get angry. He picked me up along with the pieces of his watch, which he stuffed into his pocket. "You're just like me. Neither of us knows how to fix what's broken."

One day my mother's eldest brother, Shou-tao, came to visit our house bearing oranges from the south and hard peanut candy. He gave me a wooden box with secret compartments for hiding things, which I found quite useful.

"Where did you find such nice fruit?" My mother was delighted.

"I have connections," my uncle said with a mysterious smile. Then he told us his big news.

He was dating a Shanghai movie star now. Well, an aspiring star. "She hasn't actually made any films yet. But she's being considered right now for several. She almost starred in quite a few really big ones." All the titles were similar: *Darling and the Devil, The Maiden and the Monster, Bittersweet Heartache of Spring,* pulpy things like that.

"I'm afraid we don't have time to go to the picture shows," my mother said politely. In truth, she would never think of going to see *those* kind of pictures.

Finally my uncle got to the point. He wanted to buy a car. Not just any car, although any car would have been impressive in Nanjing in those days. He wanted a Mercedes.

"How on earth will you afford it?"

"That's just it. I want to sell my share of Mother's land to you."

"You're selling land to buy a car? Don't be ridiculous. What happened to the rest of your inheritance?"

"This lady is very elegant. She's used to a certain lifestyle—"

"You're just a doctor. You can't compete with the Shanghai crooks. If all she cares about is money, she'll leave you as soon as she's spent everything you have."

(She very nearly had.)

"But Mei-en, it's time for me to marry. Both my younger brother and younger sister are married. How do you think I feel?"

"Why do you need a car?"

"She's going to be a movie star. I can't just expect her to move out to the provinces—"

"Provinces? This is the capital!" My mother was protective of her city.

"You don't understand. She has a lot of important friends. We can't lose face. It's very important to project a certain image. Her friends can help me, they'll expand my clientele."

"If her friends are so important, why is she still trying out for movies like *Darling and the Devil*?"

Her brother's lips twitched like a rabbit's. "Please, Mei-en, have I ever asked you for anything before?"

"Do you love her?"

"I'm so lucky. She's so beautiful. I want you to meet her. She's so sophisticated. She's so witty—"

"Does she love you?"

"Of course. I'm sure of it."

"Then she wouldn't want you to sell your land to buy a car. Of all things."

"Please." Her brother's face was white, he twisted his hands together. My mother had never seen her brother this way, not even when she discussed suing their father. "You'd like her. She's a lot like you," he insisted.

"If she were like me, she'd never let you waste your money so foolishly." But then my mother relented. "All right. Let me talk to my husband. We'll see what we can do."

"You'll see. You'll really like her!" Her brother looked as young as when he passed his entrance exam into high school and he ran through the family compound shooting off firecrackers though their father shouted for him to stop. It was disconcerting to see her brother turned into a teenager again, and a shiver shimmied up her spine.

This is all that I remember of life in Nanjing, our Normal Life, the life that my parents thought was full of problems and worries but that seemed at the same time so stable that we could imagine a future based upon it. We continued to think this way until the summer of my fourth year, July of 1937, when the battle that would become known throughout the world as the "Marco Polo Bridge Incident" changed our lives forever.

12

THE LAST SON

Ruth with Winberg
(standing) and Di-di
on her lap, Nanjing,
circa 1936 or early
1937.

~ *May-lee* ~

In school I was taught that World War II began on December 7,
1941, with the bombing of Pearl Harbor. Before America's involve-
ment, it was only a European war, not a *world* war. Of course. That
China was involved at all seemed distant, part of an endless series of
conflicts that had occurred in Asia for decades, a footnote compared
to the treachery of the day that would live in infamy.

But for my grandparents, as for hundreds of millions of people on
the other side of the globe, it was the Marco Polo Bridge Incident
that became the first battle of World War II in the summer of 1937.

That July the Japanese, who had stationed troops in north China
since 1931, were conducting maneuvers ten miles west of Beijing near
the ancient Marco Polo Bridge, which was strategically important
because a railway bridge linking the northern and southern lines had
been built next to it. At the time, the Japanese controlled all of Manchuria but they had not yet spread to the more industrialized parts
of north China. Control of this railway bridge would enable the Japanese to take three important northern industrial cities: Tianjin, Kal-
gan, and Taiyuan.

The militarists in Japan had been pressing the government to annex more Chinese territory because the country could hardly afford to keep importing food and raw materials and north China was rich in both oil and coal reserves. The end of World War I had decimated the Japanese economy, which had been dependent upon munitions exports to Europe. Then the American stock market crash of 1929 dried up the U.S. market for Japanese silk. However, the Japanese government thus far had been reluctant to engage in an all-out war with China for fear of international repercussions against Japan. An unprovoked act of aggression against the Chinese was ruled out as too risky.

The evening of July 7, the Japanese commander of the troops stationed near the Marco Polo Bridge reported that one of his soldiers was missing and claimed that the soldier must have been kidnapped by the Chinese troops nearby. Thus "provoked," he then ordered his troops to attack the Chinese position.

The Chinese troops fought back fiercely and, surprisingly, repulsed the Japanese Imperial Army, the best-equipped and most highly disciplined fighting force in Asia.

The next day the Chinese launched a retaliatory attack on the Japanese position but were beaten back. By July 27, the Japanese had mobilized five divisions, the Chinese four. On July 29, the Japanese began a bombing campaign over Tianjin, destroying the campus of Nankai University where the students had organized anti-Japanese rallies.

By the end of July, the Japanese controlled the entire Tianjin-Beijing region. However, Chiang Kai-shek refused to acquiesce to Japan, as he ultimately had been forced to do with Manchuria, this time vowing that China would "struggle to the last."

In August, Chiang Kai-shek ordered his best, German-trained divisions to Shanghai, where the Japanese had a marine garrison in the International Settlement, and fighting broke out immediately.

Japan sent fifteen new divisions to northern and central China.

In the ensuing battles, 250,000 Chinese troops were killed or wounded. The Japanese suffered 40,000 casualties.

Still, war had not officially been declared.

During August, the Japanese also began air raids over Shanghai. These raids would soon to spread to Nanjing, Canton, and twenty more cities in eastern China.

The Nationalist government in Nanjing ordered the populace of the capital to begin preparing bomb shelters. Officials even instructed the citizens to paint their roofs black so that the colored tiles would be less visible during a night raid.[1] By mid-August the government began staging drills: the shrill air raid sirens blared throughout the city and everyone rushed to find shelter.

Nanjing was in a state of panic, rumors rampant: many Chinese intellectuals who had studied abroad—as well as the missionaries, of course—thought that America would surely come to China's aid; others speculated that Chiang Kai-shek would be forced to ally with the Communists to repel the Japanese. Refugees from the countryside made their way to the city in ragtag caravans and set up camps in the streets. The only thing certain was the panic and grief written on their faces. Crime rose, mysterious influenzas spread through the air, soldiers from distant garrisons speaking unintelligible dialects appeared in the night.

In August of 1937, my grandmother was seven months pregnant with what she hoped would be a daughter after two sons. She was large and uncomfortable; it was the middle of another infernal Nanjing summer; she wasn't as young as she once was, as the family doctor delicately chose to put it. (She was probably in her mid-thirties.) She should be careful, rest more, try not to worry.

But the Japanese were preparing to bomb her city.

My grandparents decided it was too dangerous to stay in Nanjing and prepared to leave, hoping they could keep ahead of the advancing Japanese army.

~ *Winberg* ~

I remember the panic in our house in the days before our evacuation. It was very exciting to a boy nearly five years old. In the dark of night holding flickering oil lamps, the servants buried the family treasures in the backyard. They dug deep holes and lowered in the *Yi-xing* tea set, scrolls wrapped in oilcloth then packed in metal boxes, toys with jewels sewn inside, the good china plates, silver.

---

[1] Iris Chang, *The Rape of Nanking* (New York: Basic Books, 1997), p. 65.

Everything that could be buried safely was buried now in the dark so that the neighbors could not see. My parents trusted no one outside the family. Secretly, bags of money were deposited into the well in what they hoped were airtight boxes. My mother locked herself in her room and sewed her jewelry into the hems of her dresses, into the cuffs of my pants, in the stuffing of my little brother's quilt.

It was on our last day in the capital, with my family in a hurry to leave, when I decided to stay. The servants chased me through the house. I ran faster, I hid behind furniture. The cook tried to entice me out from under the dining room table with a sesame pastry.

I refused to obey, galloping on all fours on the polished wood floor toward the kitchen.

"Winberg!" My father snatched hold of my arm painfully. "I'll beat you to death!"

I was too shocked to squirm away. My father had never been rough with me before, never lifted his voice in anger. I was the first-and-best son. I was above reproach. I stared now in utter disbelief. Hands under my armpits, my father dragged me out of the house, oblivious to the pain in my heels, which I tried to dig into the too-slick floors.

"Ma!" I shouted, to let her know that my father had lost his mind, but then I saw that my mother was inside the sedan chair already, fanning herself and holding my annoying brother, who was naturally crying. She lifted the brocade curtain now so that my father could shove me inside. It was unbearably hot in the sedan chair, which was just a tiny enclosed box with two small windows on two sturdy bamboo poles. I tried to squirm out the window but my mother took my hand in hers and would not let go.

August was the month of stillness, the air boiling in everyone's lungs, but on this day we all wore layers upon layers of clothing, dressing for seasons to come.

Four newly hired men now hefted the thick bamboo poles of the sedan chair onto their shoulders. Others were carrying our luggage; some carried nothing as they would take over for the sedan-chair bearers when those men became too tired to continue. In those days, there were so many impoverished families in China, it was easy to hire men to work like mules. They were in need of a job, and at least traveling with a family, a fairly large entourage, was safer than living on the streets.

"Wait!" My mother waved her fan out the window.

My father and the rest of our group turned, startled, as if a Japanese bomber had just popped out of the clear blue sky.

My mother dangled a set of keys at my father. "I forgot to lock the door."

He ran back to the house and locked the front door carefully. Everyone watched him in silence. Then the sedan bearers readjusted the poles, the sedan chair lurched and swayed, like a great animal rising, and off we went as the men found their rhythm.

I watched from the window as we passed through the winding avenue outside the wall around my mother's house to the broad sycamore-lined boulevard that led directly to the city wall. It was as if the rest of the city were waiting just for this signal from our family. Now with each house we passed, each gate, each tiny wooden two-story sundries shop, more families spilled out, swirling like leaves in our wake. The streets soon filled with thousands upon thousands of families, also dressed for winter, all carrying crates and trunks and baskets packed to the bursting point, children, servants, parents, everyone walking out of the city.

We're lucky, my father told us. My uncle Huan was now the district magistrate in Anhui, he'd have room for the whole family, and Anhui was not so far away, just a few days along the river then a short trek by land.

My father said this at the very beginning of our journey, when he was still energetic enough to be optimistic.

First we traveled by boat, then truck, then by foot. I don't remember any of that. I remember my brother crying and my mother trying to sing to him as we all sat in the hot and stuffy sedan chair for what felt like an eternity, my legs cramping. I had the feeling that I was suffocating slowly.

En route my parents decided we should first visit my father's ancestral hometown, Jing Xian, to pay our respects to the family shrine, to bow and burn incense before the Chai clan tablets inscribed with the names of generations of men. As a Christian convert, my father was not supposed to believe this behavior was necessary, but with danger so near, he wanted all the help he could get, and if that meant appeasing the spirits of his ancestors, so be it.

~

Our clan temple was neither small nor large by Nanjing standards, but because Uncle Huan was a district magistrate, he'd used his influence to have the temple repaired and rebuilt so that it was now one of the most impressive in my father's tiny hometown. The temple was surrounded by a tall stone wall, its gate barred with thick iron locks, guarded on both sides by two red-faced Door Gods. Their eyes bulged, black beards swirling like snakes across their broad chests, swords drawn and lifted in the air. Their faces contorted into terrifying scowls like devils, they looked poised to jump from the door and attack whoever dared to knock. I held my father's hand very tightly as he rapped at the unobtrusive wooden door of the small house next to the temple. This was where the elderly male relative who worked as the caretaker lived.

The door opened a few inches. "Who's knocking?" a raspy voice croaked.

"It's me, Chai Chu, come with my family to pay my respects."

An old man with a round bald head shaped like an onion and a thin white beard poked his head out the door. He squinted at me, then my father. "Oh, look how you've grown! The last time I saw you, you still had a shaved head." The man had a very high-pitched voice, which made me laugh. "Oh, is that the first son?" He extended a gnarled hand with knuckles as swollen as ginger roots toward my face. I tried to squirm away but my father held me in place while the old man twisted my cheek between his dry fingers.

Now the caretaker unlocked the big gate and led us down a dark corridor, lighted only with candles. The air smelled sweet with incense and rotting fruit from the offerings set before the statues that lined the walls. A giant scholar Buddha with his second brain prominently set on top of his head smiled serenely from the shadows, as well as the Goddess of Mercy Guan Yin; the many-armed Buddha who could use his many hands to pluck up poor souls as they fell into hell; the many-faced Buddha who understood all the sufferings of man; and one portrait of several Daoist Immortals with bald heads and long beards riding a fish through the clouds. My mother had brought a small wooden cross with her, which she now laid on one altar, beside an incense burner.

"This is the most powerful symbol of our religion," my mother said.

The caretaker examined it with curiosity.

"I converted to Christianity when I married in America," my father explained.

"America." The caretaker set the cross back on the altar carefully. "All gods are welcome in the family temple, of course, even the Western ones." He grinned then, revealing a gold tooth. "The more blessings for the Chai clan, the better."

We walked past the rest of the statues, heading straight for the inner altar, which was so hot and smoky that I felt we were marching directly into a stove. My parents advanced side by side, forgetting me, leaving me in the dark hall with the frightening statues all of whom seemed to be staring at me. In the flickering light, I swore that a Buddha's lips twitched. Quickly I grabbed my two-year-old brother's hand so that he wouldn't feel afraid.

"Owww!" he whined, such a silly boy, he didn't know I was protecting him, but no matter how he complained, I wouldn't let go.

At the altar the names of all the members of the Chai clan since the second century B.C. were recorded, some names carved on the gray stone tablets that lined the walls, others on bamboo. Since the 1911 revolution ending the Qing dynasty, the names of wives and daughters had also been recorded, including my grandmother and my father's two younger sisters (and their husbands, and their husbands' titles) as well as my mother's name and that of my uncle Huan's wife. My parents now bowed three times before the altar, my father prostrating himself each time on the smooth wooden floorboards. Then they lit incense and, with the joss sticks in their hands, bowed three times again. Finally my father apologized to his ancestors for not returning to pay his respects sooner; he'd not been home to the family temple since he'd left for Beijing to attend college when he was a teenager. Now he thanked them for the ten thousand good fortunes that had come his way, for their most appreciated help in his studies, for his success so far from home in the foreign land, America, for his most fortunate marriage, for the most auspicious birth of two sons and a new baby on the way.

That was our cue to step forward. The caretaker put his clawlike fingers on my shoulder and pulled me to the altar. My father showed my brother and me how to bow. Then smiling, he showed me where my name was inscribed in ink in the large rice-paper book that held the names of the members of the most recent generations of Chais. He also showed me the clan biographies of the most illustrious members of the family, and how a book already many pages thick had been started for him. Finally, he showed me where the names of our family were carved on polished stone tablets.

"Look, very modern," he said to my mother, pointing to where her name had been included as his wife, as well as her academic achievements.

Of all the names on all the tablets, my father's name was carved especially large in an ornate style, with his title and educational background prominently displayed, because his achievements showed that the clan was strong in this century and the ancestors could be proud that their struggles in the past had not been in vain.

"Your brother hired the best calligrapher, he is so proud of his little brother!" The caretaker smiled.

Then my mother pointed to the smooth, blank portion of the tablet. "That is where your achievements will be recorded for the family," she said to me.

And misunderstanding, I pressed close to peer into the smooth stone, thinking that I would be able to read my future there.

As it turned out, nothing more would be recorded for our family. The war would scatter us all across China and then across the world, and then in the 1960s, the Red Guards would come and destroy the family temple, smashing the statues and the stone steles, setting fire to the bamboo plaques and the rice-paper books recording the history of the Chai family.

My father was much relieved after our visit to the temple, but soon we discovered a problem that no one had anticipated. In order to deter the Japanese army, Chiang Kai-shek had instructed his armies to start destroying the roads. Soldiers and local militiamen were using dynamite, and the terrifying explosions made the earth tremble. We were still nearly forty miles from my uncle's home in Wuhu. Although we had planned to travel by boat, we couldn't reach the docks anymore. Instead we had to hike for several days through the foothills.

Anhui province was renowned for its rugged beauty. Buddhist pilgrims for hundreds of years had trekked through its sacred mountains, obtaining merit by walking up the thousands of stone steps carved into the earth. A proverb promised that if over the course of one lifetime you could climb China's two most important religious sites, Mount Tai in the north and the Yellow Mountains in southern Anhui, you would live to be a hundred. But there were no such dictums to encourage us about the terrain we were crossing. Instead we felt as though we were taking years off our lives for every hundred feet we ascended. The men carrying my mother's sedan chair grunted loudly, sweat running down their backs in streams, the veins of their calves bulging, like small snakes throbbing beneath their skin.

As we climbed higher, the road narrowed into a mere path between pine trees. Strange bat-colored birds laughed from the shadows as bamboo creaked in the wind, a sound like a bridge ready to fall. We had stopped talking to each other, to conserve strength and because no one had anything pleasant to say anymore.

From the sedan chair, I watched the back of my father's head as he marched before our caravan, waving a stick at his side, like a child's play sword. My brother was asleep, his head leaning heavily against my arm. I tried to push him away. I could smell cedar on the wind, above the scent of our sweat. My mother tried to keep me from fidgeting, brushing my spiky hair from my forehead. I leaned against her side finally, trying to sleep. Inside her, the baby kicked. My mother placed a sweaty hand against her side, as if to tell the baby everything was okay, go back to sleep, but the baby continued to kick. A nerve in her back was pinched, she said, groaning a little.

The sedan chair rocked as if it were adrift in the middle of the ocean.

"We must look out for bandits," my father said aloud, surprising himself. He had not intended to speak at all. A sign of fatigue. He no longer had control over his tongue.

"What have you seen, sir?" Amah stepped closer to the sedan chair, nearly tripping the men.

"Nothing. I'm just thinking aloud." My father forced his voice to sound confident. Or at least, very loud. But now Amah was practically walking in his footsteps.

"I heard the Japanese will kill everyone in their path. Women as well as men. They cut the children up to see how Chinese babies are put together and then sew them back up with different parts inside. Animal parts. Just to see what will happen."

"That's nonsense." My father slapped a mosquito on his neck. A kiss of blood remained on his palm.

"A family from the north told me. Their nursemaid said she'd seen it with her own eyes," she insisted, her fear overriding her sense of decorum.

"If she'd seen such a thing, she'd be dead by now. They would have killed her too." My mother's voice was firm as it emerged from the sedan chair. We all admired its steadiness.

"She was hiding. The Japanese soldiers didn't see her."

"Then she's a coward who hid while children were being cut up before her. And we shouldn't trust a word she says," my mother said from behind the curtained window.

No one spoke again for an hour, and then everyone was too tired to speak at all.

Toward dusk, giant clouds unfurled from the sky. Within twenty minutes, we were enveloped in a sticky moist fog.

Then raindrops began to fall, at first with slight gnatlike stings, but soon with a force that was painful, like arrow points.

Inside the sedan chair, we listened to the rain fall in uneven drips on the roof, the grunts and pants of the men carrying the palanquin, my brother's cries. My mother stroked his forehead to calm him, but he continued to fuss. He shivered and huddled closer, making a soft animal whimpering sound, as if he hadn't the strength to cry.

I refused to look at my brother, so noisy, stealing all my mother's attention. I was sick of sitting cramped in the sedan chair for yet another day. I poked my head out the window. My mother pulled the cloth shut.

"I want to see!" I complained.

"It's too cold for your brother." But then she wondered if it were wise to keep all the fresh air out. Perhaps I would catch my brother's cold. She hesitated. For the first time in her life, she had no idea what was the right thing to do. I felt frightened.

And then miraculously, the road began to level out.

The men moved at a faster clip now, the rocking became more rhythmic rather than the uneven lurching from side to side. My father called from outside, "We're almost there. We'll be in town by evening."

My mother squeezed my hands with such enthusiasm, I cried out in pain.

After an hour, we decided to take a break so that we could relieve our bladders and try to eat some of the stale buns that remained as well as some flavored watermelon seeds that my mother had been saving for a special occasion. During our picnic, the clouds suddenly parted and thick shafts of sunlight fell to the earth like the columns of a temple, the sky a rainbow banner trembling above our heads.

A good sign, we decided.

But as the road took a bend, sloping between an outcropping of veiny rocks and soggy pine trees, the fog returned like a river over-stepping its bank, swirling around the sedan chair, enveloping us in a thick white porridge. The air was damp and hot, as sticky as sweat.

And then disaster. Two of the sedan bearers tripped and they dropped the chair with us still in it. My mother cried out, as we slid down the steep path.

"Quick, quick!" my father shouted, as the men scrambled to stop the chair's descent. Now my brother screamed unhappily, a harsh monkey shriek.

"Don't worry!" my father shouted ferociously. "You're going to be fine!" The men grabbed hold of the thick bamboo pole on the side that was in the air and pulled down with all their weight until the chair was level again.

My mother crawled out the door, holding my brother to her chest. She fell into a pile in the mud and lay there. My father wrapped his arms around her and rocked her as if she were a small baby.

After the chair was repaired enough for us to climb back inside, my mother held my screeching brother on her lap; unable to soothe him, she allowed him to cry continuously. But to me she said, "If you don't stop crying, you'll make yourself sick. And if you become sick, too, who can take care of you with the soldiers coming?"

I rubbed my eyes, but they wouldn't stop tearing.

My mother offered me the hem of her dress to blow my nose, which I did, twice. And then my eyes did stop crying, or at least they only leaked a few tears, not a stream each. I buried my head in my arms and closed my eyes tightly. The sedan chair still jerked and lurched as the men struggled to descend down the muddy path, but at least with my eyes closed, I felt safer.

And then the men dropped the chair again.

My mother lay on her side for a long time after this fall, breathing shallowly while my father bent over her. I could not hear what they said to each other, but Amah prayed loudly to God and Buddha, her keening voice scaring even my little brother into silence.

I don't remember much about the rest of our journey. Did we walk for a day or days? We must have made it to the river, reboarded a barge to the city of Wuhu. But I don't remember a boat, and for the rest of their lives, my parents only talked of the endless trek through the mountains when remembering our journey. In my memories we are walking forever and then the chair drops and my mother shrieks. Over and over this scene plays in my head until there is nothing but this moment.

It was evening by the time we arrived at my uncle's residence, a traditional compound surrounded by a stone wall and barred gate, dark and unfriendly, two iron and wood doors latched to two stone columns, guarded by two grim-faced men carrying guns. My father argued with the men for a while until finally one of them went inside to bring my uncle out.

When my uncle Huan saw us, bedraggled and muddy, he was too surprised to greet us properly. "It must be true," he said grimly. "The Japanese are going to attack the capital."

Uncle Huan and his wife were gracious, welcoming. He promised he would call his doctor in the morning to take a look at my brother, who'd developed a fever. We ate, we bathed, we were shown to a real bedroom, with a real bed with clean blankets. Huan apologized for the paucity of his home.

"It's nothing like you're used to. Not so modern," he apologized as politeness dictated. After our journey, we felt we'd arrived in heaven.

While the rest of us went to bed, my father sat with his brother in his study. He was still physically shaking, all his muscles trembling at once, too tired to sleep.

"So you've come back to Anhui." Huan poured his brother a cup of hawthorn wine to keep him from catching a chest cold. "You'll all be safe. The Japanese will never come here. There's nothing here they'd want."

"You've done very well. I always knew you would," my father said, not wanting to speak of the war just yet. "Such a big home, a beautiful wife." He gestured to a silver-framed photograph of a woman wearing a lot of makeup.

Huan lit a cigarette, then with a sigh, sat opposite his brother. "You're going to have another baby." Smoke hovered cloudlike over his head. "I can't keep up with you. Maybe a third son for you this time. One for scholar's glory, one for business riches, one to take care of his parents."

"My wife would like a daughter."

"Well, you can always have a fourth child." Huan jabbed his cigarette out angrily onto an antique ceramic bowl.

My father could not see his brother's face in the shadows. "Why don't you start a family? You're married now. No point living like a bachelor anymore. You're settled."

"There's something wrong. We can't have children," Huan said, his voice flat and even, as if he were discussing the budget for his household. Before my father could react, Huan waved his hand dismissively. "Don't worry about me. You're always worrying about something. Just be thankful you have so many children. You're a lucky man." He laughed, an angry sound. "Now you should get some sleep. We'll have plenty of time to talk later." He turned his head and blew a cloud of smoke toward the wall. "Remember, this is Anhui. Nothing exciting ever happens here."

My father allowed his brother to help him to his feet. They walked together in silence through the courtyard toward the guest bedroom.

Curled toward his wife in the soft bed, my father snored with his mouth open in a grimace, but my mother could not sleep. Something was wrong. She felt contractions. She tried to time one now, but she couldn't read her husband's watch in the dark. She knew about false contractions, they could come and go as the body prepared to give birth. But did they ever come this soon? Seven months. She couldn't think. She couldn't remember.

There was a wheeze to my father's breathing, something deep in his chest. She didn't want to alarm him, he wouldn't be able to go back to sleep if she woke him now. And it was probably nothing serious. Just fatigue. A false alarm.

Except the contractions were becoming more intense, more painful. She panted, wishing the pain would go away.

By roughly two in the morning, my mother could no longer ignore the pain. She slipped from the bed and tried to pace the pain away. But after several minutes, she only felt worse. She was almost too afraid to think what was happening.

She shook my father's shoulder. "Wake up. I'm sick."

My father stopped snoring for a minute but then sighed and continued wheezing. My mother pinched his cheek. His eyelids fluttered. "It's the baby. Coming," she panted.

"What baby?" My father sat up sleepily, rubbing his nose.

"I've gone into labor."

My father blinked. "It's too soon."

"I've got to go to the hospital. Get up." Then she curled up into a ball on the floor and began to moan in earnest.

By the time the rickshaw arrived at the hospital, her water had broken. My father ran through the halls, banging on doors, shouting for the doctor. My mother was crying out in pain, sweat soaking her dress, running down her face as though she'd just emerged from a rain shower. She was shouting too. "No, no, no, I don't want it! I don't want it! I can't bear it!" She panted, eyes rolling back in their sockets, like a mad dog. "God, God, I don't want it!"

The nurses tried to calm her, wiping her face, her back, her arms with wet cloths.

"It's your daughter," my father cooed, clutching her hand, petting it. "Don't worry. Everything will be all right. It's a daughter this time. I know it. God will help you both."

They wouldn't let him into the operating room.

He waited in the hall, on his knees, praying.

When the doctor came out hours later, blood in Rorschach splatters across his gown, my father stood up, holding his breath. My father couldn't read the tired man's expression. The doctor waited an interminable moment, as he wiped his round glasses on his sleeve, before speaking.

"You won't be able to see the baby now. We've never had a baby this premature, but we do have equipment. We'll do our best."

"My wife?"

"She needs to rest. We can't let you see her until the morning. You understand. But she's going to be fine."

My father felt the knot in his throat loosen. He almost fell down to the floor.

"There's no need to cry." The doctor looked uncomfortable. He patted my father on the arm. The doctor's sleeve was bloody, my father noticed. "Go home. Rest a little. You can't help your wife like this. She needs you to be strong. Come back later in the morning. Or after lunch. Your wife can see you then."

My father nodded. He was creeping down the hall, going to wake his brother's rickshaw man, when he remembered. He turned around. "Doctor," he called. "Is it a girl?"

The young man's eyebrows shot up. "Oh, I forgot to tell you." He ran over to my father, clapped a hand on his shoulder. "No, no. You're very fortunate. He's a son."

My father turned to go, but then he waved to the doctor again. "Please don't tell my wife. That it's a boy. Not yet. The disappointment will be too much."

The doctor looked surprised. "As you wish."

On his way back to his brother's home, my father could not forgive himself. It was all his fault. His wife had not wanted another baby. It was the wrong time. With the war coming. The Japanese. Everything so unsure. She'd wanted an abortion when they'd first found out, but he'd bribed the doctor, told him to tell his wife the baby was a girl, he knew how much she wanted a daughter. He'd tricked her into keeping this baby.

His poor wife. And the poor baby. Who knew if he would even survive? All this suffering for nothing.

Huan was waiting for his brother. He was smoking, a glass in his hand, his cheeks flushed. Now his brother's weary tear-lined face made him assume the worst. Jumping to his feet, he grabbed his brother by the shoulders. "I'm so sorry."

My father was shaking beneath his coat. "It's my fault. She didn't want it."

"Don't talk this way. What is it that you say? It's *God's will.*"

"And it's another boy. I promised her a daughter. After all this, another boy."

Huan directed my father into a chair, poured him a drink from an expensive Western bottle. Huan was not without connections, even here in the provinces.

"I don't drink."

"Think of it as medicine." Huan held his brother's hand steady as he helped him lift the glass to his lips.

My father coughed, then drank another sip. "Poor baby. Poor little baby."

"We will give him an appropriate burial. You must think of a good name. We'll inscribe it in the ancestral tablets."

My father set the glass onto the floor and dropped his head to his chest.

"Sorry. No need to talk of that now. Don't worry." Huan paced uncomfortably in the parlor, while his brother cried unabashedly, head between his knees. "I'll make all the funeral arrangements. As if for my own son."

My father looked up, blinking. "You think he'll die, then? The doctor said they'd do their best, but I knew he was lying to me. It's hopeless, isn't it?"

"What do you mean, 'hopeless'?" A dead baby couldn't be more hopeless in Huan's eyes.

"The baby," my father insisted. "Haven't you listened to a word I said?"

"Remember, you're tired. Don't get excited. So, the boy is not . . . dead yet?"

"I hope not," said my father miserably.

"I don't understand."

"The baby is two months premature."

"But alive?"

"Of course alive!"

Huan grabbed his brother's ears. "Why didn't you tell me? You're moping about as though the baby's already gone! What's the matter with you!" He shook his younger brother. "How's your wife, then?"

"The doctor says she needs to rest—"

"But she's okay?"

"Well, yes, but—"

Huan slapped his hands against his temples. "You've always been this way, so indirect. It's infuriating." He squeezed his brother's shoulder. "Don't worry. I'll take care of everything. I'll tell the hospital not to spare any expense. We'll pay for anything they need. I'll see to it that the best specialists take care of your son."

My father began to cry again.

"What's the matter now? Your son is fine. Your wife is fine."

"I made her suffer. She didn't want a son."

"That's ridiculous. Three sons. What good fortune for you!"

"No, you didn't see how she suffered. You didn't see." My father couldn't get the image of his wife's pained face, contorted and howling, out of his mind. "I've made her suffer so. I don't know how I'll tell her it's another boy."

"Listen to you! I would give anything for a son and you sit here moaning because you have three." Huan poured my father another drink but then thought better of it and drank it himself. "I'll never understand you." He drained the glass completely, stubbed his cigarette out directly on his polished wood desk, then searched in his pockets for his cigarette case.

"Why can't you have children? It makes no sense." My father sat slumped in an overstuffed Western-style armchair, his face swathed in shadow, out of the prying light. He watched his brother's back. "What if I give you one of mine? Could you love him like a son?"

Huan turned and eyed his brother coolly. "You should get some sleep. You always talk too much when you're tired."

"Could you love an adopted son as your own flesh and blood?"

"Don't—"

"I mean it. I'd give you this baby if you would truly love him. If he lives."

His brother was serious, Huan realized. He would give him a son. "The baby will live." Huan let the cigarette burn a hole in the sleeve of his robe. "I won't let him die. I'll go to the hospital right now. I'll tell them. I'll explain. This is no ordinary baby. No expense must be spared. If we have to bring in a specialist from Shanghai, my brother's son will live."

"It's in God's hands." My father's voice was a whisper, a whiff of smoke.

"We won't let our son die. Not after all he's had to suffer to get here." Huan ran down the hall to the servants' room. "Get up! Get up!" He banged on the door with his fist. "We're going to the hospital!" He ran back into the parlor. "Don't worry. I'll speak to the doctor tonight."

"He must have gone home by now." My father felt as though his body had turned to lead. His eyelids fell across his eyes. "He must be very tired."

"Tired!" Huan buttoned his long black cape as he shouted, "Our son's life is at stake! They had better have a doctor there twenty-four hours a day. Or I'll have them all fired! I'll have those incompetent doctors run out of town!" He adjusted his collar in the mirror, examined his hair. "Don't worry, little brother, I'll take care of everything." Huan disappeared down the hall. The front door closed with a bang, decisive as a gunshot.

My father could not move a bone in his body. He had melted into the chair.

During the next few days, while my father slumped from room to room, certain both his newborn son and wife were dying, Huan took care of everything. He brought in a specialist to examine the baby. He hired a wet nurse, a sturdy girl fresh from the countryside. He ordered his wife to prepare a nursery.

His wife sulked, certain her husband had merely found a new way to belittle her. First these strangers invade her home, now she's going to be stepmother to one of their brats? It didn't bode well for her. Huan threatened to divorce her—in front of everyone, no less! It was too much to bear. But she knew what was expected of her. Soon she was openly warming to the idea of an adopted son. She ordered everyone around.

Uncle Huan ordered and paid in cash for new clothes for my brother and me, many toys, any kind of sweets we wanted. Without my mother watching over me, I ate five candied apples on a skewer and twenty-two White Rabbit taffies and fourteen preserved plums, which gave me a stomachache for two and a half days.

"Your son is very tall," he remarked to my father. "I'll have to study your techniques for child rearing."

My father nodded glumly. He rarely spoke at all these days. My father was certain that the baby would die, and now he had raised his brother's hopes for nothing. He could say nothing during his brother's elaborate preparations for the baby's return from the hospital. He watched from afar, like a monk in meditation. Nothing changed his blank expression: not the excitement of the household, the fussing wife, the arrival of a wide-faced amah and the pretty wet nurse. All the servants gossiped shamelessly, but they, too, were pleased. The maids pasted red paper cutouts in all the windows. Every night Huan and his wife burned incense and bowed before pictures of their parents.

"Even if he does not live for his first month, he will always be my son," Huan assured his morose brother. "I will inscribe his name on the family tablets. Even if I have a dozen sons after him, he will always be my first-and-best son. I will never forget him."

Geomancers came to measure the *qi* flowing through the house and determine the most auspicious location of the furniture in the baby's suite, which was luxurious by any standards, absolutely imperial by the standards of Anhui. Yellow silk embroideries and scrolls decorated the walls to promote scholarship, jade flowers were set in the southeast windows to promote the flow of positive masculine energy, mirrors were placed in every corner to scare away evil spirits. Huan wanted to keep fresh flowers in celadon vases on pedestals but my father convinced his brother finally that the baby might be allergic to such things.

No one told Ruth about the preparations that were taking place in her brother-in-law's home. She still believed she'd given birth to a daughter, as the nurses had all been instructed to refer to the baby this way. "The disappointment will kill her," Charles had said to them, not understanding his wife at all. It was true enough that she looked weak, feverish, and anemic; they kept her drugged. She'd been split open and sewn together again. She looked like a balloon that had lost half its air.

It was true, Ruth was not feeling well. She felt weak, her body hurt, her body felt like a stranger's. She'd given birth in this provincial hospital, without proper anesthesia. She'd torn and been sewn together. In her moments of consciousness, she understood the situation perfectly. Why they didn't let her see it. *It.* She didn't want to see it. *It.* Not yet. Not until they were both stronger.

She couldn't yet think of the baby as a person, a she or a he. She thought of it as a tiny unformed creature like a polliwog, caught between stages. She longed to talk to the baby as if it were still inside her, as she had grown accustomed. She wanted to believe she was still a cocoon, a nest, a safe place for this growing person, not an empty broken shell with an unformed chick locked away in an incubator like a glass coffin.

As she lay on the lumpy bed with her eyes closed, the sheets smelling of bleach, the floors of harsh detergents and blood and urine, the air stagnant, Ruth imagined she could still feel the baby inside her. Her hand reached around her belly. As if she could still speak to the baby this way. "Hold on, not yet, not now," she whispered. "Wait, wait."

On the black screen of her eyelids the faint pulse of blood, a flicker. "Don't go, not yet."

The nurses came in to bathe her and found her whispering in this way. They assumed she was praying.

But Ruth was talking to the baby. So long as she did not see *it,* vulnerable as a broken egg, so long as she continued to believe in the baby's wholeness, *it* did not exist and her baby, whole and healthy, still waited, listening for her instruction.

The nurses talked among themselves about the poor crazy lady who talked to herself. They speculated on the chances of the baby's survival, so small, smaller than any baby they'd ever seen that hadn't been taken out deliberately. Like a kitten really, or a doll, not a baby, they agreed.

They whispered too, speculating about the reasons a woman from a rich household living in the capital would come here to Anhui to their hospital in such haste in such circumstances. She was dehydrated, undernourished, exhausted, sunburned. And everyone said it was because the Japanese were going to take the capital.

"Do you think it's true?" Gossip about the war replaced gossip about the sickly baby.

"I heard the Americans are sending warplanes."

"The capital will never fall."

"My mother is ill in our hometown. I only moved here because of my husband. He doesn't want me to go home."

Ruth ignored the whispering girls hovering around her bed, prodding her with thermometers and cold sponges and dry hands. She closed her eyes and murmured to her baby, urging the child not to give up, to hang on. She willed the baby to hear her and obey.

Weeks then a month passed. Newspapers reported Chinese victories, but refugees arrived daily bearing new rumors of villages burned to the ground. My family barely took notice. My uncle Huan prepared for the arrival of his son, my father prayed every hour of every day for the safety of my mother and the baby, and my mother lay in the hospital, hovering between sleep and consciousness. Everyone ignored me. Even worse, when anyone did notice me, they could only smile and say, "Aren't you excited? The new baby is going to live. So strong. A miracle!" As if that would make me happy. All I wanted to know was when my mother was coming back, but no one could tell me anything.

My fifth birthday came and went.

I broke a matched set of vases reputedly dating from the Ming dynasty. I threw rocks in the fishpond, teased the singing birds in their cages by letting the alley cats in through the kitchen window. I captured crickets outside, which I then released indoors just to hear them chirp from hidden corners, annoying everyone. Still, everyone ignored me.

Without my mother, I was but a child underfoot.

I wanted nothing more than to return to our big house where I was a prince. We never should have left home, I thought. Now everything was worse.

I was wrong, of course. Things weren't even *bad* yet. Our problems were only just beginning.

One day, cheered by the baby's progress, my father relayed to my mother all that he had arranged. How she had given birth to a son, after all, not a daughter, but not to worry because he'd taken care of everything. He explained how he'd convinced his brother to adopt this third son and how happy Huan was. How Huan had taken care of all their expenses, which were considerable. But especially how pleased Huan was to have a son finally. He'd treat their son like his own flesh and blood, she needn't worry at all.

At first my mother thought she didn't understand him. Then she understood completely . . . Her husband had given away their son!

I cannot repeat here the words she used to put a stop to that plan. But by the end of her furious outburst, my father had no choice but to tell his brother that they were keeping their son after all. My mother insisted that we move from my uncle's house. (I mean, my uncle that thief! That scoundrel! That bandit!) After being humiliated before his household and his wife—who now reminded him that she'd always thought this adoption scheme was doomed—my uncle insisted that no, we did not leave his home, we were *expelled* from his house! And he should have known better than to trust his brother's crazy wife!

Thus, we found ourselves in a small town in an economically depressed province with no means of support, nowhere to go, no family to turn to.

Now everything was worse.

13

FLEEING THE JAPANESE ARMY

Family portrait in
Hunan. Charles is
dressed in his soldier's
uniform as he is now
employed by the war-
lord General Hsueh
Yueh, circa 1940.

~ May-lee ~

Like my father's family, many Chinese in the fall of 1937 had hoped
that the United States would intervene in the conflict with Japan.
Certainly many intellectuals speculated that Chiang Kai-shek's main
reason for sending his best troops into a hopeless battle against the
better-equipped Japanese divisions in Shanghai in August was to
provoke a Western response in a city with a large international population. Still, although Chiang would lose 60 percent of these
troops—including 10 percent of his entire trained officer corps—he
refused to order their withdrawal for three months. During this time
the valiant "Defense of Shanghai" made front-page news around the
world. In America, Henry Luce's publications provided ample and
sympathetic coverage of China's battles against the Japanese, and
U.S. army officers stationed in Beijing also provided intelligence of
the conflict to the War Department. For example, Joseph Stilwell, at
this time a colonel, reported that the Japanese claimed to have killed

25,800 Chinese in the September 24 attack on the railtown of Baoding (in Hebei province) alone.[1]

But the American public was staunchly isolationist at this time, afraid of getting involved in a foreign war that they did not think would affect them. As a result, President Roosevelt did not intervene. (In fact, the United States would continue to sell Japan scrap for its war machine for a year and a half after the infamous Rape of Nanjing.[2])

While my father's family waited in Anhui province as the Battle of Shanghai raged, frightened families in Nanjing, only one hundred and fifty miles from Shanghai, also wondered what to do: whether it would be safer to wait in the capital or head to ancestral hometowns or perhaps some other inland location. Even Chiang Kai-shek made plans to move the government to Wuhan farther up the Yangtze River.

In preparation for a long war with Japan, the Ministry of Education on September 10 announced that a new national university would open in Changsha, the capital of Hunan province. The new school would consist of the three northern universities that had been taken over by the Japanese: my grandfather's alma mater, Qinghua, as well as Peking University and Nankai.[3] Of the four hundred thousand Nanjing residents who would flee before the Japanese arrived in the capital in December, many now decided to head to Hunan.

Changsha was under the control of one of Chiang Kai-shek's most trusted generals, and therefore was considered relatively secure. As the city was located off a tributary of the Yangtze, factories, universities, hospitals, and government offices now hastily packed their machinery and books and records and supplies into wooden crates and shipped them to the city via the river. Sampans and barges piled high with crates were pulled upstream by teams of hundreds of men, tow lines slung over their shoulders as they trudged along the banks of the Yangtze. Tens of thousands of refugees, including students and

[1] Barbara Tuchman, *Stilwell and the American Experience in China: 1911–1945* (New York: Macmillan, 1970), p. 171.

[2] Tuchman, p. 199.

[3] John Israel, *Lianda: A Chinese University in War and Revolution* (Stanford: Stanford University Press, 1998), p. 14.

faculty members, shopkeepers and government clerks, families and orphans, now made their way to Hunan.

Among the refugees heading to Changsha in the fall of 1937 was my father's family.

~ *Winberg* ~

Banished from my uncle's compound in Wuhu, we at first moved to a small house in the city, one room for the family to sleep in together, one room for the servants. Because my parents were arguing all the time now, I preferred to stay outdoors. Because in a house like this there was nothing for them to do, the servants had plenty of time to play with me. Some of the men were quite young, barely out of their teens, and we got into all kinds of mischief together. The servants taught me how to swear in different dialects, how to gamble, how to spit, and best of all how to eat the sugar cane that grew in the fields surrounding the town. Together we gnawed on the wooden stalks until we broke into the sweet center. Then we sucked the marrowlike pulp until our teeth hurt.

The servants knew everything. They traded wu shu martial arts moves with the locals and speculated on the progress of the Japanese army. The local boys told us scary stories, how warlords were kidnapping young men, just like us, to serve in their armies. Bands of thuglike recruiters came to small towns and villages. Sometimes these men lured you with the promise of city jobs, sometimes they offered your parents money, sometimes they merely kidnapped you, taking you far away where no one spoke your dialect and you were forced to be soldiers. Then you were never heard from again.

The young men were all very happy to have me along with them, a rich family's son, because they thought that being with me would protect them. Any kidnappers would see that they had ties to an important family, a family with money and connections, a family who would cause trouble should we disappear. At five years of age, I developed a very keen sense of my own importance, which never diminished over the years, no matter the circumstances we found ourselves reduced to.

Anyway, while I was thoroughly enjoying myself and our life in

Anhui province, my parents, on the other hand, were terribly afraid, with a kind of fear that pinched their faces and tightened their stomachs and made them grow old all of a sudden, overnight. They were afraid that we would not be able to survive here. That there wouldn't be enough to eat. That my brothers and I would fall ill. They were afraid that the Japanese might come here, after all. News filtered into our town slowly, and then it was hard to know what to believe. Chiang had vowed to protect the capital at all costs; perhaps they were too hasty in evacuating, my parents thought. They vacillated between options—should they return to Nanjing where at least they had friends and connections and the possibility of employment, or head farther inland because the Japanese were coming and no one would be able to stop them no matter what the generalissimo was claiming now?

Because my parents were afraid, they argued night and day.

One afternoon my father was pacing in the dusty streets, pretending to be thinking when he was really escaping the squalor of the small house and the crying children and his worried wife, when a miracle occurred. In a novel or a movie, such a coincidence would immediately destroy the entire verisimilitude of the narrative. But in real life, this is incredibly, miraculously, exactly what happened. My father bumped into a former high school classmate on the street and this man offered my father a job. Not just any job, but an important position. A life-saving job. A miracle.

My father's classmate was the brother of Chang Chih-chung, the governor of Hunan province and one of the most influential warlords under Generalissimo Chiang Kai-shek. This classmate happened to be in Anhui checking on family before embarking to his brother's military base outside Changsha. He was almost ready to leave, this being his last day in town, when, what a surprise, he bumped into my father. The two men laughed and exchanged pleasantries, my father spoke of the new baby, the classmate spoke of his new post. Then my father explained that, what a coincidence, he'd been looking for a position himself. And like that, his friend offered him a job. He didn't know yet what my father would do for his brother, but he was sure there'd be something. He offered to let us travel with his entourage to Hunan, where he'd handle the introductions with His Honor, General Chang.

So we packed up once again and traveled by boat, this time to Hunan province, a region known for its spicy food and its history of rebellions and insurrections and near constant warfare. Hunan's most famous general would become the Communist leader Mao Zedong, but at the time we knew nothing of him.

Here in Hunan the people spoke in a different dialect. They said *f* instead of *h* and vice versa, which took some getting used to. The tones were different too, so that words that meant one thing in Mandarin could mean something entirely different in Hunan dialect.

As we traveled along the river, I remember seeing the lush groves of orange trees whose fruit was destined to be shipped to America as Sunkist oranges, my father explained. The dockworkers carried large wooden crates emblazoned with the Sunkist logo, loaded them onto long flat barges, all heading downriver to ocean ports.

I felt somehow safer to see these oranges, these crates, these men and ships going on with business, the world of commerce continuing as if there were no war, as if to say nothing was so bad after all.

But in truth, China was disintegrating into a sea of soldiers.

Once we arrived at our warlord's camp just outside the city of Changsha, my father was awarded the rank of colonel via a gaudy paper notice covered with seals, including the warlord's, whose chop was larger than any emperor's. My father now dressed in the uniform of the Hunan army, stiff epaulettes and shiny buttons, his legs wrapped in white cloth, a cap with a visor on his head. It's a good thing, this hat, he joked mirthlessly, his hair was thinning terribly now, since our flight.

General Chang decided he wanted to establish a Western-style military academy for his officers and my father would be the head. He wanted to indoctrinate his soldiers with a new philosophy, a new approach to military-civilian relations. During the last three decades, soldiers too often viewed the villages they "saved" from invading armies—whether they be rival warlords or the Japanese—as the spoils of war. They looted, raped, and stole from the people. As a result, most Chinese were afraid of their own troops. The Communists had had much success recruiting followers in the countryside because they indoctrinated their troops successfully with a policy to "serve the people." Chang knew that the Nationalists would have to modernize their armed forces if they were to defeat such a well-equipped fighting force as the Japanese. Only by uniting as a nation instead of exploiting their own people could the Chinese hope for victory.

My father then embarked upon devising a curriculum: Sun Yat-sen's Three Principles of the People (Socialism, Nationalism, and Democracy), Dewey, Locke, Kang Youwei the great nineteenth-century reformer, Chinese—and American—legal theory. Basically, the school was designed to indoctrinate the troops with an understanding of democratic principles. My father's classmate from Anhui was very excited about this curriculum. He agreed that all this philosophy was *exactly* what a modern warlord's army officers should know.

A building was converted into a school, desks and benches, chalk and blackboards acquired. My father set about trying to put together a library. Sometimes he would copy out passages from his own books or else resort to his memory where needed. He sent out letters to former professors, classmates, trying to gather a faculty. He trawled the growing expatriate community in Hunan; as the Japanese army progressed inland, more and more refugees from the eastern seaboard arrived via the Yangtze. So long as my father was busy setting up his school, he felt pleased and hopeful.

In the meantime, my mother insisted we live in a village outside Changsha rather than in the city, explaining to my brothers and me that Changsha was too congested, too close, the houses too small. She said we were moving to a village to have more space, as if there were no war, no bombing raids, no battalions of soldiers preparing for an invasion.

As a young boy, I agreed with this logic completely. Why live in a city when we could live with fields outside our door, with a large courtyard in the center of our house, the sky for a ceiling, the sound of crickets outside our windows. I didn't realize that my mother was afraid to live in the city.

My mother had never imagined herself living in the countryside before, yet here she was, in a village outside a gray provincial city, off a tributary of the Lu River. The fishy scent of the paddies rose above the fragrance of the fruit trees. Outside her front door, the fields stretched like mirrors as far as the eye could see, the bright blue of the sky reflected in the water. She felt she had fallen onto a raft in the middle of the ocean. This was not the life she had planned for herself. She now lived in a traditional brick house, a series of boxes around an open courtyard, with a large lemon tree in the middle. The sky stared down at her head every day, unblinking.

Because there was no icebox, every morning at dawn she walked to the village market, her eldest son at her side. One of the male servants carried a pole across his shoulders with two baskets, the baby in one side, the toddler in the other. On the way back from the market, both children rode in one basket to balance the bundle on the other side: our food for the day, oranges and turnips, potatoes and leeks, pickled cabbage and smelly tofu, plus an arrogantly clucking chicken or a flopping fish. Hunan was China's breadbasket, produce plentiful, the markets a marvel. In eight years' time, due to the disruptions of the planting seasons from the war, Hunan would suffer a terrible famine, millions of people would die of starvation, and the province would become synonymous with death, but in the fall of 1937, we could not even imagine such a thing.

Just before dawn, I remember we set out from the house to the village market. The air was as still and soft and gray as the interior of a silk cocoon. Then with the startling clarity of a trumpet blast, the sun rose above the edge of the earth, piercing the sky. Pink and gold petals of light fell across the paddies, enticing the fish there to rise up, their open mouths making popping sounds as they smacked the surface, trying to swallow shards of sunlight. The shadows retreated quickly, seeping away from the dirt road, retreating faster, faster, like an inky tide.

My brothers were ecstatic. They chattered like parakeets in their baskets while I talked to my pet cricket, which I carried gingerly in a cage made from a hallowed gourd. My brothers and I loved the countryside. We couldn't have been happier.

My mother, out of her element, tried to keep active. She talked to the local schoolmaster, a wizened old-fashioned-looking Confucian scholar who believed nothing that could not be memorized by rote was worth learning. She discussed the concept of a modern curriculum, including such radical notions as physical education and foreign language study. She started to write a book on teaching English. Without anyone to practice with, she worried that she was losing her American accent. She practiced the difficult sounds—*th,* short *i, v*'s, and all the dipthongs and complicated consonant clusters—over and over to herself while knitting new clothes for the baby, called Mao-mao, who was still small for his age.

My mother asked herself what her mother would have done, what her mentors, what Eleanor would do, and she decided to open a Sunday school. She invited all the farmers in the village.

Curious, they came the first Sunday, bearing fruit and flavored seeds. My mother explained that wasn't necessary and offered tea and candy to everyone. She had set up chairs in a semicircle before the makeshift blackboard she had constructed by papering a wall. She explained now about the Bible and the promise of eternal life, the Father and the Son and the Holy Spirit, the Ten Commandments, sin and the cross. The next week only a few children arrived; they looked disappointed that there was only a little candy left. The next week even the children with a sweet tooth did not come.

Undaunted, my mother restructured her Sunday school, calling it "English Lesson School" instead. Soon parents were sending their children, dragging them to her door, urging them to study hard with a slap across the back of their heads. Happily my mother taught them about the Bible and God—but in English. They repeated all the strange words dutifully because everyone wanted to learn English. Even the farmers in this village—perhaps especially farmers in a village—wanted their children to have a good education, even if that meant a foreign education, a better chance for a better life.

When she told her students that if they studied the Bible and accepted the word of God, they would be born again, they nodded in agreement. But they were thinking of a new life in a big city, where shopgirls and clerks with good English could earn in one month more than a farmer could earn in a year and never have to sleep on a dirt floor or walk behind an ox, knee-deep in gelatinous red mud. But if she suspected that she was saving few souls, my mother did not for a moment lose her self-confidence, the feeling that she was doing exactly what God intended.

One morning we were walking as usual to the village market when there was a sound like thunder. The ground shook. The sky was perfectly clear, a pearly gray, the sun still hidden below the horizon. Then we heard the whine of the "Zeros." Japanese fighter planes were bombing Changsha.

"Stop! Don't move!" my mother called out. She clutched my hand painfully. We stood frozen on the road, crouching instinctively, illogically, as we squinted into the softening sky. We couldn't see the fighters, but the thunder roared again from the cloudless sky. We waited, holding our breath.

Soon Chinese fighters appeared, like tiny metal stars in the sky. We could hear nothing but this metallic dragonfly drone as the planes gave chase to the Zeros.

I thought of my father in the city.

But there were no more bombs dropped. The Japanese planes had left.

My mother continued to stand frozen in place, facing Changsha, as the sun flung arrows of gold into the sky, rending the soft gray silk, light flooding across the fields, every surface glittering.

A water buffalo careened suddenly from a drainage ditch, startled. By what? The bombs? Us? Something it could smell that we couldn't? He lumbered toward us and the servant set the baskets with my brothers down and chased the buffalo back into the fields with his pole. "*Aiya!* Get back! Shoo!" he shouted at the beast.

Laughter. The farmers had been watching this spectacle, the city folk scared by an ox.

My mother exhaled slowly. "Let's go," she said calmly. "We don't want Winberg to be late to school."

"I hope the professor's all right in the city," the servant said, meaning my father.

"Of course he's fine," my mother snapped. "Do you think the general would allow his officers to be hurt?"

We walked in silence to the village.

Every morning a "chauffeur" came from Changsha to drive my father to work, that is, a soldier on a motorcycle with a sidecar attached. On weekends all five of us—my parents and my brothers and me—squeezed into the sidecar, and our chauffeur drove us through the city, to go shopping in the multistory department stores, to eat occasionally in the fancy city restaurants.

Later our days in Hunan, in our village, would seem like a dream, like a hallucination. While others suffered, starved, died atrocious deaths, we lived in our village, safe and snug, visiting the city like tourists. If not for my father's uniform and the occasional air raid, my parents' anxious whispers, I would not have known that my country was at war.

But while we were living in our village, our beautiful village that smelled of fish and fruit, the earth and smoke from the farmers' stoves, red peppers and fresh rice, while we were safe in our village, the world outside was dying.

News filtered slowly into the provinces along with rumors and speculation. At first none of us could believe the news of the Japanese strike on Nanjing in December and then no one could deny the reports that were circling the globe. Chiang Kai-shek, despite his promises, had pulled his troops out of the capital, fleeing inland to Wuhan, leaving the capital's defense to another warlord. The troops that remained had barely enough ammunition for their weapons and no heavy artillery.

The Japanese navy sent minesweepers down the Yangtze, cutting off this route of escape. Tanks stormed the city gates. That the Chinese defense—underequipped and undermanned—lasted a day not to mention a week was a miracle, a testament to the soldiers' resolve. Many civilians who could afford to leave had already fled, but the Japanese promised clemency to those who remained, dropping leaflets over the city declaring, "Though harsh and relentless to those who resist, the Japanese troops will be kind and generous to noncombatants and to Chinese troops who entertain no enmity to Japan."[4] But once the Japanese entered the city on the thirteenth of December, they began a wholesale slaughter of the inhabitants, young and old, women and children alike. The Yangtze was reported to have run red with blood.

The worst accounts wouldn't come until later. They'd trickle in with refugees and survivors, with Western news reports translated in the Canton newspapers. Bodies piled a meter high. Tens of thousands of women and girls raped then photographed nude before they were bayoneted. Fetuses ripped from the wombs of pregnant women. Decapitations, firing squads, rape squads. Total war.

A third of the population of Nanjing would be killed during the Japanese occupation, more than three hundred thousand people, according to Chinese sources.

---

[4] *The Rape of Nanking, an Undeniable History in Photographs,* edited by Shi Young and James Yin, (Chicago: Innovative Publishing Group, 1997), p. 32.

And then there was the flood.

After the Japanese took Nanjing and began advancing inland, Chiang Kai-shek ordered dikes on the Yellow River to be blown up to keep the Japanese from reaching Kaifeng, and thus the rail line leading south. The resulting flood destroyed more than four thousand villages, drowning countless unsuspecting Chinese—farmers and soldiers and refugees who'd received no advance word of their government's plan. The flood kept the Japanese at bay for only three months.[5]

Because of Changsha's strategic importance—the air force was temporarily concentrated here and it was a primary depot on the river lines south of the Yangtze—the Japanese were planning a big attack on the city, definitive, and everyone knew what that meant now, after what happened in Nanjing. But no one knew where to go. Where in China would be safe? Our warlord decided he would do as Chiang Kai-shek did not dare, he would defend his city to its last man, he would do anything to keep Changsha from falling into enemy hands.

In the morning of November 13, 1938, when it seemed that the Japanese were approaching, General Chang allegedly ordered his troops to set fire to the city. There was no warning. His soldiers started on the outskirts and moved inward.

It was an inferno. From the village we could see the black smoke rising like thunderheads, we heard the faint wail of sirens, the roar of the fighter planes dropping water bombs across the city. Animals in our village seemed to lose their minds. Water buffalo brayed and ran through the rice fields, trampling dikes. The roosters crowed at midnight, the chickens refused to lay, a sow ate seven of her piglets, one after the other. It rained ashes for three days.

My parents spoke about the fire in hushed tones when they thought I wasn't listening, when I was playing with my cricket, whistling at the birds my father kept in bamboo cages.

"He's a madman."

"He thinks he had no choice. At least he kept the Japanese from attacking the city."

"Why do the Japanese even bother to fight us? We Chinese will kill ourselves fast enough!"

---

[5] Spence, p. 449.

"Everyone says you were right, you know. How clever of you."

"What?"

"To live in this village. I've seen the damage. It's atrocious. The poor people. If we lived in the city, we could be dead, too, or all our things burned up."

"Sshh."

"What's wrong?"

"Remember the children."

My parents whispered all the time now. I could remember when our house was filled with their friends shouting their views about Chiang Kai-shek and the fate of the Chinese republic and the character of the Chinese people. Now no one came to visit and my father returned from his institute every evening too tired to play with us, his face a mask of his former face, too tight to smile, his forehead wrinkled like crumpled paper.

The KMT official history of the Sino-Japanese War recorded the event this way: "In the morning of November 13 [1938] when a big fire broke out in Changsha, our air defense units participated in the fire fighting and suffered no losses."[6] There's no mention, of course, that the fire was deliberately set.

Not too long after the "big fire" in Changsha, General Chang was replaced by a new warlord named Hsueh Yueh. My father was worried; perhaps with his connection gone, his job would evaporate as well. However, General Hsueh liked my father so much, proclaiming him an "honest intellectual," that he promoted my father to major general and gave him even more responsibility at the Officer Training Institute.

As my father's duties increased, he returned home later each night. I grew too tired to wait for his return. Sometimes I awoke in the middle of the night to the sound of my parents whispering, but I fell asleep again and dreamed of battles.

One of my father's new duties as major general was to invite cultural troupes—singers, puppeteers, traditional opera companies, and

---

[6] *History of the Sino-Japanese War, 1937–1945,* compiled by Hsu Long-hsuen and Chang Ming-kai, trans. Wen Ha-hsiung (Taipei, Taiwan: Chung Wu Publishing Co, 1971), p. 274.

acrobatic groups—to perform at the school, to promote the students' appreciation of the arts and to promote Chinese culture. As part of their contracts, my father required each troupe to perform in our village as well. I loved the martial operas with the elaborate sword-fights, the acrobats who reenacted the story of Sun Wu-kung the Monkey King battling the forces of evil, the piercing folk singers whose songs seemed to shatter the sky. But best of all were the movies. Even my mother, who had taken to frowning all the time, smiled when the picture shows came to our fields.

On movie nights, we arrived early, with the farmers, well before dark. Chickens fluttered through the dusk air, mother pigs rooted through dry fields, my crickets chirped in my pocket. We all waited in awe, the farmers and their children sitting on the ground, our household on the small wooden chairs we brought with us. In a hush as if in one of my mother's churches, we watched as the soldiers first set up the bamboo poles like a giant scaffolding then brought out the great white canvas sheets that would serve as a screen. They fluttered like the wings of a flock of enormous geese.

Soldiers steadied the screen while another group readied the generator brought here from the city, a great whirring mechanical beast. Some children clambered near only to run away shrieking once it started up, belching smoke.

And then the show began. Mostly they were silent movies from Shanghai, old stories of families separated by war, young maidens tricked into slavery in the wicked city, families reunited at the death-bed of a mother. They always ended tragically, a single tear adorning the white moon-face of our heroine as the hero too late rushes home to be at her side. Giant shadow faces flickered across the billowing sheet, and we sighed, we gasped, we cried, as unrequited love went unanswered, as mothers and sons were reunited only in death, as families lost everything to the chicanery of the wicked in the heartless streets of the city. Long after the picture ended and the animals had all gone back to the houses, bored with the humans' folly, we continued to sit awestruck, staring at the empty screen, as if we could conjure the characters back to life with our persistence.

But the very best pictures were the American comedies. In American pictures, the heroes always won, the good were rewarded, the wicked were exposed, the pretentious had pies plopped in their faces, the little tramp always got the last laugh.

Chinese pictures exposed the secret fears in our hearts but American pictures made us laugh.

After watching the movies, I dreamed in black-and-white.

In my memories, the war mixes with these films, flickering ghosts across a fluttering sheet.

My daughter is looking through my old pictures, old papers, her dictionaries spread around her like a wall. I don't know why she likes to look at these old pieces of paper. She is quite serious about translating the names of the photography studios, the commemorative banners printed across the tops of the photographs, even though the print has faded and is difficult to read. She squints through her glasses. When I was her age, I liked to sing and dance, I liked to get out and enjoy myself. She likes to look at these old pieces of paper. Who can understand the young?

She shows me one picture, darkened so that it is brown, the paper brittle. My mother, brothers, and I sit in the middle of a group of people wearing large white crosses hanging from ribbons pinned to their shirts. It's a commemorative photo taken of my mother's church group in our Hunan village. The inscription across the top identifies the scene as Easter of 1939.

"It says, 'Lu Xi Christian Association,' " my daughter says, checking her translation. "So was Lu Xi the name of the village?"

I don't recognize the name. I have to take off my glasses to read the small characters. Holding the picture close to my eyes, I see my own face staring back at me. I look miserable. So does my middle brother. My youngest brother, still small for his age, is cradled in the maid's arms, asleep. My father's not in the picture. He had to work all the time so he escaped my mother's Sunday school.

"Don't you remember?" my daughter asks now in her persistent way.

"Remember what?"

"The name of the village!"

" 'Lu Stream,' it says. That means we are by the Lu Stream," I offer hopefully. "Maybe that's the name."

"You have no idea what the village was called then?"

"No."

She sighs.

My daughter likes to worry about these little details. I tell her about our village outside Changsha, why Nai-nai wanted to live there and not in the city, how Ye-ye brought movies to the village on weekends for us to watch. Still she's not satisfied.

Now she shows me an old book she's found describing the Three Battles of Changsha. "What about them?"

"I don't remember."

"How can you not remember? Weren't you scared?"

But I don't remember being scared. I remember racing crickets with boys in the village, it was so much fun. The cockfights and New Year's fireworks. I loved going to the market every morning, I could walk barefoot all year long. "We were rich," I say. "We were safe."

"What about *this* picture, then?" She points emphatically, serious. All her gestures are serious.

It's the only picture of the entire family from our Hunan days. My father stands in his uniform, rigid, his bones poking through the cloth. I am dressed in a kiddie uniform imitating him. My brothers are dressed in homemade baggy jumpers, much too big for them, clothes made to last through several growth spurts. My mother's *qipao* is cotton, rumpled, not elegant, not like her Nanjing dresses. This is a formal portrait before a curtain in a studio. We are all wearing our best clothes. It's not how I remember us. In my memories we are grand.

"Things couldn't have been so good." My daughter points to my mother's face in this Hunan photograph and then to another one taken just a few years earlier in Nanjing.

My mother has changed, it's true. I see that now. My mother has aged, she is no longer a young woman, her hair is unkempt, her face lined. I'd forgotten. I'd forgotten how she looked in Nanjing, how beautiful, young and confident. In her Hunan photograph, she almost looks the way I remember her now.

My daughter has a point. I must think like an adult, not remember like a child. Things must have been very difficult for my parents. They protected me, my brothers, sheltered us from their worries.

My father had many worries in Hunan, it's true.

Sometime after 1941 when Chiang Kai-shek moved the capital again, this time to Chongqing, my uncle Huan came to work for a very high official in Chiang's cabinet. My father didn't know. After the adoption fight in Anhui, he hadn't kept in touch with his brother at all. However, someone else found out and told our warlord Hsueh Yueh. Hsueh was incensed. He thought my father must be spying on him for Chiang Kai-shek, reporting his doings to his brother. Not all of Hsueh's activities conformed to official policy. For this kind of act of disloyalty, a man could be executed on the spot. It had happened before.

Hsueh called my father into his headquarters. He was escorted by guards carrying guns, men who looked straight ahead and did not meet his gaze. My father knew something was wrong. He'd never been treated this way before. He didn't understand. His old friend the general now looked at him with narrowed eyes, his expression like a mask across his face.

Then General Hsueh confronted my father with his new intelligence. He accused my father of spying for his brother. My father was shocked. He had no idea what his brother was up to. My father now pleaded his case. He said he'd had a falling-out with Huan, he truly did not know that his brother was even in Chongqing, much less working for Chiang Kai-shek. Miraculously, General Hsueh believed him. But because of Huan's position, he explained now, my father naturally could no longer work for him; there was a conflict of interest. However, the general would not have my father killed. He'd decided just now: seeing how honest my father was reminded the general how much he liked him. Instead, the general would allow my father to resign and "accept" a new position in the south of Hunan, at Hunan University. He could be dean of students there.

General Hsueh nodded, satisfied with his decision.

My father understood that the offer of this job was not a suggestion; it was an order. He accepted the new post on the spot, and as soon as he returned home that afternoon, we began to pack.

14

FLEEING THE WARLORD

Southern Hunan. Ruth (seated at center in light gray dress) is serving as a judge at a local school competition, around 1941.

~ *May-lee* ~

En route from Changsha to Sunxi, my grandmother nearly got my grandfather killed. By the time I first heard this story as a child, it had reached nearly epic proportions

They were moving south so that Ye-ye could assume the post of dean of students at Hunan University. What's more, they were in a rush, unsure whether their warlord patron would have my grandfather assassinated after all for some imagined disloyalty.

They traveled by boat on the Yangtze, known in Chinese as the *Chang Jiang,* the "long river," the third-longest river in the world, the lifeline for so many families during the war. They were a large party. There were house servants and the amah, and hired men to do the heavy lifting because their servants were not used to such tasks. My grandparents splurged on a private cabin, using my grandmother's gold and jade jewelry as currency. My grandmother understood that it was essential to look important when traveling, so important that bandits would see that it might be dangerous to rob or mistreat them.

It was a lot of money, this sudden boat trip, this cabin. My grandparents argued about the cost. Their tempers were short. Everyone remembered their arguing, even if no one could recall exactly what they argued about. Perhaps Nai-nai wondered aloud if Ye-ye didn't give in just a little too easily on the price instead of bargaining harder. Perhaps Ye-ye suggested that Nai-nai should have just taken care of it herself since nothing satisfied her. My grandparents argued so much during the war that their children stopped listening to them. Instead my father played with his brothers in the cabin.

He liked to tell them his mother's stories about America. Because he was conceived in Chicago, he considered himself practically American. "If I'd only been born there," he sighed, "I could be president someday."

His brothers laughed as if this were the funniest thing they had ever heard. "You!" they snorted. They held their sides as if their mirth made their ribs hurt.

"You don't know anything about America! You don't know anything!" Now it was my father's turn to laugh at their ignorance, loudly. He called to his parents for confirmation but they weren't listening.

Suddenly there was singing. Loud masculine voices. My father and his brothers were enthralled. The voices pounded the air. They'd never heard songs like this. They were wonderful. Not like their mother's church hymns. Not like the patriotic songs they learned at school. These were bouncing, rocking, rolling songs. The men's voices were strong. My father and his brothers wanted to join in.

My grandmother slapped the tabletop at their noise. "Stop that!" Her voice was stern, her face a thundercloud. The children fell silent.

"Do you hear that?" she asked Ye-ye.

"Hear what?" He shrugged.

"That—that—" She searched for the word. "That obscenity!"

"The soldiers have been drinking."

"Someone should order them to be quiet. It's indecent."

For a while my grandparents stopped arguing.

The men continued singing. They were most likely indulging in a last night of revelry before being shipped to a new battlefield. Perhaps they were afraid of leaving home, of dying, of suffering.

But my grandmother had no sympathy, she was merely horrified. Their songs were undoubtedly quite obscene. Hunan is renowned for its bawdy folk traditions. Nowadays such songs are collected by oral historians, preserved, analyzed, deconstructed even. Academic books are written about them. Here's one sample:

> *In the skies, clouds are upon clouds;*
> *On the ground, graves are upon graves;*
> *In the kitchen, plates are upon plates;*
> *On your bed, a man is upon a woman.*

And another:

> *One thrust, two thrusts, three, four, and thirty-six thrusts.*
> *Each pierces the heart of my peony flower.*
> *Have mercy, oh please, have mercy.*
> *I just can't go on any more.*

Both of these examples were collected in a very respectable book by a renowned scholar.[1]

But at the time my grandparents didn't think, How interesting, the folk culture of Hunan! What traditions these songs represent!

My grandmother said something like, "Our Father in Heaven, protect my sons' ears, close their ears firmly to this filth. I am your faithful and humble servant."

The singing did not abate as the night wore on and the river grew rough. The boat tossed and pitched on the waves. With each passing hour, if anything, the soldiers seemed to gather strength.

My father and his brothers could not sleep. They fought grumpily. One of the boys may have broken down into frustrated, screeching sobs.

"They are drunk!" Nai-nai announced. "That is why they are singing."

"Of course," said Ye-ye wearily, his head propped on his arm on the table. "They're soldiers."

Nai-nai paced angrily. "It's not right. This is against God's will. The Chinese people will never be strong so long as we tolerate this drunkenness, this obscenity. This is why we are so easily defeated.

---

[1] Jerome Chen, quoting the novelist Shen Congwen and a folk song journal, in *The Highlanders of Central China* (New York: M. E. Sharpe, 1992), p. 193.

We do not keep God's commandments." This was the way she always talked during the war.

She folded her hands now and prayed loudly to God to forgive the soldiers, they did not know, they were ignorant and uneducated. The boat pitched violently and everyone was tossed like so many coins in a rich man's pocket. The children whimpered.

"There, there's your answer," my grandmother said.

She shook my grandfather's shoulder now, waking him.

"You have to go out there. Tell them to be quiet. The children cannot sleep. These drunkards are keeping everyone up. And God is not pleased with this kind of disrespectful talk. You must tell them."

Ye-ye blinked at her sleepily. "What do you mean?"

"You're a major general, aren't you? They'll listen to you."

Ye-ye naturally did not want to go out to tell the soldiers to be quiet, and he said so.

"You have to set an example!" my grandmother insisted. "How is China going to survive if our soldiers have no discipline?" My grandmother pressed her hands together to pray. "Come on, boys. You must pray. Close your ears now. Pray with me."

She led the children in the Lord's Prayer.

Every marriage has its crazy moment, the fight that ends with one or both partners behaving in an illogical, sometimes suicidal fashion while the other shouts to God for deliverance.

So while my grandmother prayed, my grandfather dressed and, taking a strong male servant with him, left the cabin to tell the soldiers to be quiet.

When he came running back, minutes later, smelling of grain alcohol where the soldiers had doused him, he was shouting: "Quick! Quick! Open the door!"

My grandfather had a preternaturally loud voice so that the family could hear him shouting well before he actually burst into the cabin, wild-eyed, followed by the servant, who was beating back the soldiers with a walking staff. The other male servants jumped up, threw a chair out the door at the mob, then pulled the two men into safety. Then they slammed the door shut.

But the soldiers threw their bodies against the door. The wood frame cracked in one corner. Now my grandfather and the men dragged the furniture across the floor, barricading the door with the beds and the remaining chairs.

"Get down! They might shoot!" my grandfather shouted, his voice bouncing off the walls.

My grandmother crouched in the corner behind an overturned table with the children and their amah. She led them in prayer again, clutching at their hands until my father could no longer feel his fingers.

My grandfather beat on the wall, trying to wake the neighbors in the cabin next door.

At last the men in the neighboring cabin came out. "Don't you know, that's General Hsueh Yueh's right-hand man!" they shouted, trying to make peace. They convinced the soldiers that Ye-ye was an officer, that they'd better not break into the cabin or they'd be executed for insubordination, and finally the soldiers went away, although everyone continued to hear them singing drunkenly from afar.

Of course no one slept a wink all night.

I've always liked this story because it was never hard for me to understand. My grandparents' personalities had not changed that much over the years; I could picture them on this boat, Nai-nai praying, Ye-ye dressing to confront the soldiers. The events seemed crazy but familiar. Years later, when my father or grandfather brought up the boat incident at family gatherings, far from being chagrined, my grandmother would laugh.

However, it took years before I understood what a warlord was, what it really meant to live in such times.

When I was a little girl and we first began studying World War II, probably in junior high, I asked my father once which side they'd been on. "You liked Chiang Kai-shek, right?"

My father shook his head in disgust, more at me than at Chinese politics. "No," he said. "We just followed our warlord."

I had no idea what that meant. I couldn't even imagine.

I began to understand the concept of warlords only when I was a student at Nanjing University in 1988 and I was able to vote in a U.S. presidential election for the first time. I'd made arrangements to vote by absentee ballot and so I followed the election debates and campaign via Voice of America radio broadcasts and whatever newspapers and magazines were mailed to me by relatives. I was starved for more information, but in those days in Nanjing, as in most Chinese cities, it was virtually impossible to buy American newspapers or magazines anywhere, only Chinese official government publications such as *China Daily* and the *People's Daily*.

I'll never forget one conversation I had with a young man who worked in the fancy Jinling Hotel. He was very well educated, with a degree in English literature, but the best job he could find at the time was to work at the counter of the pharmacy for tourists. After I bought cough syrup from him, we started talking about the upcoming presidential election. He wanted to know whom I preferred, Bush or Dukakis. Then he asked, "What if the army decides to follow Reagan?"

"What do you mean?"

"Well, the president is also the commander in chief, isn't that right? What if Reagan's army decides they don't want a new commander?"

I laughed then because the idea seemed so absurd. "It's not like that in America. The armed forces will have to obey whoever is elected."

"But the president can send all the troops of the United States into war. The president can order the army to invade even little countries like Grenada if he desires." The young man had obviously been paying attention to world events. "How will the generals feel to be commanded by a new man? What if they don't like Bush or Dukakis as well? Aren't you worried?"

"No, not at all," I blithely insisted. "It just doesn't happen like that in America. Every four years there's a presidential election. It's been this way for more than two hundred years."

"That's not a very long time," he said. "But I hope you're right."

This conversation forced me to examine my own assumptions about what constituted political power. For example, certainly in 1988 everyone in China knew that Deng Xiaoping still held power because of his strong ties to the military even though he had officially retired from his political position as secretary general of the party. Because Deng was already quite old, people worried who would succeed him if he should die. Would it be an economic reformer who would continue Deng's more open policies or would he be succeeded by a political hard-liner who had strong ties to the military? Because the process of political succession was completely secret, speculation about perceived shifts in the political climate was practically a national pastime in China.

Before I lived in Nanjing, I never understood the extent to which I took America's peaceful transition of power every four years for granted.

In my grandparents' day, generals held both civil and military power, which is why they always referred to these men as "warlords."

The general for whom my grandfather worked, Chang Chih-chung, was also governor of Hunan. Only such generals had the power to enforce laws and to "keep order." By contemporary standards this kind of military rule would be viewed as one of oppression, but such generals were also the only people who could protect the people of their province from the armies of another general or from the advancing Japanese army.

Although Chiang Kai-shek portrayed his regime as a republic, as if he were the single ruler over a peaceful nation, in fact he had only nominal control over much of the country. The warlords of the various regions had signed allegiance to him, making him the leader of the republic, but they might at any time feel the need to act independently. They kept their own armies, and he was extremely paranoid, worrying that his generals would betray him.

One such general, Chang Hsueh-liang, actually kidnapped Chiang in December of 1936, in an effort to force Chiang to vow to fight the Japanese instead of concentrating on killing Communists. Chang demanded that Chiang Kai-shek save the nation by instituting reforms that included putting an end to the civil war and reorganizing his corrupt government. Chiang tentatively agreed to the demands, and Chang Hsueh-liang voluntarily returned to Nanjing with Chiang to prove the sincerity of his motives for the kidnapping. But Chang was then court-martialed and placed under house arrest. Even after Chiang Kai-shek and the rest of the Nationalists fled to Taiwan in 1949, Chiang brought Chang Hsueh-liang with him as a prisoner and kept him under house arrest on Taiwan until Chiang's own death.

As a result of such political and military plots, Chiang Kai-shek's regime was marked by extreme paranoia. He had two secret police organizations for spying on his advisors and generals, and perceived disloyalty was dealt with swiftly. Political executions were carried out in public as a lesson to others who might be tempted to cross Chiang. The warlord-generals who ruled the provinces also had their own spies and internal secret police to ferret out Chiang's spies, anyone who might be disloyal to them, anyone who might be plotting against them, even anyone who might be unlucky enough to be suspicious.

It was this atmosphere of political intrigue, of paranoia, of assassinations and executions, that I needed to understand before I could begin to comprehend my grandparents' life.

15

THE MILK INCIDENT

Contemporary Chongqing, 1998.

~ *Winberg* ~

Life was much harder in southern Hunan province where we had
moved after my father fell out of favor with his warlord than it had
been in our village so my parents decided to relocate the family again.
This time we moved to Chongqing, which was now the wartime
capital of China. It must have been around 1942 when my parents
decided to leave Hunan.

My father had been offered a post in Chiang Kai-shek's government as his personal assistant on legal affairs after he had met the
generalissimo at a National Youth Corps Conference. Chiang had
been impressed by my father's speech on the need for legal reform
and invited him to come to work for him in Chongqing. Unfortunately, after we arrived, a jealous classmate of my father's, now
working as Chiang's confidential secretary, claimed that he had no
record of the appointment and refused to allow my father to see
Chiang to straighten up the snafu. As Chiang was frequently traveling and quite secretive about his whereabouts, my father had no
way to reach him.

He had no choice but to seek out his brother's help. Although Huan was still angry about the failed adoption, he did help my father meet with the right people at National Chungking University and my father was named the first dean of the newly inaugurated law school. My mother also was hired as a professor in the English department, but to be truthful, these positions did not provide much in the way of salary or provisions. We were all housed on campus, and because food was rationed, we were required to eat in the university canteen.

There was very little food. Meat was rare. After the bounty of life in our village in Hunan, we were little prepared for the deprivations of life in Chongqing. We were always hungry. In the university canteen each table was given only a few bowls of vegetables and rice, which had to be divided among everyone at the table. One family was notorious for its piggy children; we called them the Five Fatties. Although families were supposed to sit together, the parents were very clever and instead had each of these hungry ghosts sit at a different table. As soon as the bowl of food was set down, the Fatty would start grabbing with his chopsticks, thrusting giant clumps into his mouth. The parents had taught their children how to swallow without chewing. Like a cloud of locusts, they could polish off an entire bowl of food before anyone else at the table could stop them. They were very young kids so we couldn't just hit them to make them stop; it was really their parents' fault, after all. Yet if you complained to the parents, they threatened to report you or cause all kinds of trouble, accusing you of being abusive to their child. It was a nightmare. No one could convince the parents to be fair and reasonable and no one could eat faster than their children. We all dreaded when one of the Fatties tried to sit at our table.

Only my mother thought of a method to stop them.

Normally, every table had to have six people at it in order to be served. These were the university's rules to ensure that there was enough food to go around. As there were only five of us in the family, it was inevitable that one day one of the Fatties would try to join us.

Sure enough, one evening, a Fatty planted himself at our dinner table. His tiny eyes barely visible in his doughy face, he stared with a wolf's concentration at the empty tabletop, licking his dumpling lips, ready to pounce when the food came. At the sight of him, my brothers started to cry. We were all very hungry. There was barely enough to eat when everyone ate like a normal person. We couldn't bear the thought of having to make do with even less.

However, when the food came, my mother put her hand on the Fatty's ear and twisted the fleshly lobe severely. He dropped his chopsticks and tried to free his ear, but my mother wouldn't let go. Not for nothing had she been the principal of an elementary school.

"We are Christians at this table. And as Christians, we do not start eating until we have said grace."

She made the Fatty bow his head while my father said the blessing. While everyone prayed, she divided up the food equally.

Then the Fatty cried.

Later his father came up to my mother to complain, but she explained all about God to him and why it was against His will not to say grace and that no one at her table could violate God's will. Eventually the father gave up trying to intimidate my mother and none of the Five Fatties ever tried to sit at our table again.

In fact, inspired by this episode, my mother then used every meal as an opportunity to explain about grace and God and Jesus to the unwitting sixth person to sit at our table. After a while, no one wanted to sit at our table, and we could divide the six portions among the five of us.

From time to time the Americans would send in relief supplies for the populace: sometimes crates and crates of leather shoes, sometimes various dried and canned foodstuffs. Once the Americans sent sacks and sacks of powdered milk "for the starving Chinese children." Most Chinese children did not drink cow's milk, of course, and many were lactose-intolerant, which meant that the powdered milk would give them diarrhea. However, because my mother had gone to school in America, she had always believed in making me and my brother drink cow's milk in Nanjing, and she knew that at least two of her three sons could tolerate milk. When she heard the rumor that milk was coming to the city, she had my father keep his eyes and ears open. Many of the American-sent supplies—if not most—were not regularly distributed but were illegally sold to middlemen who then sold the war-relief supplies on the black market, which meant that everything would be too expensive for most people, including us, to afford.

My father did manage to procure three sacks of the powdered milk, but unfortunately, he was tricked by his best friend into giving all the milk away. In those days, you couldn't trust anyone.

~ May-lee ~

I remember very clearly one Thanksgiving when I was a child, Nai-nai gazed across the table laden with holiday foods and suddenly her face changed. She shook her head, pursing her lips. "He gave away all the milk," she said cryptically, pointing at Ye-ye. " 'What will the children eat?' I asked him. 'What will we feed them?' The boys all cried. They sat on the floor and cried. He gave their milk away."

My father hacked at the turkey as fast as he could, the buzz of the electric carver temporarily drowning out Nai-nai's voice. My uncles passed the platters of food as quickly as hot coals, they dangled her favorite dishes before my grandmother's nose, but Nai-nai would not be bribed into silence.

She saw everything as it had once been, her hard life spread before her like the leaves of an illuminated manuscript. She adjusted her dentures with her tongue and launched into the story.

The family was starving in Chongqing, refugees in their own country. A wheelbarrow of money wasn't enough to buy a sack of buns. Then, thank God in heaven, one day they managed to get hold of some dried milk powder. American airlift rations, three bags full. She'd had to surrender some of her best gold and jade jewelry, but she didn't mind the cost, giving up her mother's jewelry like that. No, that wasn't what made her angry, even now, some thirty-odd years later. It was the ease with which her husband gave the milk away, all three bags, to his good-for-nothing friend, just because the friend came begging, playing him for the fool, saying he needed the milk, he had a sick baby, he didn't know what to do, and so Charles had given away his own children's milk, just like that.

Nai-nai took a deep breath. She'd remembered something else, just this minute. Her husband had not only given away the milk, but also his only coat.

"But I can't walk on the street like this," the friend had said, his rat-face twitching, his tongue darting at his thin lips. He gestured to the sacks of milk under his arm. "I'll be robbed."

Charles had nodded. Then he took off his only coat and gave it to the man to wrap around the milk, to hide it from thieves.

"I'll bring your coat back tomorrow. Don't worry," the friend said.

"Of course, of course." Charles nodded.

And, of course, he never saw his coat or his friend again.

Oh, how she'd cried, how she'd ranted and raved, shouting at her husband, never mind if the boys cried now, afraid because their mother shouted that they would all starve to death, that their father would be the death of them all, and she would die too, how could she live with this knife in her heart, how could she continue to live if she had to watch her three sons starving slowly but surely to death?

She'd acted like a fool, she declared, silent while he gave away the milk. She was mad at herself, livid, murderous that she had stood there mutely and allowed the swindle to happen under her nose, just because a wife must never contradict her husband in public, before his friends, and she hadn't wanted her husband to lose face.

What else could she do but cry?

Despite the decades that had passed, Nai-nai spoke of all this, the Milk Incident, as if it had happened yesterday.

Silence fell across our Thanksgiving table like a blanket of fresh snow . . . until Ye-ye laughed gently, and, smiling, took Nai-nai's hand in his, patting it, until everyone could eat again.

My family lived with the Sino-Japanese War long after it had officially ended: my grandparents, my father, and by extension—through their flashbacks and mood swings—my cousins, my brother, and me.

But as a child, I didn't understand my grandmother's moods, which frightened me, the sudden way her memories would intrude upon the present, bringing any family gathering to a complete halt. She didn't speak in complete sentences, of course. She didn't provide any context. She would talk about these stolen milk bags and my grandfather's coat but wouldn't mention the war. The adults knew what she was talking about, but my brother and cousin and I had no idea. It seemed as though Nai-nai, with her half-told stories, was losing her mind.

The other difficulty in understanding Nai-nai's mood swings was my father's insistence that nothing bad had happened to the family during the war. In fact, the way my father described the past, it seemed as though there had been no war at all. He talked about his mother's grand house, their servants, his parents' prestigious positions.

It was very confusing.

After I went to college and studied Chinese history, I had a better understanding of what went on during the war years and what my grandparents must have experienced. But I still couldn't answer why my father refused to talk about the war years. I wasn't sure if he had blocked these memories or if once he started to think about the past he was too overwhelmed by emotion to talk.

He grew angry whenever I asked him questions.

My brother and I were never allowed to listen to music in the house when we were growing up. The sound of drums made my father fly into an inexplicable rage. Rock and roll or pop music was the worst, but even classical music upset him. Finally, when I was ten, my mother got him to admit that the sound of drums reminded him of the sound of bombs falling. From the ages of nine to thirteen, he had lived in Chongqing in Sichuan province, and the Japanese had bombed the city frequently. The family had had to flee into caves dug into the mountainous terrain of the city in order to survive.

And although I could then understand why he didn't like drums, I still didn't understand why he couldn't explain this to us, why he was so reticent to share his memories or even to explore his memories. His silence was a wall between us, and I had no idea how to penetrate it.

In the fall of 1998, my father and I traveled together to Chongqing. It was his first trip back to the wartime capital of the Republic of China since 1945. I'd convinced him we should go to see what had become of the city.

We arrived in a blur of fog. Our little China Southwest Airlines plane was buffeted in the air, shaking our water glasses and sending my stomach into my throat.

Although on U.S. airlines this kind of turbulence would have sent the flight attendants to their seats and prompted the captain to put on the fasten-seat-belt signs, here the flight attendants were still in the aisles serving drinks. As I gripped the armrests tightly, one flight attendant laughed cheerfully. "Don't worry," she said, shrugging. "It's always like this."

We landed in a vertical descent that can only be described as a testament to the power of gravity. As the brakes screeched and we bounced along the runway, one passenger remarked (in awe or in terror, I don't know which), "The pilot must be retired from the military!" If so, someone should have reminded him that he was no longer flying a fighter jet.

Once safely on land, my spirits picked up immediately, whereas my father fell into a deep silence.

It was a muggy day, typical weather for mid-autumn in eastern Sichuan, and we were sweating by the time we'd dragged our suitcases outside of the unair-conditioned airport where a line of new-looking minivans and taxis waited to take everyone into the city.

During the half-hour ride to Chongqing, we passed emerald mountains terraced with paddies that reflected the sky. Water buffaloes placidly waded in the ditches, impervious to the traffic. But lest I forget this was the nineties, the sides of the highway were lined with numerous shops with large signs written in English: California Restaurant, California Bowling, California Number One Shop.

Sichuan is home to some 84 million Chinese, making it China's most populous province. But crowded living conditions in its cities and overworked farmland had historically made it a prime source of immigrant labor to other countries, including the United States. Perhaps this phenomenon explained the popularity of naming things after California, I thought, as some forty percent of all Chinese immigrants to America have settled in the state.

But when I asked our driver, he insisted there was no connection. " 'California' just sounds good. New. Western. People like that. They think it will make their business more popular," he said with a shrug.

As we entered the city limits, I was surprised to see the rampant construction under way. Building cranes dotted the horizon, all of the city's streets seemed to be in the process of expansion.

In 1997, Chongqing had been designated as a special economic development zone. That meant, like Shanghai and Shenzhen, the government was pumping in funds for development and offering foreign businesses incentives to set up in Chongqing. As a result, neon was popping up green and red and blue everywhere, there were skyscrap-ers and pedestrian malls, Taiwanese department stores, and even a four-star Holiday Inn. Judging from the pedestrians I saw, I gathered that this fall leather miniskirts in colors not found in nature were all the rage, while even men were dyeing their hair orange.

Every boulevard, every street, every alley, was clogged with buses, taxis, and motorcycles. (Chongqing is too hilly for China's most common form of transportation—the bicycle—to be practical.) Bill-boards advertised everything from computers to Sprite. As our taxi weaved through the congested streets, I had difficulty imagining Chongqing as a city of starving refugees so desperate that they'd steal milk from their best friend. Chic new restaurants abounded, dump-ling shops, Pepsi stands, and the ubiquitous Kentucky Fried Chicken franchises that have been expanding to every major city in China.

I was startled, too, by the presence of large (and extremely healthy-looking) nude statues, male and female, seemingly at every traffic circle, every plaza, in front of every new building. The figures looked like Chinese versions of the athletes on the old *American Gladiators* TV show—all bulging muscles and enhanced bosoms. In front of a senior citizens' center, someone had painted green pants and halter tops on the cavorting bronze nudists.

I was gawking, but no one else in the city was. I could remember a time, not so long ago, when people in Chinese cities used to stare at foreigners, at unusual fashions, at anything new. Now, I had be-come the country mouse.

Finally, I had to ask our driver, "Why are there so many nude statues everywhere?"

He explained that there used to be only statues of Chairman Mao but they'd been torn down. These new statues were tributes to two decades of open-door policies. "Chongqing is very progressive," he said enthusiastically.

My father and I were both sticky by the time we reached the hotel. The weather was a lot warmer than we'd expected. Before embarking on our sightseeing expedition, we decided to eat and change out of our layers of sweaters. Although I'd begun to relax now that we were settled, my father was completely strung out, pacing and irritable. He'd been silent during the entire ride from the airport, barely glanc-ing out the minivan's windows. Now we argued in our room, over nothing, over the placement of our suitcases. Then he pouted, settling into an armchair. "You're the one who likes to see sights," my father said bitterly. "I don't want to see anything."

I knew he hadn't come all this way to China just to watch CNN on the hotel TV, but I had learned not to snap back. "We can always come back to the hotel early if you get tired," I said to placate him.

Although I managed to convince my father to leave the hotel after lunch, he was still tense, taciturn, as we sat in the back of the small minivan, while our guide, Mr. Ye, zipped through the crowded streets.

Our first stop was the campus of Chongqing University, where my father's family had lived during the war. Ye-ye had been dean of the law school and Nai-nai a professor in the English department. Now the university was one of China's "key" universities, roughly equivalent to America's Ivy League, with twelve thousand students, but no longer any law school.

My father shook his head as we passed the pastel-colored dorms, students on motorscooters dashing around us. Almost everything had changed. He recognized nothing. "I was only a child," he said, trying not to sound disappointed.

Finally, in a thicket of gingko trees opposite the basketball courts, we found one of the old classroom buildings, built prior to the Communist victory in 1949. Constructed of gray bricks with a tile roof and sweeping eaves, the building was dark and deserted. I found the traditional-style architecture charming, so much more attractive than the generic cement-block rectangles that now constituted the campus, but our guide shook his head. "They should tear it down." Mr. Ye scowled. "So old."

Like many people in Chongqing, he was impatient for the city to modernize, even if that meant razing all remnants of the past, even a solitary building in an obscure corner of the campus.

But finding this building had a remarkable effect on my father. "Yes," he said, almost enthusiastically, "my father taught in a classroom just like that." We'd found a piece of his history, waking my father from his torpor, his curiosity overwhelming his anxieties.

Now he asked if we could go to see the *shan dong*, the mountain caves that his family hid in during the war.

Our guide nodded and announced that it would be a day trip as it was four hours by bus.

THE GIRL FROM PURPLE MOUNTAIN 199

"What?" We were shocked. It seemed so inconvenient for a city's bomb shelters to be located so far from the center of town. Perhaps only these distant caves were left, we thought, and all the others had been filled in, built over.

But just as we were leaving the city limits, my father began to talk. "We were just kids. We thought it was fun to run to the caves. The sirens went off and we got out of school early."

Mr. Ye suddenly burst into laughter. "Oh, you mean the *fan kong dong*, air-raid shelter caves, not Shan Dong." The latter was now the name of a mountain resort. "Why they're all over!" He turned the minivan around and headed back into the city. "Why do you want to see them?"

My father replied that he wanted *me* to see the caves. "My daughter was born in America. She doesn't believe anything I tell her." Though I winced, I knew my father didn't want to talk about his feelings, his own need to find his past, so I didn't contradict him.

"It's good for young people to see," Mr. Ye agreed. A wiry man in his mid-forties, he told us that he used to be a soldier in the People's Liberation Army. However, a heart condition had forced him into early retirement.

He shook his head as if in astonishment. "Young people today don't know what real suffering is," he sighed.

Now as we drove through the city, Mr. Ye pointed to the man-made air-raid shelter "caves" everywhere. Some tiny shelters were just large enough for a person to crouch in: they were dug into the rock behind single-family shops. Others were so large that they'd now been converted into motorcycle showrooms, noodle shops, clothing stores. We'd driven by them all morning on our route throughout town and never taken notice. Now we saw that these caves were practically everywhere.

We stopped at a particularly large series of caves, the personal air-raid shelter of Zhou Enlai, who later became premier under Chairman Mao. Large enough for trucks to drive through, the tunnels now housed a subterranean metalworks factory.

Mr. Ye said we could go in for a look. My father surveyed the entrance of the cave, moss and vines hanging in tendrils. Then he refused to go inside, instead pacing by the side of the road. "I need to stretch my legs," he said. But I happily disembarked from the van and ran into the cave. It was dimly lit with a series of exposed lightbulbs hanging from wood supports along the ceiling. I was surprised how deep the cave went into the mountain. One end was blocked off by a metal grate. Mr. Ye explained the authorities were afraid it might collapse, but as I peered through the grating, I could see that the tunnel continued for what looked like several hundred feet.

I tried to picture what it must have been like to stay in such a cave, without any lights, listening to the vague drumlike thuds of falling bombs reverberating through the stone walls. Suddenly I became aware of the presence of someone standing directly behind me, startling me out of my daydreams.

Turning, I found a young man staring at me. Sporting a chic black turtleneck and large black-rimmed glasses, which greatly magnified his eyes, he looked like a troglodyte version of a Left Bank intellectual. He asked me something in Sichuan dialect, which I didn't understand. Mr. Ye came up to us now and began talking to the man. He pointed to me and to the cave. The young man smiled then, nodding.

"I told them you're a tourist from America come to see Sichuan's culture," Mr. Ye explained in Mandarin.

Now a woman suddenly appeared, and I realized she and the young man had emerged from another small cave carved out of the wall, just large enough for three or four people to sit inside. I hadn't noticed it before. It was the office of the factory, lit by a single bulb dangling from the ceiling. The office was decorated spartanly with a rather large desk with a red thermos on top, a long wooden bench and a filing cabinet.

The employees agreed to give me a tour. Their main work was conducted down another tunnel, where I could see a series of large machines. A young man wearing a blast helmet was welding something. He waved at us cheerily.

I asked my guides if they liked working in a cave factory. It seemed a little dark and claustrophobic to me.

"Oh, no, it's better than most buildings," the woman laughed. "Cool in summer, warm in winter."

After I took a few pictures, I thanked the factory workers for their tour then went back outside to see how my father was doing. I thought he might have become irritable again because we had abandoned him, but he greeted Mr. Ye and me pleasantly as we emerged from the cave. "So now you know," he said to me pointedly.

After we piled back inside the van, Mr. Ye decided to take us to see something "more interesting," he said. He wanted us to see Chongqing's new pedestrian shopping mall, part of what he called "the New City." My father remained quiet as we drove away from Zhou Enlai's air-raid shelters.

Because Mr. Ye did not speak English, he and I were both obliged to speak in Mandarin. As I speak with a very strong American accent and Mr. Ye with a very strong Sichuan accent, I could tell that there were times when neither of us knew quite what the other was saying. As our guide, he seemed to feel it was his duty to be entertaining by telling me amusing stories and jokes, after which he laughed and nodded at me encouragingly in the rearview mirror, clueing me in that he'd reached the punch line. I smiled and nodded too, but unfortunately all his jokes sailed right over my head because they were dependent upon puns between dialects. As I knew only one dialect, I never caught the allusions.

This charade continued for some time: Mr. Ye valiantly slugging away at his puns as I desperately pretended to laugh at the appropriate moment, while my father looked out the window silently.

"The fog saved us," my father said suddenly. "Chongqing is always foggy. I'd forgotten about that until we got here."

"That's right, that's right," Mr. Ye agreed, too relieved that my father was talking again to wonder what on earth my father was talking about. He chattered on happily. "Hot in summer, foggy in winter. The clouds keep the heat in, so it's never too cold. No snow here."

It seems that talking about the weather is an acceptable way of filling an awkward silence the world over.

"The Japanese bombers didn't have radar," my father said, continuing his train of thought. "Because it was so foggy, they couldn't find their targets."

My father told us now what he remembered about hiding in caves when the Japanese bombers came. "We heard the siren that meant a plane was spotted. We were so happy! That meant school was canceled." My father, a grandfather in his sixties, now smiled mischievously, recalling the boy he'd once been.

"The only bad thing for us kids was that there was no electricity in the caves, so it was very dark at night." My father smiled ruefully. "That's how a kid thinks."

Between October 1938 and the end of the war, the Japanese flew more than 9,500 sorties, dropping nearly 22,000 bombs on Chongqing, according to Chinese records. More than 11,800 civilians were killed and 14,000 wounded.

Sometimes my father's childhood memories seemed more like nightmares than anything real, so vastly different were my experiences growing up. I admit that I had been afraid that going back to Chongqing would be traumatic for him, but as we left the caves behind us, my father seemed almost pleased by our discoveries, as if, finally, he could say he wasn't crazy, his memories were real.

After listening to my father's reminiscences, Mr. Ye decided not to take us to the new shopping malls but instead to one of the older sections of the city that had not yet been demolished and rebuilt. When we arrived at this neighborhood facing the juncture of the Yangtze and Jialing rivers, Mr. Ye wrinkled his nose. "This area is still very poor," he said sadly.

However, we were thrilled to discover still intact whole sections of the city wall of Chongqing, made of ancient brown bricks centuries old, towering above us at the top of the cliff overlooking the rivers. Beneath the wall, along the entire face of the cliff, traditional wooden houses clung to the mountainside.

"All the houses used to look like that," my father said, pointing. Because there was not enough level ground to build on, the people raised platforms on wooden stilts off the side of the cliffs and built their houses upon them. The wooden posts had been replaced by stone sometime after the war. Now many of the old houses were being torn down completely. A modern ten-story apartment building made of cinder blocks was already half-finished just off the multilane highway.

Mr. Ye waved now at what looked like a sandbar in the middle of the river.

"That's an old Chiang Kai-shek military airfield. Children like to fly kites there on the weekend now." But he added that soon it would be completely underwater once the Three Gorges Dam was completed.

I took several pictures, but what once must have been the pride of the Nationalist forces now appeared to be nothing but a soggy field, drifting in and out of the fog, like a blurry black-and-white photograph.

Below us ferries crossed the river, a round trip for one yuan. Such ferries were once the only way to cross the river from the peninsula of Chongqing, but now cable cars arced overhead, carrying passengers more quickly for twice the price.

Mr. Ye was growing weary of my preoccupation with the past. He pointed with pride to the new award-winning "Number One Yangtze River Bridge," four lanes and nine spans long. "Don't you want to take a picture?" he prompted.

We gazed across the Yangtze. The river had nourished Chongqing throughout the war, supplies were ferried in off the Burma Road, fresh troops arrived from the provinces, refugees poured in from occupied areas on sampans and barges.

Chongqing is a peninsular city, located on a mountain at the confluence of two rivers. Because of its location on these transportation lines as well as its position far from the Japanese bases in Shanghai and north China, Chiang Kai-shek had decided to move the capital of the republic to Chongqing in 1938. From then on, refugees and soldiers migrated to the city during the war years, swelling its population from 300,000 to more than a million by 1940. The capital became the center of the Allied Forces' China Theater Command, which meant that America's advisors to Chiang—including General Joseph Stilwell; Colonel Claire Chennault, officially retired from the U.S. Air Corps but head of the Chinese Flying Tigers air force; Roosevelt's Vice President Henry Wallace—as well as British military leaders came to the city to aid Chiang. The Communists, too, sent representatives, including Zhou Enlai, in an attempt to form an alliance with the Nationalists, the better to fight the Japanese troops.

I rather naïvely expected some commemorative obelisk at the bridge, this potent symbol of modernity on China's longest river, but for the moment I had forgotten that Chiang belonged to the losing side of the Chinese civil war from the Communists' perspective and the official history blinked at events that focused on the Nationalists. In some ways, this lack of acknowledgment struck me as sad. But, of course, politics always determines what events a nation chooses to celebrate or to censor.

So perhaps it was a positive sign that rather than some pompous historical monument to an unhappy and tragic past, there were instead four giant, übernudes—two male and two female—adorning each end of the new Yangtze River bridge.

I asked Mr. Ye about their symbolism.

He seemed surprised that I would need to ask such a stupid question, so obvious was the answer. "The statues represent our modern future! The blend of Western and traditional styles," he explained patiently.

As he faced the muddy Yangtze, my father was nodding now, lost in thought. I wondered if he were on the verge of sharing another memory, another wartime anecdote, but as we climbed back into the minivan, all he said was, "I thought I'd forgotten everything."

16

TREACHERY IN CHONGQING

Zhou Enlai's wartime air raid shelter cave has been turned into a metal-works factory.

~ *Winberg* ~

My mother's conversations with me in Chongqing consisted primarily of lists of Things to Be Worried About. She warned me always to be on the alert for kidnappers. Children were routinely sold on the sides of the road by impoverished relatives or people claiming to be their relatives. Once kidnapped, a child could be taken far away and sold and never heard from again. The desperately poor were rumored to have turned to cannibalism, and while a family would never eat their own son, they might eat someone else's. Gangs of renegade soldiers and bandits reportedly lived in the mountains; they committed all manner of atrocities. I was never to talk to strangers, stray into the woods, the mountains, alleys, or docks, and certainly I should never go anywhere alone. Because of the Japanese bombing raids, I was not to play too far from the air-raid shelter cave where we could hide. Never forget, she reminded me. The world was fraught with danger, survival was dependent solely upon miracles, no one was to be trusted.

Because my mother frightened me, I did my best to avoid her and spent as much time as possible with my friends.

In addition to kidnapping, cannibalism, thievery, and barbarism, my mother worried that my brothers' and my growth would be stunted and all our teeth would fall out because of our poor nutrition. She thus devoted most of her time trying to find food. She did everything she could to raise extra money, cultivate connections so that my brothers and I would have better food to eat. She gave private English lessons for additional money, for example, and was tutoring the daughter of Sheng Shih-tsai, the warlord of Xinjiang province, among others.

In 1943, Lord Louis Mountbatten arrived in Chongqing to try to broker a peace between the American General Joseph Stilwell and Generalissimo Chiang Kai-shek. Vinegar Joe and Peanut—as Stilwell referred to Chiang in his journals—were feuding again and the Allies were concerned that China would be lost, to the Japanese, to the Communists, lost forever if the situation were not amended. They were hoping that the British admiral could persuade Chiang to work with Stilwell.

As a professor of English, my mother was chosen to be Lady Mountbatten's interpreter. The Chiangs entertained the Mountbattens lavishly; cakes and dim sum, all manner of meats and sweets, wines and exotic teas, abounded at every meal, which were twenty-, thirty-course banquets. The Chiangs knew how to be charming when it pleased them. At the one banquet my mother was permitted to attend, she thought she'd faint at the sight of such food.

She dared not eat freely, she did not devour the food before her, savoring the last grain of rice, the way the family ate in the school cafeteria. She did not want Lady Mountbatten to know how poor she was, how desperate. She wanted the British to go home with a good impression of the Chinese. So following Lady Mountbatten's habit, she did not clean her plate but merely tasted each course of the official banquets as if she, too, were a dainty Royal, as if she were not hungry at all. But when the Lady wasn't looking, she slipped buns and pastries into her purse and pockets for my brothers and me at home.

My brothers and I were so happy when we saw all the wonderful treats that she had brought home for us, we started to fight.

"Ssh! Do you want the neighbors to hear you? What if they come in and see all the dim sum? Do you want to share with them?" As usual, my mother knew exactly what to say to make us behave.

She made us sit nicely at the table and let us eat three dumplings each. I had forgotten how delicious barbecued pork tasted, how soft rice-flour buns melted on the tongue, how sweet was red-bean paste. We licked our fingers afterward, trying to savor even the grease that remained on our skin.

Although we begged her to let us eat more, my mother insisted we save the other cakes and candies for breakfast. She managed to parcel out the goodies as supplements for three days, any longer and she was afraid the food would be spoiled. It was only after I had gobbled down the last third of the last onion cake that I realized my mother had not eaten any of the food she had saved herself.

After the war all my mother's teeth went bad, as well as my father's, because of their paltry diet during these years. After she died, my father moaned and moaned about how much my mother had suffered during the war, how she would take but a few mouthfuls of food and give the rest to her children. It is true, thanks to her fervent efforts, that my brothers and I suffered no serious health consequences.

During the twenty-plus years that they lived together in New York after the war, my father cooked every meal for my mother—she didn't know how to cook after all, she'd always had servants her entire life. He tried to make her delicacies, remembering the recipes that the imperial chef had taught him when he was a teenager, but because her gums hurt, my mother preferred soft, bland foods.

The air raids gave me something to think about besides food.

As soon as the first warning siren blared, my brothers and I ran straight from our classrooms to our parents' apartment on the campus of Chongqing University. The household was usually in a state of turmoil. My parents shouted at everyone at once, the servants grabbed the bedding, the cots, food supplies. There was no telling how long we'd have to stay in the shelter and we all had to carry something.

While I walked with my friends, we speculated what kind of plane was coming—a Zero, which would drop bombs, or a reconnaissance flight, which would cause no harm. Our parents followed, sweating profusely.

"Did you bring your schoolbooks?"

"No lights allowed," I reminded my mother happily. "Can't read!"

I ran ahead now, oblivious of my parents' worries, enjoying my unexpected playtime.

We'd know it wasn't a reconnaissance flight when we were packed into the air-raid cave if the ground trembled and the air took on the distinct odor of dirt. My mother clutched me and my brothers to her, praying aloud. My brothers cried then, but I was a big boy, at least ten, so I tried to push myself free. However, the more I squirmed, the more she tightened her grip.

Sometimes we had to wait all night in the caves, in the dark, too afraid to leave even to relieve ourselves. The musty air began to smell of urine, or worse. Babies were shrieking, their cries echoing off the walls. Only then did I wish that there was no such thing as air raids. I prayed with my mother, I promised God I'd be grateful, I'd never complain about school again, if only the Japanese bombers would leave and we could go home again.

Sometimes the explosions were distant and beautiful, the fires leapt up against the night sky, flames like fingers tearing black flesh. Sometimes the fog was too thick to see anything, smoke hung in the air, the earth trembled, no one could sleep.

During one raid nearly a thousand people suffocated in their cave when the entrance collapsed. My teacher told our class. He was a bitter old man who delighted in scaring us. From then on, we all thought of the collapsing cave every time the ground trembled.

However, neither the food problem nor the air raids were the worst thing that happened to our family in Chongqing.

The worst thing, as far as my mother was concerned, occurred because of my uncle Huan.

Although my father's brother had an important position in Chiang's cabinet, as chief aide to the head of the Ministry of Organization and Education, Dr. Chu Chia-hua, we still did not have much to do with him and he made no effort to help us with our food situation although his connections gave him access to supplies.

However, one day Huan came to visit my father in his office at the law school. My father was startled to see his brother. He'd been working on his class lecture notes when the door opened and Huan strode into the tiny office as though he came to visit so frequently that there was no need to knock or call in advance.

My father blinked at the man dressed rather dapperly in a military-cut wool topcoat and felt fedora.

"Aren't you going to greet your brother?"

Charles hastened to his feet. "It's good to see you," he said, sincerely. My father was incapable of holding a grudge. "Can I get you some hot tea? I'm sorry I don't have anything else to offer you. We're a rather—"

"Just a glass. Would you like some bourbon?" Huan pulled a small silver flask from his breast pocket. "It's very good. Imported."

"No, no, no. I don't drink."

"That's right, I always forget about your . . . religion." Huan made an exaggerated display of disappointment.

Charles quickly removed some books from the office's one spare chair and offered it to his brother now. Huan dusted the seat with a gloved hand then gingerly sat down.

"So what brings you here?"

"What?" Huan looked hurt. "Is it so surprising that I would want to visit my own brother?" But then even he realized how that sounded. He cut to the point. "I have an idea. A brilliant idea. A matter of national security. To save our country. You'll like it." Huan folded his hands neatly over his knee. "And I need your help to pull it off."

Charles recognized his brother now, always so ambitious, fond of bold gestures. "Mm-hmm." He tried to sound as neutral as possible.

Then Huan recounted his brilliant idea. He and his colleagues wanted to convince Zhou Enlai, Mao Zedong's right-hand man, to defect to work for Chiang Kai-shek.

Charles thought this was very funny. He was pleased to see that his elder brother had not lost his sense of humor.

But Huan was serious.

Zhou was, in fact, currently in Chongqing. Huan explained that Zhou had come to act as a liaison between the Nationalists and the Communists, who had established strongholds in the north. The Communists knew, just as Stilwell had known, that the only chance China had of defending the populace was if the Chinese armed forces fought as a united front. Currently, Chiang spent as much energy trying to fight the Communists as he did the Japanese. Meanwhile the Japanese had embarked on what became known as the "Three Alls" campaign across the Chinese countryside: kill all, burn all, destroy all. Zhou was trying to hammer out an agreement with Chiang, the terms for a new alliance.

"But what makes you think he'd even consider such a thing?" Charles shook his head.

"Because he has no choice. The Communists must be desperate if they'd trust Chiang again," Huan explained. During the previous "united front" between the Communists and the Nationalists, Chiang had suddenly ordered a purge on the Communists, and killed many student activists, union organizers, and workers in Shanghai in April of 1927. "Zhou must know that the Communists are doomed without American aid and weapons. And the Americans will never give them a thing."

Charles still did not see how that would make Zhou ready to defect. Zhou Enlai was highly respected, considered a brilliant strategist as well as a diplomat; he was popular with foreign leaders. Mao needed him.

"Yes! That's just it," Huan exclaimed. "If he can be convinced to join Chiang, the Communists are finished. They won't survive without him. And think what he could do for the KMT! We need a man like Zhou. To save the country."

"What does Chiang think about this idea?"

"Are you crazy? If he thought for one minute we were negotiating with Zhou Enlai, with the Communists, he'd have us all killed." Huan laughed at his brother's naïveté. But it was exactly this political innocence that had made Huan think of his brother, for this . . . project.

Because Huan himself naturally could not be seen talking with Zhou or his people, he had thought of Charles. My father was not a member of the government after all, he was neutral, dean of the law school. He could approach Zhou, make overtures, see if he'd be willing to switch allegiances. "You're so articulate. You've always been good at explaining your ideas. I've heard you talk. I know."

Charles put his index fingers to his temples. He still couldn't quite believe his brother was serious. He examined his brother's bloodshot eyes. Maybe Huan was drunk?

"Well?" Huan leaned forward.

"My wife won't like it," Charles said automatically. Ruth did not approve of the Communists' ban on religion, the so-called opiate of the people.

"That's the brilliance of my idea. No one would ever suspect you of talking to a Communist!" Huan explained. "I'll do whatever I can to help you, of course, but you know, under the table. I'll consider you one of my staff. I'll compensate you for the extra work. What do you need?"

Charles was on the verge of laughing and telling his brother that he'd have to find someone else for the job, when he had an idea. Huan had access to American rations, to food. He could use his brother's connections to get more food for the family.

He agreed then, to this crazy scheme. "I have an idea," Charles told his brother. "I can't talk to Zhou outright. My wife would be furious—"

"No, no, of course not. Besides, if Chiang got wind of it, he'd have to have you killed. No, you have to think of a subtle approach."

"Yes, as I was saying—"

"Don't tell anyone that I came to talk to you either." Huan looked worried suddenly. "I thought you understood—"

"I do! Listen. I have an idea." Charles raised his voice, easily overwhelming that of his brother.

"Ssh!"

Charles sighed. "As dean of the law school, I can invite Zhou to be a guest lecturer. He can offer a class on the administration of law under the Communists' soviets. No one has to know anything about our other 'discussions.' It can all seem very innocent and academic"—he smiled at his brother—"and *boring*."

Huan clasped his hands together, pleased. "I knew you'd think of something."

"There's just one thing," Charles said. "I'll need some compensation. All the time I don't spend teaching or preparing my classes—"

"Don't mention it. Of course, I'll get you whatever you need—"

"The boys need better food. They're growing—"

Huan stood up. "Don't worry. I'll help you. What are brothers for?" He tipped his glass of bourbon and drained the contents. "*Gan bei*," he said.

Although my father did not for one minute believe that this scheme would work, he did invite Zhou to lecture at the law school. However, because he did not want to be seen talking to "that Communist," as my mother called Zhou Enlai, my father did not attend his lectures. Instead, he sent his favorite students to attend Zhou's class and report back to him what was discussed.

Zhou turned out to be a remarkable lecturer and soon many patriotic students wanted to leave Chongqing to join the Communists in their stronghold in Yan'an in the north. My father, inspired by Zhou's gift for rhetoric, sent him long queries: If private property is abolished, what will prevent the state from assuming the role of absentee landlord? Have the Communists drawn up a constitution? How would they ensure that the laws were enforced?

He carried on this proxy debate for many weeks, then several months. My father grew excited and cheerful, staying at work for long hours, enjoying himself for the first time in years. My father loved a good debate.

During this time, our family food supply also vastly improved. We even ate meat from time to time. My father led our mother to believe that he had made some new connections at the law school; he did not mention Huan's scheme at all.

One afternoon Huan showed up at his office unannounced. He placed his dapper hat on Charles's desk but began his questioning before he'd even bothered to unbutton his topcoat. "So have you talked to Zhou yet?"

"He's brilliant, but devious," Charles exclaimed. "The Communists have already implemented their agricultural reforms in the areas they control. He agrees that education is essential if their plans for soviets are going to work, but so far as I can tell they're only inculcating the people with their propaganda. Still, they seem to be sincerely intent on building an egalitarian society—"

"Have you talked to him about defecting?" Huan interrupted coldly.

Charles was startled. "Well, not yet. It's too soon. I'm still trying to understand his—"

Huan exploded, slamming his palm against Charles's desk, sending a pile of students' papers fluttering across the floor. "You realize how important this is to us? You always have your head in the clouds—"

"I'm establishing a relationship," Charles defended himself. "I can't just blurt out, 'Leave Mao! We'll give you American arms and a high position!' I have to convince him we're worth joining first."

"Worth joining? Listen to your talk. This Communist is converting you." Huan picked up his hat and turned to go. "Just remember, I'm counting on you. We need Zhou. Chiang isn't going to win on his own. I could lose my position."

"*We* could lose the war to Japan," Charles reminded him archly.

"Don't lecture me." Huan left, letting the door slam behind him.

As pressure, Huan decreased the amount of American goods that he had been secretly giving to Charles.

My father did not know exactly what he should do. It was clear to him that Zhou would never leave Mao. If he were to broach the subject, Zhou would clearly see through this whole lecture scheme. He might even complain to someone in Chiang's cabinet.

Chiang was growing increasingly paranoid as the war dragged on and the Japanese continued to score victory after victory. He periodically purged the ranks of his cadres, demoting men left and right, leaving them no face and no means to support their families. Anyone who was thought to be sympathetic to the Communists was in danger. Even Americans who were sympathetic to Mao were persona non grata with the generalissimo and his cliques. Even Stilwell. His service to the Chinese was above reproach, he'd trained Chinese troops in Burma, he spoke Chinese, he loved Chinese culture, but Chiang complained to Washington, tirelessly campaigning for Vinegar Joe's removal. (Eventually, FDR did recall Stilwell to the United States in October of 1944, replacing him with a man more to Chiang's liking, General Albert Wedemeyer, a fervent anticommunist.)

Students warned my father that strangers had been spotted on the campus, suspicious-looking men whom they suspected were part of Chiang's secret police, sent to spy on the populace and keep "order" in the capital.

Finally, my father turned to my mother for help, confessing his part in Huan's plot to convert Zhou Enlai.

"Don't you realize, Chiang could put you to death!" she gasped. "Don't you understand anything? He hates them. He hates the Communists. He'll kill anyone he thinks is sympathetic to them. How could you do this? How will we live if you die? You may not love me enough, but think of your sons! How could you?"

She insisted that my father have nothing to do with Zhou, that he never even be on campus on the days Zhou was to lecture. She told him to be sure to speak out against the Communists in faculty meetings. He followed her advice.

Huan eventually realized his brother was stonewalling and called off the whole project. He had the university cancel Zhou's course, mid-semester, much to the dismay of the students, and then cut off the special food supply that he'd been funneling to my father. For the duration of the war he had nothing to do with us.

But Huan's anger paled before my mother's fury.

She could never forgive my uncle for this last act of treachery, as she saw it. Huan had put his brother's life at risk, just to further his career.

My father tried to explain that his brother was acting in the best interests of China, that an alliance with the Communists was necessary if China had any hope of defeating the Japanese, even some of the Americans thought so.

"Your brother only cares about his career. He was using you to make himself look good. 'The best interests of China' had nothing to do with it!" My mother, never blinded by patriotism or ideals, could always see straight to the heart of any power struggle.

My mother forbade my father from having any further contact with his brother. And she meant it. Even after the war was long over, even after my family had immigrated to America, she could not forgive my uncle Huan.

~ *May-lee* ~

My grandmother's anger used to frighten me. I couldn't understand how anyone could be so unforgiving. A memory for past injustices so long.

I've tried to understand. I've tried to find a point of comparison. The closest American analogy I can think of to the atmosphere in Chongqing in the 1940s would be the McCarthy era, of course, except that more people in Chongqing met the fate of Julius and Ethel Rosenberg, and being merely blacklisted would have been a benign fate for those Chinese accused of Communist sympathies.

The political paranoia did not end with the Communist victory. Mao proclaimed the founding of the People's Republic of China on October 1, 1949, in Beijing, then systematically began taking over city after city until Chiang was forced to move the capital of the Republic of China to Taipei on the island of Taiwan in December of 1949. From Taiwan, Chiang vowed to "recover the mainland." His secret police kept close scrutiny on the populace, made up of some two million refugees from the mainland and some six million Taiwan residents. Anyone caught making openly critical comments against his government might be spirited away in the night by the secret police, never to be seen again. He declared martial law, forbidding contact with the mainland by residents on Taiwan; even reading a mainland newspaper or sending letters to family members separated by the civil war were prohibited. (This ban on direct travel and mail was not lifted until 1987.) Schools were not permitted to teach subjects related to the mainland, such as modern Chinese history. Chiang even insisted upon calling the mainland government in English "Chicoms," a slur for "Chinese Communists." All throughout his twenty-five-year reign as president of the Republic of China on Taiwan until his death in 1975, Chiang insisted that someday the republic on Taiwan would "take back the mainland."

In reality, despite Chiang Kai-shek's tough talk, the only thing that saved Taiwan from being quickly conquered by the Communists was the outbreak of the Korean War in 1950, when the United States decided to intervene. President Harry Truman reversed his neutral stance and ordered the U.S. Seventh Fleet to prevent any attack on Taiwan. It was the start of the Cold War and Truman was unwilling to let another country fall to communism. Then in 1954, the U.S. Congress passed the Mutual Defense Treaty, which stated:

> The government of the Republic of China [Taiwan] grants, and the Government of the United States of America accepts, the right to dispose such United States land, air and sea forces in and about Taiwan and the Pescadores as may be required for their defense, as determined by mutual agreement.

To this day, the civil war between the mainland and Taiwan has never officially ended. The tense state of affairs was made clear to the rest of the world when China fired three missiles at Taiwan in a "weapons test" in the spring of 1996 and the United States had to send two aircraft carrier groups to the Taiwan Straits to prevent war. Most recently, Chinese leaders issued threats during Taiwan's presidential election in March of 2000, promising military retaliation if the winning proindependence party candidate Chen Shui-bian sought independence for Taiwan.

Even if I will never fully appreciate my grandmother's rage, I have to admit now that I admire how well she appraised the political situation in Chongqing, how she understood the degree to which the war between the Nationalists and Communists would endure, passionately, well beyond the war with Japan.

17

THE UNFORGIVEN

Charles giving a calligraphy demonstration in one of his classes at the New School in New York, circa 1970.

~ *Winberg* ~

I did not see my uncle Huan again until shortly before his death.

In 1972, long after we'd immigrated to the United States, my father received a disturbing letter from his older brother, who had fled to Taiwan after the Communists' victory in 1949. Huan was dying of a liver disease. Huan wrote that his wife, tired of his philandering ways, had left him years ago. Their only child, an adopted daughter, had become a flight attendant and flown away, never to return. Huan had many regrets. He had behaved selfishly his whole life, treated his family shabbily, thought only of himself. He could admit that now. He would die soon and heaven would judge him. There was no point wishing the past away now. However, he did have one final request: he would like to see his brother again once before he died.

My father sighed. He knew that my mother would never forgive him if he went to see his brother, even now. She would only say that Huan was finally getting what he'd deserved. Charles had promised never to have anything to do with his family again, not after all the trouble they'd caused. He could hear Ruth's voice in his head as clearly as if she were actually speaking: Where was Huan's pity when they were starving in Chongqing? Huan had put his brother's life in danger, he'd refused to lift a finger to help them. Huan's wife was gone because he'd never been faithful to her, unfaithful in war, then in peace. His daughter was gone because he'd never treated her like a real daughter; she was lucky to escape him. A selfish man. A spiteful man. An evil man meeting a just fate.

He's never helped you without a price, Ruth would have reminded him. Why do you still trust him after everything he's done to your family?

My father called me from his office. He was now working as an account auditor in the legal department for the City of New York. I was surprised to receive the call. He'd never called me from work, and never during the day. Ever thrifty, my parents called at off-peak hours, late at night, on weekends. Now this unexpected call mid-morning.

By this time, I was a married man, with two children, a professor at the University of Redlands in southern California. This morning, I had not yet left for my classes when the phone rang. The sunlight was warm as it filtered through the kitchen windows, but my skin chilled as my father's voice buzzed in my ear. He'd had a heart attack recently and my first thought was that he was ill.

"Winberg, I need you to do something for me," my father whispered. His whispering was an illogical thing for him to do, I thought, as he was speaking in Chinese in his office, and who would understand him?

"What's the matter?"

"I need you to go to Taiwan. To see your uncle. My brother is dying. I need you to talk to him. I have something to tell him. A special message. I can't go, you know."

"Of course I'll go," I agreed immediately. I would do as my father wished, whatever he asked of me.

"But you must promise me that you'll never tell your mother," he whispered, his voice so low that it was a mere tickle in my head.

"Don't worry," I said. "I won't say anything." Full of glib confidence, I had no idea then what the consequences of my promise would be.

Because I'd left Taiwan at age seventeen and never gone back, when I thought of Taiwan in America, I remembered my life there with a schoolboy's preoccupations: first of all, high school and studying every hour of every day. Second, I remembered our relative poverty, the anxiety of having to buy food on the black market, of always feeling hungry. We ate pineapple every meal, every day, because we had pineapple plants in our yard. We all had canker sores, our gums burned with acid, but still we had to eat more pineapple. (Although my family considered me statuesque, when I first arrived in America to attend college I was five feet eight inches tall and weighed exactly ninety-eight pounds.)

Finally, I remembered waiting for the Communists' army to attack. Everyone assumed they would storm the island. Taiwan is only a little more than one hundred miles from the coast of the Chinese mainland. Living in Taiwan in 1949 was like living atop a time bomb without knowing when it was set to go off; you heard the ticking of the clock every second of every day.

Now returning as a man, I found Taiwan changed, or at least Taipei the capital almost unrecognizable. The heat was the same, but the congestion, the purposeful traffic, the honking cars and motorbikes, the budding skyscrapers, the smell of exhaust of the wind, reminded me of New York. I was temporarily in a state of sensory confusion, caught between worlds and ages in my life.

But the sense of dislocation ended immediately when I arrived at my family's house. My uncle Huan was now living with my youngest aunt, Orchid, and her businessman husband from Shanghai, the man whom my mother had always referred to as "the Gangster." (My father's eldest sister, called "Gu Mu" by my daughter, had returned to China with her husband years earlier and at the time we did not know how she had fared.)

My aunt greeted me warmly, welcoming me into the house, a traditional one-story compound along one of Taipei's back alleys. As she apologized that her husband was not yet home from his office, he'd had some business to take care of, she had me sit in the sitting room, in the best chair, stiff straight-backed cherrywood, while she bustled about, bringing me a steaming cup of tea and a bowl of licorice prune candies. I felt like a little boy again. Only after my auntie Orchid and I had exchanged pleasantries and she had congratulated me on my Ph.D. and the births of my children (in that order), did she bring up the subject of my uncle Huan.

"He still understands us, I think." She fanned herself briskly, wrinkling her short flat nose. "Just tell him who you are. Squeeze his hand. Don't worry. He's not contagious. At least, I don't think so."

Just then her husband came in the front door. He was a large man with a round pumpkin face and a melon belly, quite plump for a Chinese man of his generation. He was sweating profusely and slightly out of breath. When he saw me, his eyebrows shot up and he slapped his forehead. "*Aiya!* You're here already!"

"You're late!" my aunt charged back. "How embarrassing!"

"You should call me and tell me my nephew's arrived." He rushed over to pump my hand, American-style. "Look at you! So handsome. So tall. Look at him! Takes after his mother. She was quite a looker."

Orchid sniffed. "Eat some snacks," she said, offering me the bowl of candies. "Didn't you pick up the red-bean-paste buns I asked you to get?" She shook her head at her husband. "My nephew's just come all the way from America. Don't you think he's hungry?" She sighed and scurried toward the kitchen.

"I'm fine, I'm not hungry," I insisted, as was expected. I was relieved that my aunt and uncle were so pleasant. This trip wasn't going to be so bad after all, I thought. No hard feelings at this end at all.

Now my uncle eased himself into the chair next to mine, setting his attaché case carefully at his feet. He took out a handkerchief from his pocket and dabbed at his face delicately. "Now Winberg, we have to talk about your uncle Huan." He licked his lips nervously. "I know in the past we've had some family disputes, some little differences of opinion—"

"The past is the past," I said quickly.

"Yes, that's right!" My uncle laughed happily. He clapped his hands together. "Did you hear what our nephew said, Orchid? That's the way to think," he called toward the kitchen. He turned his attention back toward me. "Now I don't suppose you've had a chance to see your uncle—"

"How could he? He just arrived!" Orchid returned bearing a tray of fruit, bananas, pears, and Taiwanese pineapple, of course.

"So I want to prepare you," my uncle continued. "Remember, he's very weak. He had a stroke a few days ago, you know."

"I didn't," I said.

My uncle nodded gravely, leaning very close to me now. All his features were larger than a normal person's, which made his expressions more pronounced. Now his face seemed to be in the process of melting in the heat, his eyebrows covering his eyes like hairy parasols, his nose drooping toward his jowls. As he spoke, I felt as though I were shrinking, my forty years melting away too, as I became a little boy again, while his face seemed to grow larger and larger. "He won't be able to speak to you. So I'll tell you. He loves your father very much. His only brother. He's always loved his little brother. You know that."

I nodded, my words caught in my throat.

"Of course you do. You're a smart boy. I've always known that. We've been following your career. Your father keeps us informed. You've got your Ph.D. That's great, great. A family of scholars. Your uncle Huan was—is so proud of you. You know that?"

I nodded again.

"Good. Good." Then my uncle reached into his attaché case and took out a thick wad of American hundred-dollar bills and handed them to me.

At first I thought that my uncle was giving the money to me, a reward for coming all this way, and my mouth must have dropped wide open. But then my uncle leaned toward me, his large mouth opening as if he meant to swallow me, as he whispered, "Give this to your uncle Huan. Tell him it's from your father." Then he winked. "I know how it is, professors don't make a lot of money."

Before I could speak, my uncle raised a hand. "We'll let this be our little secret. No need to tell your father."

I nodded. I knew my uncle meant well even if his methods were more flamboyant than my father would have preferred.

Then Orchid led me to my uncle's sickbed.

Huan lay in a back room, shades drawn against the fierce midday sun. He looked nothing like his former, handsome self. He lay shriveled and jaundiced in the gloom, covered with a blanket despite the heat.

"He suffered a stroke a few days ago," Orchid said in a stage whisper, as she turned to go. "Don't expect too much from him. He's practically a vegetable."

I liked my aunt, but I could now see why she had irritated my mother. Orchid was many things, but sensitive was not among them.

"Uncle," I whispered. Huan looked at me, but blankly, his eyes glassy. All at once, I lost my voice completely. It was too hot, too stuffy, in this little room. I looked around for my aunt, but she'd gone. I knelt beside my uncle's bed for a moment until I could speak again with the words that my father had instructed me to say. "Uncle, my father regrets that he could not come to see you, but he's sent me, your firstborn nephew, to represent the family."

Then I held out the thick wad of money so that he could see and placed the bills in Uncle Huan's palm, wrapping his fingers carefully around the bundle. "A gift. From my father. He remembers that you helped him when he was a boy. You smuggled him out of your father's house so that he could take the college entrance examination. You did not marry my mother so that he could marry her. You gave him this life. He has never forgotten."

Miraculously, Huan nodded. He opened his mouth but nothing but air came out.

I knew then that it was time to deliver the special message, the real gift that my father had intended for me to deliver, the secret message that I must never disclose to my mother. "And now my father gives me to you. He has sent me to tell you that he gives me to you as your son. I am now your son too."

Huan's eyes were tearing. His lips moved soundlessly as he reached out to me, his trembling hand clutching at my arm. I took his hand in mine, a surprisingly soft hand for a man so old and sick. His flesh was cool.

"I am your son, Father," I said. "I am your son."

After Huan died, my name was engraved on his tombstone alongside his. I am identified as his firstborn son.

As a rather old-fashioned Buddhist, Huan believed that if he died without leaving any offspring, he would be condemned to walk in hell. He and his ancestors would be forgotten by the living. No one would burn spirit money for him, no one would leave offerings for him at temples; he'd wander in the afterlife an impoverished lonely ghost, nothing to bribe the judges of hell with, nothing to ensure that he'd be born again as a human. But with a son—and such an illustrious son, his own flesh and blood, his brother's firstborn, already with two children to ensure the family's continuity to please the Chai ancestors, a Ph.D., a secure future in America—Huan could die in peace.

My father had converted to Christianity long ago, of course, and was not supposed to believe in any of this. Technically, according to my father's new religion, my uncle Huan would be condemned to hell, son or no son, just because he had never accepted Christ as Lord before his death. My father knew how Christians were supposed to think. But my father loved his brother.

After I returned to America, I told my brothers what had happened to our uncle Huan. After their initial surprise at what I had done, they told my mother. How her firstborn son went to visit her enemy. They told her, and she saw now how her husband had conspired against her, had planned this act of treason.

My mother was furious. Charles had reneged on his promise to her to never have anything to do with his family again. He had lied to her. He'd arranged all this behind her back. He knew what was going on and yet every day he looked her in the face and talked of his work, the weather, the news on TV, as innocently as ever.

My mother wrote a long letter to me then, reminding me of the special bond she had expected to share with me, her firstborn son, how she had opened her heart to me throughout her life, how she had raised me like a prince, sacrificed for me, lived for me. She reminded me of the sins of her enemy, her brother-in-law. How he had allowed us nearly to starve in Chongqing without lifting a finger to help us, his own flesh and blood, although he was wealthy and important. How he had nearly gotten my father killed with his crazy scheme to woo that Communist Zhou Enlai over to "that bandit general" Chiang Kai-shek. How Huan had coveted her youngest son and tried to take him when she was at her weakest, still in the hospital, suffering.

She could never forgive this act of betrayal, my mother wrote; I was no longer her son.

18

BEST INTENTIONS

Nanjing street scene, circa mid-1940s.

~ *May-lee* ~

"Your older sister used to pick on you all the time. When your mother wasn't looking, she would pinch you and make you cry. Whenever you tried to play, she would take your toy away for herself. When you tried to say the alphabet, she would interrupt you, never let you finish. She made fun of you. She told you that you were stupid."

My middle uncle's face flushed red from the heat of his memories. "You were too young to remember. But I remember."

He sat next to my brother on the couch of our family room in our house in New Jersey. My brother, seven, held two dolls—that is, two action figures—on his lap, but he was no longer playing with them. He listened raptly, with equal measures of fascination and horror, as my uncle recounted a childhood that my brother did not recall.

"She made you cry." My uncle shook his head. Then he squeezed my brother's shoulders. "Don't let her pick on you. You're smart too."

After my uncle went back home to New York, my brother refused to play with me. Then he confronted my mother about these injustices. "May-lee was mean to me!" he shouted indignantly.

My mother looked at him in surprise. "What are you talking about? You and your sister always got along."

My brother looked unconvinced, but my mother was offended now. "I would never let anyone treat you like that."

Then my brother realized she was right. Our mother did not tolerate bickering or bullying. Other mothers had held us up as examples to their squabbling brood: See how they get along? We'd been especially proud of ourselves.

But once again, one of my uncles was taking preventive measures to guard against the tyranny of the firstborn.

Because my father was the firstborn son, my grandparents had treated him like a prince. He'd behaved like one. And there was nothing his younger brothers could do about it. While they were forced to do household chores, he was allowed to give orders. When the three of them got into trouble, only his brothers were punished.

When my father first came to America, he made up for his war-torn adolescence by joining a fraternity and partying his way through his undergraduate years. He spent his parents' money on fashionable clothes, including white patent-leather shoes. When he sent home a picture of himself in his fraternity jacket with the infamous shoes, his parents were so alarmed, they immediately sent him more money. "Winberg, why didn't you tell us you didn't have winter shoes?" They didn't want their son, their representative in America, going around in what they assumed from the photos must have been cotton slippers.

When his brothers came to America to study, they worked diligently in school, no parties for them, noses to the grindstone, as the family's resources were no longer sufficient to support the fraternity lifestyle.

My father was the first of his brothers to marry, and the first to give his parents a grandchild. Me. As the first grandchild, the first Chai to be born in America, the first girl after all those years when my grandmother had wanted a daughter, I was apparently a source of great pride for my grandparents. They alarmed my mother when, shortly after my birth, they began to discuss which college I should attend. My grandfather immediately went out and splurged on a silver-and-porcelain antique tea set, "for the firstborn."

My uncles could see the pattern of their childhood repeating. But if they could not openly criticize their brother without being disloyal to their parents, they could do their best to ensure that I didn't follow in his bossy footsteps.

When I was eight, I won a decoupage kit because I was the first in my third-grade class to memorize the multiplication tables. None of us exactly understood the concept of decoupage, even after we studied the illustrations of magazine pictures (not included) being burned onto wooden plaques (included in the kit), but a prize was a prize. My parents told my grandparents all about it when they came to visit for Sunday dinner.

"That's nothing," my youngest uncle said at the table. "Do you know algebra? If you don't know algebra, you don't know math." It was well-known in the family that he was a mathematical genius, so I listened to his every word.

"What's algebra?"

"If A equals B and B equals C, what does A equal?" he said in his rapid-fire way.

"What? What do you mean A?"

"Ha!" He repeated the equation. "Don't you get it? C!" he practically shouted. "A equals C!" He shook his head now. "You don't know math if you don't know algebra."

My mother explained that I wouldn't study algebra until I was in high school, but I thought my grandparents seemed disappointed at my failure all the same.

Despite the ribbing I regularly took from my uncles, they also gave me a hundred dollars every Christmas and for my birthday. My youngest uncle taught me chess and poker. He gave me good advice on college. My middle uncle played with me and my brother and cousins when we were children; he told us jokes and never failed to bring us fun gifts whenever he came over for the holidays; he invited us all to be in his wedding party.

It's inevitable in any family there will be rivalries and hurt feelings. Do siblings feel they are ever loved enough? Can we forgive the disappointment we experience? Certainly, these afflictions were as much a part of my father's family as any family, and yet I think they would all say they loved each other.

~

The year after my father went to visit his uncle's deathbed, after his mother supposedly had broken all ties with him, we moved from California to New Jersey. My father was teaching at City College in New York. We visited my grandparents every weekend in Manhattan. Over the holidays, my grandparents came to stay with us. While Ye-ye and my father discussed their new book projects, Nai-nai sat in the kitchen with my mother and talked about her hard life.

Nai-nai periodically sent my father long letters instructing him how best to live his life. Sometimes she told him about a new promotional offer at a city bank: open a new account and get a toaster or a vacuum cleaner. She gave precise directions how to get to this branch and when the promotion ended. Sometimes she would relate an incident from their war years, something emotional and horrible, something she wanted him to remember. But my father would become so upset that he would rip up her letters immediately. My mother tried to restrain him, telling him that someday he'd be sorry he hadn't saved his mother's letters, but he couldn't stop himself.

When I was a child, my father acted as though he could make the past go away.

~ *Winberg* ~

It's hard to explain to your children so that they understand your motivations.

I did not make my children study Chinese when they were young and joyful. But are they grateful? In front of family friends, my daughter points a long finger at my nose. "He wouldn't teach us Chinese." She says this as if it were a punishment, as if studying Chinese when you're a child is a fun thing, like going to Disneyland.

No child wants to study Chinese, not really, not after the first one hundred characters. Does my daughter think children in China enjoy studying Chinese? She's wrong. They're forced to study by their parents. I remember when I was young, oh, how we hated to go to school. The teacher carried a long thin stick and he could beat your hands or the backs of your legs if he wanted, if you couldn't memorize well, if you forgot how to write a character. My youngest brother was forced to stand all day long in the corner of the school in our village in Hunan. He couldn't memorize. He was too young to be in school at all, just a toddler really, but he was very clever, precocious, and our mother thought he should go to school. But because he was too young to speak properly, he couldn't recite, of course, and the teacher punished him every day. He began to cry and cry every morning, begging to stay at home. It wasn't until my mother discovered what was happening that she took him out of school.

All my friends who sent their children to Chinese school in America reported to me that their children hated it. They hated memorizing so much, they didn't like having to go to school on Saturdays or after the regular school day was over. They wanted to play, they wanted to participate in extracurricular activities with their non-Chinese friends, they complained all the time.

So I spared my children this misery, and now my daughter points the accusatory finger.

When my daughter was still a little girl but beginning to be a bigger girl—I have no idea what age she was, only my wife could keep track of the children's ages—she came home from school one day, angrily pointing her index finger at me. "You lied to us!" my daughter charged.

"I never lied to you!" I could say this with some certainty, even though I had no idea what she was talking about, because I knew that it was impossible to lie to a child. What did a child understand? I never discussed important things with my children when they were young, what was there to lie about? I'd never even bothered with inventing white lies about Santa Claus and the Easter Bunny although it is quite socially acceptable to do so.

But my daughter would not be placated. "We are studying human biology now," she announced, enunciating the syllables importantly. "And today we started the unit on the digestive tract." She paused as if I should immediately grasp the significance of this. "Don't you remember how you always told us that if we jumped up and down after we ate, the food would go down the acid tube in our stomach and we would die?"

I nodded. I didn't remember saying this but it sounded like a reasonable, fatherly thing to say. After all, who wants their children to jump up and down after eating?

"Well, the science teacher showed us a film about the stomach today!"

"How terrible," I said.

"No, no, no. It's good. She showed us and there's no acid tube! I even asked her. You won't *die* if you jump up and down after eating. You'll only get *indigestion*" She pronounced the word with triumph in her voice.

"Yes," I said.

"You lied to us!" My daughter now had her brother at her side, encouraging him to feel incensed as well. "You said we'd die!"

"Well, well, well," I said, stalling until my wife could rescue me from this conversation. I still couldn't see where the problem lay. My daughter should have been grateful that I was so concerned about her and her brother's health that I wanted to spare them stomachaches. Some parents would have merely allowed their children to find out the hard way. Let them jump until they feel sick, then they'll understand, these parents think. But I wanted to spare my children even this pain. And what thanks do I get?

I think that there will always be this gap in understanding between parents and children. It is because our perspectives are so different.

It's very hard to explain to my children how I think. The logic is self-evident, what's to explain? I'm sure all parents feel this way. My parents must have. My mother certainly. I try to remember this when I think about their lives, the decisions they made.

It occurs to me that I have forgotten to say how kind my mother could be.

After the Americans dropped their atomic bombs on Japan and the Japanese were defeated in August of 1945, we moved back home to Nanjing. We didn't recognize the city at first, the wall was missing, gone in huge sections. Now it was broken like a smile with no teeth. Large portions of the city, entire neighborhoods of wooden shops and houses, had been burned to the ground. The buildings that remained were no longer grand, but stooped and crumbling.

We found our house, dilapidated, ruined. The half that had been my mother's school was now inhabited by the prostitutes and their Russian pimp. I cried seeing it. The whole journey from Chongqing,

I'd grown more and more excited at the thought of returning to our lovely, warm house, as if moving in again would restore the life we once had. But though my mother herself banged on the front door, the pimp refused to let us in.

We installed ourselves in the adjoining quarters, which were quite run-down now, while my parents tried to think of a plan.

My father was now working four jobs, as no single position's salary provided enough money to survive on: professor of law at National Central University, counselor of law in the Judicial Yuan, adjunct professor at Nanjing Christian Girls College (which my mother's parents had helped to found), and dean of administration at National Cheng-chi University, which had been established originally in Chongqing for Chiang Kai-shek's cadres. The campus needed to be rebuilt in Nanjing from scratch, a faculty, a library, a student body. My mother ostensibly was professor of English at both National Central and Cheng-chi, but her salary was a pittance. She spent most of her time trying to procure food and fix up her house. Even so we were better off than many families.

Somehow members of our old household found us, servants that had once been associated with my grandparents' household or with the missionaries as well. Cousins whom we hadn't seen in years, and who we thought might have been killed, suddenly appeared at our doorstep. They all wanted one thing—my mother's help.

She may have had a reputation for being difficult—that is, for being an opinionated woman—but everyone knew that my mother was smart and tough and if anyone could find a way to survive, she would.

Their faith was not misplaced.

After my father convinced his law students to rally against the pimp in the name of nationalism and bodily remove him and his prostitutes from our house, my mother used my father's connections to procure building supplies and construction crews to repair her dream house. At night when the workmen had gone home, we dug holes in the backyard trying to find the treasures we had buried there. The money we had hidden in the well was gone, but my mother did find the *Yi-xing* clay tea set her mother had given to her for her graduation so long ago. She'd buried it near the wall and neither the Japanese officers who'd been stationed in our house nor the Russian had found it.

My mother held the clay teapot in her hands as though it were a tiny animal that needed to be comforted. It was then that she became quite obsessed with the idea of finding our treasures. She hired men to dig holes in the backyard, everywhere, looking and looking. She herself searched through our house, picking through the rubble, the piles of broken bricks, the holes in the walls and floors and the ceiling. She ignored me and my brothers for hours as she searched and searched, but she never found what she was looking for.

Only later did we learn that she was looking for her graduation present, her mother's pebble, an irrational act. Only my father could make her stop, convince her of the futility of looking for a lost rock amid rubble. And then she cried.

Just as our house was repaired and made livable again, to my dismay, my mother rented it to some of the Americans who had come to advise Chiang Kai-shek in rebuilding the postwar Republic of China, and we moved out of my mother's house again. I was sad, I cried even though I was a teenager, too old to cry anymore, and that made my brothers cry too, because I had told them stories about how wonderful it was to live in our big house; they were, of course, too young to remember anything but the war.

But my mother explained that we had to be practical. The Americans had money, money that was worth something. On the deed my uncle had signed with the pimp, I see that my mother's house had rented for over a billion Chinese yuan. I'm sure she got more than that from the Americans, perhaps as much as three hundred U.S. dollars per month. She'd built a comfortable house, I knew. And they were grateful to live in such a residence; they didn't want to live like Chinese people, filthy and cold, everyone packed together in one room. My mother understood what Americans expected from a house.

With the rent money, she had the construction crews build us a more traditional-style Chinese compound, no money for a fancy American house anymore. Enclosed within a tall brick wall were clustered four small houses, one for us, another for the servants, a third for one of her cousins, and the fourth for my uncle Shou-tao (her eldest brother) and his family, even though he was the one who'd rented her house to the pimp in the first place.

My uncle had stayed in the city during the entire occupation and he had been witness to the infamous Rape of Nanjing. He didn't like to talk about it, certainly not in my presence. He could only shake his head and say, "It was very bad." I could tell from his tone of voice that I shouldn't ask any more questions. He himself had been spared because he could speak a little Japanese and the soldiers needed someone to translate for them occasionally. My uncle, with his starlet wife acting as his nurse, was able to find work as a doctor with the American missionaries, who kept their hospitals running as long as possible, flying the American flag to show their neutrality. At that time in 1937, Japan had not yet bombed Pearl Harbor and the soldiers held no enmity toward the Americans. The missionaries had tried to save as many Chinese as they could, he told us, taking refugees secretly into their compounds, treating the wounded, but my uncle's grim manner suggested that their efforts had not been much help to most of the populace.

It was Uncle Shou-tao who told us that some of the Japanese officers had used my mother's house as their quarters.

Once my uncle took me to attack some Japanese soldiers. It was in the very beginning, right after the surrender. Because my father had obtained a governmental position, as a counselor in the Judicial Yuan, we were all allowed to fly back to the capital on military cargo planes. There weren't enough seats for all of us on the first flight, so I was allowed to fly home while my parents and brothers waited for a few weeks for a plane with space enough for them. My parents had discovered a very distant member of the Chai family was also taking this first flight and so he pretended that I was a member of his family just so that I could travel with them. I was only thirteen but my parents considered me to be quite mature for my age.

The plane didn't have normal seats, I remember. It was a large hollow shell, and I sat on a crate next to my unknown uncle and rows of grim-faced KMT officials, everyone sitting on his luggage. The whole trip the plane bucked and shivered, the engines' whine a roar in my ear. My uncle sat with his eyes closed, his fists clenched over his kneecaps, but I was disappointed when the ride ended after only a couple of hours.

A military jeep took us from the airport back to my uncle's official residence. As an official legislator, he'd been "awarded" one of the Western-style homes still in good condition after the Japanese occupation. In fact, the returning government officials were all occupying whatever good houses they could find, whether they owned them or not. For this reason, my mother had wanted me to rush home to claim our house before the KMT tried to requisition it.

Although my uncle and his family treated me quite kindly, I was quite relieved when my mother's eldest brother, Uncle Shou-tao, came to pick me up the next day.

He brought me to my mother's house, which he had already rented to the pimp because only such people had any money under the Japanese occupation. My uncle had installed himself in the servants' quarters. Although the pimp wouldn't let us in, I tried to peek into the boarded-up windows, but someone had hung thick curtains in every one, cutting off the view entirely. Standing on my uncle's shoulders, I peeked over the wall into my former nursery school playground next door, but the swing set and teeter-totters had all been carted off, perhaps turned to firewood. An extremely obese Russian woman sat on a stool smoking. I climbed down quickly, thoroughly depressed.

However, my uncle promised that he knew of a way to cheer me up.

During the next week or so, my uncle took me and some of the male servants, who had come by the house to see if our family had returned yet, to the work camp where the Japanese soldiers were being held while they awaited repatriation to Japan. Chiang Kai-shek's soldiers forced the Japanese to do public works, helping to clear rubble, clean streets, repair walls, that kind of menial labor, and my uncle knew where they would be this day.

I was very scared, my heart beating rapidly in my chest. My parents had warned me not to go anywhere near the soldiers, not Chiang Kai-shek's and especially not the Japanese. But my uncle explained that it was our duty as Chinese to defend our city's honor. The servants and I thought this was an excellent idea, but to be honest honor had very little to do with it. I was thirteen years old, the young men who had worked in our house were probably only in their early twenties now at most. We were young men, looking for trouble.

As we approached the boulevard where the Japanese soldiers were marching in columns to their latest work detail, clearing rocks from the remains of a bombed department store, we stopped to hide behind the wall of a building across the street. We were so close to the

Japanese soldiers, I could see the sweat on their faces. They did not look like devils, as I had imagined, but a lot like Chinese boys, only heavier, better fed. No Chinese looked very healthy after the war, it was true.

We watched as they moved methodically, slowly, seemingly without vigor or fatigue. Like sleepwalkers.

"What can we do? What if they attack us?" I whispered excitedly.

"They can't do anything. Our soldiers will shoot them," my uncle said.

"One of them might break loose," one of the servants said thoughtfully. "The Japanese are like demons. They are very sneaky and cunning."

"We'll run and hide," another said. "Have a plan. Think where you'll run first. Then go there. We must all run in different directions. One soldier can't chase all of us."

I swallowed then but held my tongue. Because of my stiff ankle, I was not a very fast runner, but I didn't want anyone to accuse me of cowardice and so I didn't dare back out now. Furthermore, I grew even more anxious as I realized that since the Japanese were moving rocks, they had plenty available to throw back at us, but I knew it was too late to stop our attack.

Now my uncle said, "Be sure to shout at the soldiers, 'Baka yaro!' That's a terrible swear word in Japanese."

"What does it mean?" I wanted to know.

"It doesn't mean anything in Chinese. Only the Japanese have this term."

"Oooh!" I was very impressed.

"On the count of three. One. Two. Three!"

Then we all ran out from behind the wall and started shouting at the Japanese soldiers.

"Baka yaro!"

"Baka yaro!"

"BAKA YARO!"

We spit on them as well. I hit one soldier in the back and another in the arm. One of the servants, a very talented young man, struck a soldier directly in the face. He stopped working for a second and shook his head as if to chase away a mosquito, then he continued to bend and load more rubble into a wheelbarrow. We continued to shout at the Japanese, some of the servants threw rocks, but no matter how hard the rocks struck them, their heads, their faces, leaving bruises and deep bloody gashes, the Japanese did not defend themselves. They did not glare back or even cover their faces to protect themselves. They merely hung their heads and hunched their shoulders, utterly defeated.

They continued at their work.

Even though more than fifty years have passed, I can still see these soldiers as clearly as ever. I have never forgotten that once defeated, their emperor having surrendered, the soldiers of the mighty Japanese Imperial Army allowed us to spit on them and call them names with impunity.

After my family returned to Nanjing, I bragged to my brothers about what I had done. I knew that my adventure would make them jealous. But when my mother found out, she was quite angry, at both my uncle and me.

She yelled at her brother fiercely. "What on earth were you thinking? Taking my son to the Japanese! What if one of them had tried something?"

My uncle tried to explain. "Chiang Kai-shek's soldiers were there. What could the Japanese do?"

"Chiang Kai-shek's soldiers? How dare you! Never take my son near any soldiers!" She continued shouting like this until my uncle apologized and promised that he would never do anything so foolish again.

After he left, she turned on me.

"What were you thinking, Winberg? Spitting at people. Throwing rocks. How could you do such a thing?"

"I didn't throw anything. Besides, they're Japanese!" I retorted defensively. "They're devils!"

"You will do as I say!" she shouted now. She'd never raised her voice to me before; I was shocked. "You will never do such a thing again. This is uncivilized behavior! Do you understand? You are my son! You will never behave like a barbarian!"

I have never forgotten the look on my mother's face then. Her disappointment in me.

Quickly, I promised that I would never spit at the Japanese soldiers again. I would not call them names or taunt them. Ever. And I didn't.

19

STONES

Winberg, Di-di, Mao-mao, and Ruth on Purple
Mountain, outside Nanjing, circa 1946.

~ *May-lee* ~

Every weekend when I visited my grandparents in Manhattan, they
would give me stones. Before I arrived, they would place a tiny box
of polished rocks on the third shelf of their china cabinet, a tall
wooden cupboard with glass doors, filled with all their treasures from
Nanjing. If I stood on tiptoe, I could just see the box of stones at the
very edge of the third shelf.

Ye-ye would take me by the hand and stand me in front of the
cabinet and say dramatically, "You can have anything inside.
Choose." There were many unusual objects on the glass shelves: a
miniature silver temple under a clear dome, two blossoming trees
made of jade, cloisonné bud vases—the colors muted with age, several long silver hairpins, paintings rolled tightly into scrolls, and odd-
shaped porcelain vases covered with dragons and chrysanthemums
and frightening devil faces. And without hesitation, I always chose
the box of pretty rocks.

My grandparents had purchased these stones at various stops
along their great American road trip, which they'd taken together
with my uncles and father after my father won money on *Name That*

Tune and bought a car. The only disaster occurred in Salt Lake City, when what they thought were crystals started to melt on the dashboard. They had mistakenly bought rock candy. "How terrible, how terrible," my grandmother said, laughing, shaking her head at the memory of the melting rocks.

My grandparents and I may have had our problems communicating, but our love of stones was something we shared.

I thought this stone-collecting was a family peculiarity until I went to live in Nanjing in college and I discovered the hobby was shared by a city. A museum was even devoted to housing a collection of especially pretty rocks. The stones were displayed in little porcelain bowls of water to bring out the colors. How charming, I thought.

When my friends at Nanjing University found out that I liked to collect stones too, they took me to the Rain Flower Terrace Park, where the most beautiful stones used to be plentiful, like flowers after the rain. However, although we scoured the grounds, we could find nothing but granite and bits of flint and chunks of abandoned cement blocks from a nearby construction project. Apparently during the ten years of the Cultural Revolution, the park had been picked clean of its famous stones, either by Red Guards out of spite or poor people looking to use the stones for barter, my friends speculated.

"How terrible," they sighed.

I knew exactly what they meant.

~ *Winberg* ~

My mother used to take us hunting for stones, after the war with Japan had ended and we thought that the peace was real. We had no idea that the Communists were trying to wrest control of the country, province by province. Chiang Kai-shek permitted the newspapers to print only positive news, glowing reports of national reconstruction. Mao and his soldiers were referred to as mere "village bandits."

In 1948, my mother's second brother, living in Fujian province where he was commissioner of health, wrote to my mother and asked that she take in his daughter. He wanted his daughter to get a good education and he assumed that the schools in the capital would be better than in the provinces, even if Nanjing was as changed as he had heard. My mother agreed, and for the first time in our lives, my brothers and I knew what it was like to have an older sister.

My mother was thrilled. She called this girl her "daughter," and my cousin and she spent much time together. Because she was a girl, about seventeen or eighteen years old, my cousin helped my mother with many chores—from sewing to shopping in the markets. As boys in those days, my brothers and I never had to do such things.

In the summer, every Sunday we would take a picnic to Purple Mountain to look for stones and escape the terrible heat of the city and the dust from all the massive building projects—Chiang Kai-shek was spending millions of dollars of American aid money to rebuild his capital. In the mountains, among the cool pines, we could believe that our lives would return to normal someday.

In the Nanjing tradition, my mother showed us how to find the best stones. She liked unusual shapes, textures, but color was especially important. She had us take our rocks to a nearby stream and test the color in the water, to see what was revealed.

"Like magic," my mother sighed, as she sat on the bank, cooling herself with a bamboo fan shaped like a palm leaf.

I found a rock that looked gray and dull but when placed in the stream revealed veins of deepest red.

Delighted, my mother bent closer to the water. "You can call it your 'Heart Stone'." She dangled her feet in the cool stream. "I used to like to come here with my mother," she said dreamily, "when I was a little girl."

"You can still remember?"

She laughed. "Oh, yes, as far back as that. Even further. Boys forget, don't they?"

"No, I can remember everything. Our house, your school . . . I remember . . ." I tried to think of something that I had missed during the war. "I remember eating Nanjing eels!" Fried with scallions. My stomach gurgled at the mere thought of this tasty delicacy.

"Well, then we have nothing to worry about." My mother smiled, which surprised me. I wasn't used to her smile.

My cousin sneaked up from the reeds and splashed me, kicking water furiously until I was soaked. Even though she was a girl, she was quite bold, not at all what I imagined a sister would be like. I jumped up to give chase.

"Wait! Don't forget your stone!" My mother held it out to me on her palm.

"You can have it, Ma!" I shouted and dashed off after my incorrigible cousin.

That evening, when I went to bed, I lay back on my pillow and struck my head on something hard. It was the Heart Stone. My mother had placed it in my pillowcase so that I'd be sure to find it. She'd wrapped a note around the rock, written in her strong calligraphy, which I now discovered:

THIS STONE CAME FROM PURPLE MOUNTAIN,
OUTSIDE THE CAPITAL OF THE REPUBLIC OF CHINA,
NANJING, 1948.

20

THE RIGHT DECISION

Ruth's niece, Mao-mao, Winberg, and Di-di on
Purple Mountain, circa 1947.

~ *May-lee* ~

I've found all these pictures from Purple Mountain in my father's
albums: my father and uncles and their cousin posing between the
giant stone statues of animals that lined the path to the Ming dynasty
emperor's tomb, in front of the white stone steps leading to the Sun
Yat-sen mausoleum, before giant bronze bells and other antiquities.

My father and his brothers and cousin look like typical teenagers—bored. They don't want to pose for pictures. They glare at
the camera. Looking at the two or three photos of my grandparents
from this period, I am shocked by how much they've changed. My
grandfather is a bone of a man, his Western-style suit appears far
too large for his frame. My grandmother, in her early forties at most,
looks ghostlike, ravaged. Deep black shadows ring her eyes, her
cheeks are hollow, she wraps her arms around her body as if she is
always cold.

My father insists that after the Japanese were defeated, the family
never once doubted that the war was over; America was firmly behind Chiang Kai-shek, everything would one day be normal again.
My grandfather worked in the Judicial Yuan under Dr. Wang Chung-

hui (who was also a returned student, from Yale) along with American advisors, including the famous American jurist Harvard Law School Dean Roscoe Pound. They worked to construct a new democratic Chinese constitution, a thorough revision of the 1936 draft. For the first time in my grandfather's lifetime, it seemed that China was finally going to become a democracy after all. The republic had survived. All the KMT newspapers said so.

In the spring of 1948, the National Assembly promulgated the new constitution and Chiang Kai-shek was officially named president. However, he did not name his vice president, allowing the Assembly to vote for candidates. My grandfather campaigned for Li Tsung-jen and was overjoyed when his candidate was elected on the fourth ballot.

Only in 1949 did the family become aware that the political tide had changed. America no longer supported Chiang. A decade earlier, *Time* magazine had featured Chiang and his wife, Wellesley graduate Soong Mei-ling, on the cover as "Man and Wife of the Year" in January 1938. Chiang had been proclaimed "the greatest man in the Far East" and the "Ningpo Napoleon" (*Time*, November 1936), and Madame Chiang, Western educated and a Methodist, was once lauded in the *New York Times Magazine* as no less than "the awakening of Chinese womanhood" (March 15, 1942). In 1943, Madame Chiang had addressed the joint session of the U.S. Congress, requesting more money and support for the KMT in Chongqing. She'd embarked on a month-long tour across the United States, drawing crowds of tens of thousands of admirers. Glowing reports of "China's First Lady" appeared in every major newspaper and magazine, including a fashion spread in *Vogue*.[1] However, by the late forties, reports of gross corruption under Chiang had sullied their reputations in America. When Madame Chiang embarked on another fund-raising trip to the United States in November of 1948, she was not invited to speak before Congress and newly reelected President Harry Truman pointedly refused to allow her to stay at the White House. By this time, the United States had already given Chiang's government some $3.8 billion in aid.[2]

---

[1] T. Christopher Jesperson, *American Images of China, 1931–1949* (Stanford: Stanford University Press, 1996), pp. 96–98.

[2] Sterling Seagrave, *The Soong Dynasty* (New York: Harper & Row, 1985), p. 433.

In January of 1949, the Communists defeated Chiang's troops in central China, taking 325,000 soldiers prisoner. Chiang reportedly ordered the air force to bomb his own troops in order to keep their weapons and supplies from falling into the Communists' hands.[3] Now Chiang's top generals began to sign pacts with the Communists, defecting one by one. Those who allied with the Communists included my grandfather's former boss, General Chang Chih-chung, as well as Fu Tso-yi, the commander in chief of Manchuria; Li Chi-shen, president of Chiang Kai-shek's Military Advisory Council and a Guangxi warlord; Li Pin-hsien, warlord from Guangdong; Lung Yun, warlord from Yunnan; and Tu Yu-ming, Chiang Kai-shek's former student at the prestigious Whampoa Military Academy and a hero in the battles against the Japanese.

Refugees began to pour into Nanjing again, from the Communist-controlled north, reporting atrocities, mass executions of the so-called landlord class, of people with educations, with ties to the West, with religion.

No one knew what to do. It was never obvious that Chiang was preparing to leave, sending his best troops to Taiwan, to secure his power there rather than fight for it on the mainland. In fact, there had been some talk of a possible reconciliation between the Nationalists and the Communists. However, Mao refused to negotiate with Chiang. Chiang "retired" on January 21 and my grandfather's friend Li Tsung-jen became acting president. However, because the Communists were winning, they no longer felt the need to negotiate and the Nanjing government all but collapsed. By the end of April, Li moved the government south to Canton, where many refugees were fleeing, awaiting their permits to travel to Taiwan.

My father's family fled first to Shanghai then headed south to Canton to await their permit to travel to Taiwan. Here the family found itself torn: Ye-ye thought the family should stay in China.

Acting President Li Tsung-jen had offered my grandfather an important post as Deputy Minister of Justice, the position of a lifetime, a real opportunity to shape China's judicial system. Li was planning to move the entire Nationalist government back to Chongqing, just as Chiang had done during the Sino-Japanese War. He figured that he could lead the Nationalists in the civil war from the mountain

---

[3] Seagrave, pp. 432–433.

hideaways until it was possible to negotiate a truce with the Communists, and he wanted my grandfather to join his government. "The Communists need us," Li insisted. "They have no background in government. How will they run the country?"

At the same time, Ye-ye received a counteroffer from the Communists, who had sent spies to Canton to investigate Li's plans. One of my grandfather's former students from his Officer Training Institute in Hunan had defected to work for Mao. He now promised my grandfather amnesty if he returned to Nanjing. "I know you are an honest man," his former student said. "I know you want the best for China. We could use a man like you."

But my grandmother insisted that the family had to go to Taiwan. There was no way the family could stay under the Communists. "No matter what they say," Nai-nai reminded her husband, "you were educated in America, you're a Christian, your family owned land. They will never trust you."

Because my grandparents had no ties to Chiang's army, like many other Chinese, they were afraid of following Chiang to Taiwan, where they had never been before. They imagined the island to be a desolate place, like the end of the earth. But at my grandmother's insistence, the family left China for good in the late spring of 1949.

As it turned out, Li was not able to establish his Chongqing stronghold. The city was quickly overrun by the Communists before the end of the year and Li himself was forced to flee to the United States. Most of his government officials were not so lucky. They either died when the People's Liberation Army "liberated" the city or they were imprisoned as enemies of the state.

As for the former student who had promised my grandfather amnesty, nothing he could have done would have protected the family from the vicissitudes of the regime, as the Cultural Revolution would prove definitively for my grandmother's side of the family.

~ *Winberg* ~

Nothing is ever as simple as the right decision seems in hindsight.

My mother's brothers both decided to stay on the mainland. They were surgeons, they couldn't have cared less about politics. "China will always need doctors," my eldest uncle, Shou-tao, told my mother. "I survived under the Japanese, didn't I? The Communists can't be worse." Besides, he'd spent all his inheritance long ago, his wife had had expensive tastes. He had no desire to live in poverty on some tiny island.

However, my mother's second brother, who was living in Fujian province now, wanted my mother to take his only daughter with us to Taiwan. Just in case. He wasn't sure how the Communists would treat a young woman. He'd heard rumors of communal living, of free love, of the destruction of the family. No one knew what the Communists were up to really. My second uncle wrote that he would stay put with his wife and his two sons, because he'd never trusted Chiang Kai-shek and, besides, he was a German-educated surgeon and how many well-educated physicians would elect to stay? He figured the Communists needed him, they'd never be so foolish as to give him any trouble. And he wasn't worried about his sons staying. He was more afraid that if they moved to Taiwan, Chiang might conscript all young men into his armed forces, in some crazed bid to continue the civil war. But as for his only daughter, he worried about raising a girl under the rule of these morally dicey atheists.

"I know you've always wanted a daughter," he wrote to my mother. "I'll let you take mine."

I remember my mother asking my cousin if she would miss her family too much, but my cousin insisted that she wanted to go with us to Taiwan. "You always said I was like a daughter to you. I can be your real daughter," she said.

And so my mother agreed to take her niece.

We began to pack up our house in Nanjing, or rather my mother and my cousin began the frantic process of packing up; my brothers and I watched from afar as we played games in the halls. They packed boxes and suitcases and crates, choosing only those essential items that we could not live without or that we could sell in a pinch. Everything else my father would try to sell before we left. They were busy all day long. A dutiful daughter now, our cousin no longer had any time to play with us at all.

Sometimes we called to her to get her attention, made faces or rude noises, just to see her jump up in anger, stick her tongue out. We liked to tease our sister. But when she ignored us, obviously preferring to work alongside our mother, we moped about our rooms, fighting among ourselves.

Was it two or three days that passed like this? My mother and cousin moved through the rooms like ants, the servants carried huge wooden crates of our things away, our house emptying into a shell. My father struggled to sell what he could on the black market, and my brothers and I said good-bye to our friends. In our busy blindness, we all believed that we would remain a family, despite the war.

I remember the last day that my cousin stayed with us.

It was abnormally hot that April, the rains were late, the air heavy with steam. We sweated without moving. Because this day was unbearably hot and humid outside, my brothers and I were inside the house, too lethargic even to play. Our cousin was dressed in shorts and a loose blouse, some girlish combination of pink cotton sprinkled with flowers. She was beginning to develop, and we could see the shape of her bosom through the thin cotton. We giggled as we watched her bend over the crate, her thighs exposed.

The male servants also stopped their work to watch her.

My mother came into the room carrying an armload of clothing. "Get back to work," said she, nodding at the men. Sheepishly, they obeyed.

She looked at my cousin, worriedly. "You should put on more clothes," she said. "You're not a little girl anymore."

"No, it's too hot," my cousin complained.

My mother stopped and stood completely still, as if she were seeing my cousin for the very first time. Later she would say her heart had skipped a beat, so startled had she been to realize how dangerous this was, that my cousin who looked like a woman still thought like a girl.

Then the moment seemed to pass. The two women went back to work.

The male servants, however, spent the rest of the afternoon stopping by frequently, to gawk, while pretending to ask my mother for instructions.

My cousin was a few years older than I, about eighteen or nineteen years old by this point, and she had inherited the Tsao family looks, the good cartilage, the long bones, the slim but strong figure. When my mother and cousin went on errands, men liked to stop and look at my cousin. Even Chiang Kai-shek's soldiers, who normally marched through the streets as though they wouldn't stop for anything. They eyed my cousin. Sometimes, she smiled back at men, glancing at them from the corner of her eyes.

My mother had not thought about this problem before. How much attention a pretty young woman attracted. Her brother had told her what had happened in Nanjing when the Japanese took over the city. She had seen with her own eyes how soldiers could do as they pleased if they thought their supervisors were away. Men with guns were capable of anything and they usually wanted one thing most of all.

That night my mother did not sleep. She felt tired and old. Her self-confidence deserted her. How could she have been so foolish as to take on this extra responsibility, to take a girl among soldiers? She prayed for strength, but she grew more afraid.

The next morning she was grim at breakfast, her eyes puffy.

My cousin asked brightly what they should pack today.

My mother said that she would like to talk to her. Just the two of them.

My cousin proudly stuck her tongue out at my brothers and me and went with my mother into the sitting room, flaunting her privilege as my mother's daughter.

With the door closed, my mother explained that she had realized that she had been too selfish to take her brother's only daughter for herself. Too greedy. She wasn't thinking properly at all. A girl belonged with her family. Taiwan was an island of soldiers. How could she move a girl to such a place?

My mother explained that she had sent Charles to purchase a train ticket to send her home to her parents, her brothers, in Fujian province. Amah would go with her to make sure she was all right. They would telegram her parents immediately.

As my cousin began to understand what my mother was saying she started crying. We could hear her in the next room, her voice high and desperate, begging. "I'm your daughter, I'm your daughter!"

But my mother had decided. She couldn't take a girl to Taiwan. It was too dangerous.

My mother was a strong woman, but even she felt her strength had limits.

That afternoon, my mother accompanied my cousin and Amah to the train station, with the bags that they had packed together, and sent her daughter home.

In the last picture of my cousin in my album, she's wearing a plaid *qipao* and high-top sneakers and we're all squinting into the sun in front of some Ming dynasty stone tomb markers on Purple Mountain, my cousin, my brothers, and me. I'm wearing a mock soldier's uniform, my brothers appear to be in their schoolclothes. None of us looks very happy, but this had everything to do with our age—we were in full adolescent angst—and less to do with the war situation. Japan had been defeated and we had absolutely no idea that the Communists would be coming soon and take over our city. None of us knew that this would be the final picture we'd take together, so here we are, scowling together for posterity.

I wouldn't see her again until a few years after my mother had died and I returned to China in 1985. The last time we'd seen each other, I was sixteen and she was a young woman with short, black hair that framed her full face, and now she was a mother with graying hair in a bun. We recognized each other immediately.

"Your mother always said I was her daughter," she said straightaway, even before we'd finished saying, Hello, have you eaten yet. Then she smiled, a little anxiously, as if after everything she'd been through during the Cultural Revolution and the disaster of being from an educated family had taken away her self-confidence. But I assured her that I remembered very well.

For twenty-some years in America, my mother had continued to talk about my cousin, "her daughter," and her decision to leave her behind in China. Sometimes my mother would talk about it out of the blue while we were driving through the City looking for a parking space, pricing crabs in Chinatown, in the middle of a meal. "I had to leave her. How could I protect a girl?" she'd say suddenly, but we all knew what she was talking about. We nodded our agreement, of course, it was crazy during the war, but my mother never seemed completely convinced.

In fact, my mother almost decided to stay in China herself.

We left Nanjing in April of 1949 to go to Shanghai where we were scheduled to board a boat to Canton, then apply for a special permit to enter Taiwan. But in Shanghai my father was severely injured when the rickshaw he was riding in one afternoon was struck by a car. The rickshaw puller was killed instantly and my father was hospitalized for several weeks. During this time, we were forced to live with Auntie Orchid and her husband—the Shanghai gangster, as my mother referred to him—and once more the family fights started up again.

Orchid and her husband were quite wealthy and lived in an elegant town house in the French Concession. Every meal in my aunt and uncle's home was a formal affair, attended by a variety of white-gloved uniformed male servants: one to bring in a platter, one to serve the food, and one to clear away the bowls and plates after each course. If a servant should drop even a little food or sauce on the linen tablecloth, my uncle would jump up and shout, "Damn you! I should have your clumsy hands cut off, you oaf!" Or at least, that's the G-rated version of what he said.

My mother was quite appalled at the language. "Boys, close your ears," she'd say.

My uncle seemed to like my mother, however. Whenever she grew upset, he would redden and apologize. "Excuse me, I've forgotten how to behave in front of a lady."

"What do you mean?" Auntie Orchid chimed in at once. "I'm a lady too!"

Sometimes my uncle tried to tell us amusing stories about people he knew, stories that often revolved around teahouses and singing girls, a euphemism for prostitutes. I tried to nod, knowingly, as though at sixteen I were a sophisticated Shanghai capitalist as well. My brothers, still just boys, thirteen and eleven years old, giggled like crazy. My mother, however, would quickly clear her throat and fold her hands primly until my uncle felt uncomfortable enough to stop.

"Sorry, sorry," my uncle said, flustered.

"Some people think they're superior just because they went to school in a foreign country," Orchid sniffed.

When Orchid wanted to have one of the servants beaten for a minor transgression, my mother intervened. "As a Christian, I do not believe in beating our fellow human beings." She turned to my uncle. "I'm sure a man of your sophistication does not condone such barbaric behavior."

My uncle then pardoned the servant, infuriating his wife.

Soon my aunt and my mother were not speaking to each other at all.

I don't know what triggered their final fight. Perhaps my mother had caught my aunt and her servants going through our crates of things we wanted to take to Taiwan. Perhaps she merely caught my aunt in her room and assumed the worst. At any rate, we could hear their shouts through the entire house.

"What are you doing! Stealing from me once wasn't enough?"

"How dare you? I'd never take any of your silly things. Nothing but books and old knickknacks. You see how I live? You think I need your things?"

"That's what I can't understand! Why do you need my things on top of your things!"

"You're a fine one to act so proud. Here you are practically begging for our help. Your husband's in the hospital, you have nowhere else to go. I'm only letting you stay here in *my* house because I love my brother! Don't think I've forgotten how you threw me out of your fancy house. So rude! My poor father, all he wanted to do was see his son and you put us out on the street!"

"First you steal from me, then you lie. I let you stay in my house, but you were the one who stole from me. You fired my servants. You stole the gifts I bought for my mother!"

"You—you—you—"

"You can't say anything because you know I'm telling the truth!"

Orchid picked up a centuries-old Ming dynasty vase and dashed it against the wall. "I want her out of our house!" she shouted. "I will not be insulted in my own home! You hear how she treats me!"

When my uncle heard the shrill voices of the women arguing, he grabbed his hat and ran quickly out the front door, with a finger on his lips, signaling my brothers and me not to say a word.

Finally, after enduring a number of these arguments, my mother decided nothing was worth being treated like this. She'd rather take her chances with the Communists. She'd grown increasingly pensive since leaving Nanjing. Now she questioned her decision to leave her city and her family. What would she have if she left China? At least if we stayed, she'd have her brothers and cousins, and her niece, to back her up. Finally, she told my brothers and me to pack one bag each. We're going home, she said. She herself prepared only a valise of her most treasured items: the deeds to the land she had inherited from her mother, her teaching certificates, her blueprints to our house in Nanjing, and the *Yi-xing* tea set, which was all that remained of her mother's gifts to her. Then the four of us secretly left my auntie Orchid's home early one morning and took the first train back to Nanjing.

From Nanjing my mother sent a telegram to my father's hospital room. She wrote that she could bear all the hardships of the war without complaint, but really these family fights were the most painful thing in life. Charles could have her or his family, but not both. If he wanted to stay with his family, she would not leave her city. He was free to go to Taiwan without her. But she was keeping the boys.

"I can no longer bear this heartache," she wrote. "Choose."

My father then spent the rest of his days in the hospital composing his reply. For nearly ten pages, he declared his love for her, he apologized for his family's behavior, for all the times during the war he had caused her grief. He apologized for giving away the children's milk and for getting involved with the Zhou Enlai plot and for trusting his brother when he knew he shouldn't have. He apologized for many, many things, things that I don't remember anymore. But in the end he declared, "You are my life. I cannot go on without you. I cannot bear to live without you. Please come back to me. If you do not come back, I will tell the doctors there is no need to try to heal me. I do not wish to live without my wife." And then my father solemnly swore an oath to her, that he would have nothing to do with his family from then on.

Moved by his love letter, my mother decided she did not want to live without him either. She immediately telegrammed him that she accepted his apology and his promise. We returned to Shanghai that afternoon. The next day we discovered that we had taken the very last train out of Nanjing, period. That very evening after our departure, guerrillas with the People's Liberation Army blew up the tracks outside the city limits, and no one else could escape.

I remember my father's letter very well because my mother sent it to me for safekeeping in 1965. She explained to me that this letter outlined all the suffering she had had to endure in her life and she wanted me, her firstborn, to know. But when I read the letter, I became so emotionally distressed, remembering things I thought I'd forgotten, that I ripped this letter to shreds and threw it away.

21

EXILE

Ruth and Charles in
their Manhattan
neighborhood, late
1960s.

~ *May-lee* ~

I remember how she spoke, but the sound of my grandmother's voice
eludes me completely. I think I lost these sounds once I began to
study Chinese in college. My first professor of Chinese was an American man, and although he spoke Chinese well, he did not sound like
my grandparents, with their soft, Nanjing accents. I know that when
I first began to study Mandarin, four years after my grandmother's
death, I tried to imitate her rather high-pitched voice, her forceful
and lilting intonation. But later these sounds were drilled out of me,
replaced by the flatter, harsher sounds of Northern Mandarin, which
is considered "standard Chinese," the language that all Americans
are taught when they study Mandarin in college.

Now Nai-nai's Chinese voice is completely gone from my memory.
The only voice that remains vivid is the one she used to speak English
with my mother in the kitchen, when she imitated her friends from
the senior citizens' center, how they called my grandfather's name.
Nai-nai let her voice rise and fall, cooing, "Oooo, Charles, oooo!"
But this is not my grandmother's true voice, only her imitation of
other women speaking.

I don't know why I can't remember anymore.

I do remember, however, her mannerisms: the imperious way she would wave a hand when she was displeased; how she held her head perfectly erect while listening; the graceful way she adjusted her silk embroidered shawl, which she wore over everything, casual or formal, whether sitting on the couch in our family room to watch TV or attending a formal banquet with my grandfather.

I remember my grandfather's voice very well, in English and in Chinese. His Chinese voice was deep and soft, like tilled soil, the syllables were rounded and pleasing to the ear. He never seemed to lose his temper, although he always spoke very loudly. My brother and I could imitate the way he called our father, "Wen-bo! Wen-bo!"

But Ye-ye's English accent was British. When I was very young, we perplexed each other, because although we were supposed to be speaking the same language, we didn't understand what the other wanted.

Once on a trip to Virginia when I was about four, I was left in the care of Ye-ye and Nai-nai. I don't know where the rest of my family went, my parents and my brother, but I remember walking with my grandparents through a grocery store, enjoying the air-conditioning while we awaited a thunderstorm. None of us could make heads or tails of the funny southern accents of the other people in the store, so we stuck to ourselves, browsing the aisles, testing samples from the ladies manning their electric frying pans. We were enjoying ourselves, as far as I can remember, until the point when I tugged Ye-ye's hand and announced, "I have to go to the potty."

He responded in his crisp British vowels, "There's no PAH-rty here," and proceeded to pace with me and my grandmother through the cool aisles.

"But Ye-ye," I insisted, "I have to go."

"No, no, not now." He patted my hand. "You can go to the PAH-rty later."

But I dragged my heels and bit my lip and acted so contrarily that finally Ye-ye and Nai-nai agreed to look for this "party." Maybe in the parking lot, they suggested. There was a sample lady set up with a barbecue offering hot dogs and relish, but that wasn't what I wanted.

I kept insisting that I *had* to go, now!, and Ye-ye kept insisting that I could go later, after my parents came back, after we got home to California, for my birthday perhaps, all these horrible long-term possibilities, until finally I could bear it no longer. To my grandparents' great surprise, right there in front of the barbecue crowd, I peed in my pants, standing up, although I was supposedly much too old for this kind of thing. Thus humiliated, I burst into tears.

After my parents finally returned, driving up in their Buick to pick us up, my father explained to my grandfather that "potty" meant "W.C." Naturally, Ye-ye felt quite bad for the misunderstanding. For all their studies in America, my grandparents had never come across this bit of American slang. Ye-ye apologized to me over and over, but I could only cry, "I told him I had to go and he said I couldn't!"

After this early failure, my grandparents never felt confident enough in their English to try to take care of either my brother or me alone again.

Only three letters remain of all the thousands of letters my grandmother wrote in her lifetime. All are in English. One is brief, a New Year's card she had sent to one of her sorority sisters, Louise Romig Haas, in Wittenberg around 1937. "I am always thinking of you altho' I cannot write often. These two children of mine became naughty. Winberg is in kindergarten. He can sing and play. The second one walks around and keeps me busy. With best wishes and love, Ruth." She enclosed two small photos, two by three inches, black-and-white. One shows the school she built, with a line of fourteen children standing in the American-style playground, between the wooden porch swing and the seesaw. My father stands in the center of the line. She has drawn a small arrow under his feet. In the second picture, my grandmother sits on a stone bench with my middle uncle, a fat baby, on her lap, and my father, a toddler with an eye patch, standing to her left. My father is dressed in expensive-looking clothes, knickers with suspenders, a long-sleeved formal shirt, a dark buttoned vest, and a miniature tie knotted at his throat. My grandmother's face has not yet lost the plumpness of youth. She appears happy, serene.

We have this letter because her classmate saw my father's name in a Wittenberg alumni magazine and sent it to him in 1999. She was ninety years old and had kept the card all these years.

The second letter was the one my grandmother wrote in 1970 to the president of Wittenberg College to bequeath a $3,000 scholarship:

Dear President Andeen:

It is my pleasure to inform you that I wish to donate $3,000.00 to Wittenberg University and to establish a Ruth Tsao Chai and Chu Chai Loan Fund for the purpose to assist students to meet emergency needs. I wish to make this donation at this time especially because of our 40th wedding anniversary. I was the first Chinese student at Wittenberg to marry at the Fourth Lutheran Church in Springfield in 1930 with the late President Tulloss who presented my hand in marriage.

First of all, I wish to emphasize that I am not a wealthy person. Since my marriage 40 years ago we have endured many hardships. Due to the Sino-Japanese War as well as the Chinese civil war against the Communists, my husband and I were forced to flee innumerable times and each time we lost all possessions and had to begin anew with the bare essentials. We are thankful to God and indeed fortunate that we and our three sons escaped with our lives and were able to return to the United States.

Despite such hardships and pain, I can never forget my happy experience at Wittenberg and the many friendships that have endured since my school days in Springfield . . .

To save the money for this scholarship loan fund, I have made personal sacrifices throughout the years: For example, I never patronized a beauty shop or clothing stores but instead have always worn Chinese dresses which do not change style through the years.

I realize that with today's inflation, $3,000.00 seems a small amount. But I have faith that my children and grandchildren will contribute to this fund as they are able in the years ahead.

With deep gratitude . . .

Sincerely,

Ruth Tsao Chai, '29 M.A.

The third letter is her will, which she had my grandfather type for her on their letterhead stationery and which she sent to each of their three sons in 1978. It begins: "The contents of the suitcases, which I have kept for many years as my treasures, should not be disposed as cabbages; I sincerely hope that they will remain as they are until the time when my grandchildren grow up, and then these things will be given to them as tokens of my love." She concludes in the next paragraph that the contents of her safe-deposit boxes should be equitably distributed and then kept "as memorial gifts of your dear mother. This is my heart-felt wish! God bless you all!"

I like this phrase "should not be disposed as cabbages" as well as the exclamation points. This is exactly how my grandmother always spoke, with much strength and conviction.

This much I remember.

~ *Winberg* ~

I lived on Taiwan for less than a year before leaving for America, but I remember even today the constant humid heat, the hunger, the terrible pineapples, the fear that the People's Liberation Army would arrive any day and take over the island too. My parents grew quite cross. I can still hear the sound of their voices battling, the pitch of my mother's voice rising as my father's voice boomed off the thin walls of our small house, as they debated what we should do next.

A thief came one night. My father spotted a flickering shadow in the yard, heard a footstep just beyond the lacquer screen by the front door, and knew he was no longer alone. Thieves were desperate and dangerous. People were starving. Food was controlled by Chiang's soldiers. The prices on the black market were beyond the reach of most families. The secret societies organized gangs to rob homes. A thief who was spotted by a homeowner and later identified had no hope of mercy: he could be executed by the soldiers or executed by his gang brothers to protect their boss. Better to kill the person who spotted you, a thief thought, than risk being caught.

My father heard the thief and began to talk to himself, "as if I were sleepwalking," he told me later.

"We are so poor. I don't know how we are going to survive. I am just a professor and I cannot find a post. A teacher has no patrons. My three sons need food. I do not know how I can afford to feed them and pay for their education. If I cannot afford to send my eldest to college, he will surely be drafted into the army and his life will be wasted to fight the Communists. I am a bad father, I cannot provide for my family. My wife is weak from the journey and tired. She has worked her entire life and now we are refugees. First we fled the Japanese and now we must flee the Communists. Our lives are like dust motes. Why must the fate of a Chinese be so hard?"

The thief took pity on us that night, hearing my father speak, and he did not steal from us. But the next morning, when it was light and my father felt it was safe to go outside, he discovered a pile of human feces by the corner of the fence. Then he knew that truly the thief had been there; he had not been hallucinating from fatigue and hunger after all. My father explained that it was bad luck for a thief to leave a property he'd targeted without stealing something, and so as a form of protection, he had to defecate there instead. I did not understand this, but my father with his Anhui village background understood many folk beliefs that I, a city boy, had never heard of.

In the years to come, all the houses around ours would be robbed, many times, but never once did the thieves touch our house after that night.

My father had not been lying to the thief. Because my mother's money was invested in property in Nanjing, we were relatively poor on Taiwan, for the first time in my life. We were entirely dependent on my father's connections to survive. Fortunately, he had been a good teacher, and his former students—now generals and officials in the government—eventually came to his aid. With their ration coupons and offers of teaching positions, my father was able to support us.

My mother continued to tutor students in English and served as an editor for the Ministry of Education. She coauthored with my father a series of English-language textbooks. But mostly she spent her time writing letters to all her friends in America. She'd lost track of her mentor, Eleanor, who had left China sometime after the Japanese occupation of Nanjing. My mother had a few partial addresses that she'd collected from people who thought they might know where Eleanor had gone, but the addresses proved to be false leads. She had to content herself with writing now to her sorority sisters at Wittenberg at their last known addresses, to professors, to friends of friends. She kept careful track of her correspondence, telling everyone her sad story, the story of the war and our survival. In 1949 on Taiwan, we were all certain it was only a matter of time before the Communists would invade and we, too, would be absorbed into the People's Republic.

After a year of her letter-writing campaign, I was awarded a scholarship to study in America. I remember when I announced to my English class that I was going to the United States, they all burst into laughter. My English was the poorest of all. But I had tremendous self-confidence. I never had any doubts that I would be all right, although I was only seventeen and for the first time in my life I would be living away from my family.

"Just remember, you are my son," my mother told me. "You are a high-class person. You are as good as anyone in America. Don't let anyone tell you otherwise."

I was in my room trying on the clothes that my mother and father had saved and scrimped for months to buy for my trip overseas: a new Western-style blazer and matching pants, a wide turquoise-blue tie, and shiny leather shoes. My brothers had only their school uniforms to wear these days, shorts and white shirts; they had to shave their heads in a crew cut like all Taiwanese schoolboys. But I had a new American wardrobe plus my head of thick black hair, which I slicked back into a wave because this was the way all the men in American movies wore their hair. I gazed happily at my image in the mirror. "I like America," I said. "No problem."

"Remember, you are our representative. What people think of you, they will think of us." My mother's voice and face were worried, her forehead lined. "I'm counting on you. It may be several years before the rest of us can join you."

"I'm not worried." And I wasn't. In the last picture taken of us all together in Taiwan, on the airport tarmac, just before my flight left, I'm wearing my new duds, hair as bouffant as usual, and I look completely self-confident. My parents look sad, however. I see that now. The way they cling to each other and my brothers while already I am standing separated, slightly ahead, facing the camera and not my family.

It would be five more years before I saw them again. First I went to study at Hartwick College in Oneonta, New York, where my mother's former thesis advisor, Dr. Henry J. Arnold, was president. Although they weren't yet used to Chinese in the town and groups of boys would follow me down the street, calling me names, laughing, I was completely unperturbed. I merely stuck my tongue out at them and went about my business. I lived with the president, he made the homecoming queen accompany me to dances, later I joined a fraternity and enjoyed myself immensely. Unfortunately, I enjoyed myself too much and my grade point average fell precipitously. As a result, my mother began a new letter-writing campaign and I was awarded a new scholarship to attend her own alma mater, Wittenberg. There I had no choice but to be diligent, and I graduated in 1955.

By this time, my father had been offered a teaching position at the New School for Social Research in New York City. Thus, my family became 4 of the 568 Chinese admitted to the United States in 1955. After five years in America, I could barely speak Chinese, and when my family and I were finally reunited, they laughed at me when I met them at the airport because I couldn't remember how to say the simplest things.

I suppose this could have been the happy ending to any number of stories, of immigrants fleeing war and political strife, reuniting in America, finding a new life and new opportunities.

But life in America was not as my parents had hoped.

There was a growing expatriate community of prominent Chinese intellectuals living in Manhattan in the mid-1950s. Every weekend they gathered in Dr. Hu Shih's plain three-bedroom East Side apartment on East Sixty-fifth Street, which was paid for by Chiang Kai-shek. They gathered to gossip and debate the future of China and the course of action they should take in America to save their nation. Dr. Hu was the most famous of all the expats, credited—which is only a slight exaggeration—with inventing the Chinese vernacular written language. A leader of China's Literary Renaissance of 1917 and later the May Fourth cultural movement, he had early on espoused equal rights for women, including education and divorce. (He himself had an arranged marriage to an uneducated woman with tiny feet.) He had been dean of National Peking University from 1930 to 1937 and served as China's wartime ambassador to the United States from 1938 to 1939. Author of numerous books, holder of more than thirty honorary degrees from America's most prestigious universities, in the 1930s he had been feted across the United States on a lecture tour. This was the man *Time* magazine had once proclaimed as "China's greatest living sage."

Occasionally I accompanied my parents. Dr. Hu called me "Didi," Little Brother, but even I felt intimidated in his illustrious presence.

During these visits, my mother refused to play mahjong in the kitchen with Mrs. Hu and the other wives. Instead she stayed in Dr. Hu's study and talked politics with the men.

They agreed that the Korean War had been a blessing for Taiwan. If not for the war and Truman's vow to protect Taiwan from the spread of Communism, the island would have been taken by the Communists now.

They worried whether Chiang would be able to govern Taiwan. He'd declared martial law, no one on the island was allowed to communicate with family left behind on the mainland, and the Taiwanese were not pleased that the mainlanders had taken over.

But inevitably the talk turned to jobs, or rather their lack thereof.

Because currently China's Greatest Living Sage, Dr. Hu Shih, was unemployed.

My father had his teaching job at the New School, but it was only an adjunct position, not tenure track. My mother hadn't found a position at all.

Everyone sighed. What was to be done?

This job situation was a tough problem. Americans weren't interested in China the way they used to be. Universities didn't feel the need to expand their foreign language and history departments, as if they believed there was nothing more to learn about China, this country the West had lost, or so the McCarthyites now claimed, as if China were a key chain or a bauble that had been misplaced. There was no hope for missionary work, the Communists didn't allow foreign companies to invest, what was the point of Americans studying Chinese anything?

Eventually Dr. Hu was hired by Princeton University to act as curator for their East Asian library. Everyone was shocked, aghast. He should hold a chaired professorship at Princeton, not act as a "curator" in a library, they said. They were horrified because they knew that if Dr. Hu couldn't find a teaching position, their chances were even worse.

Prominent Chinese writers and artists, scholars and lawyers, all retrained now, were trying to find a way to make a living in America. My father and a friend decided to study accounting at NYU, and finally after years of adjunct positions and piecing together a career, my father found full-time employment as an auditor in the legal department for the City of New York.

In 1960 my parents applied for citizenship. My brothers and I were still in graduate school. I worked part-time in an advertising agency while completing my Ph.D. at NYU. In 1961 my father and I wrote together *The Story of Chinese Philosophy*, published by the prestigious Washington Square Press. Now our lives began to look brighter. We would write eight more books together: *The Changing Society of China* (1962), *The Sacred Books of Confucius* (1963), *The Humanist Way in Ancient China* (1964), *I Ching* (1964), *A Treasury of Chinese Literature* (1965), *Li Chi: The Books of Rites,* two volumes (1967), *Confucianism* (1973), and *Asian Man* (1977). *Changing Society* became a best-seller, selling more than 100,000 copies in several editions, and was translated into six languages. *A Treasury of Chinese Literature* became a standard college text for a decade; and our edition of the *I Ching* was a popular hit, selling more than 200,000 copies in paperback.

With the book royalties, my parents invested in stocks and property and generously helped their sons, including me, as well as friends and relatives who had remained in China. However, my father continued to work at two or three jobs in the city, teaching part-time in addition to his accounting work. He suffered a heart attack in the mid-1960s and a second one a few years later, he lost all his teeth (as did my mother), but he seemed happy, busy with his work and his research. He'd spent his entire life trying to reform China, and now he wrote about every positive thing he could recall about China.

My mother found no appropriate position and did not work.

My father, my brothers, and I all told her that she should rest now. She'd earned this vacation, we argued, hadn't she worked hard enough in her life already? We assumed that she was happy too—or if not happy, at least resigned to the way her life had turned out.

I thought this way until April of 1981 when my mother died in her sleep, and we discovered her burial plans.

22

LEGACY

Ruth in her fifties.

~ *May-lee* ~

At first my grandmother hardly missed working, there was so much to do managing the family affairs.

In the first version of her will, written in 1957, Ruth made sure to specify how much money she expected the family to continue to send to her brothers and aunt back in China should she die first: between $250 and $300 each per year, "depending on what you can spare." At the time, Charles's salary for teaching at the New School hovered around $4,000 per year. Her sons were graduate students, working to earn money for their educations, so $900 sent annually back to China represented a considerable financial strain, she knew. But family was family. Besides, she was managing the money, she knew the meaning of thrift, she'd make sure there was enough left over.

Thinking over her sons' forgetfulness, she decided to add a line at the end of the will, stating that any extra clothing should be sent to her niece and nephews as well.

Slowly, miraculously, the family's finances improved. Her first-born son won a small fortune on *Name That Tune* and bought the family a car. Her husband's books sold well. Charles found full-time work as an auditor, a city job, with union wages and benefits!

By the mid-1960s, for the first time in her life, Ruth experienced leisure. She sat at home, watching television so that she could keep up on the world, following the soaps, which showed how the world really worked, all these unhappy men and women falling in and out of love, families cheating each other then reuniting again and again.

Now that she had leisure to think of spiritual matters, she went to the Christian church down the street and was rejected, made to feel strange, like an outsider, Ruth Mei-en Tsao the missionaries' prodigy, the woman who had once memorized the Bible! Walking down the street with Charles, who must walk every day after his heart attack, Ruth happened upon the Jewish temple's senior center and found acceptance. At first the widow factor didn't trouble her. She liked her new friends; they understood each other, they all knew the value of a dollar, the true meaning of suffering. They complained together. Oy! Who could believe the price of a cup of tea these days? And the way their children liked to spend money! Did they think it grew on trees maybe? They traded investment tips. Ruth invested her husband's money, bought property, opened bank accounts to take advantage of new interest rates and giveaway incentives like free toasters, although neither she nor Charles ate toast. But her husband in his college days had studied under an imperial chef, Charles could make anything taste good, he'd think of something to do with it, Ruth knew; nothing need go to waste.

In 1965, her eldest son moved to California for his first tenure-track position. He phoned after a month to say that he'd found a bride. An artist and television journalist, he said. She wasn't Chinese.

Ruth didn't mind. She wasn't prejudiced. This was America after all, how many Chinese girls were there to be found? She understood about the modern ways of marrying. Hadn't she been quite the fire-brand in her day, requiring Charles to write her a letter every day of their engagement, to sell forty *mu* of his family's land to buy her engagement ring? And it was she who had chosen him, over his older brother. What did she care for musty traditions?

Then her eldest son let the bomb drop. His bride-to-be was a Catholic.

In China the missionaries translated the term "Protestant" as *ji du jiao* to mean "Christian," which consequently excluded Catholicism, which was translated as *tian zhu jiao*. Ruth remembered well the sermons of her youth, the pastor's warnings about the Catholics with their strange cult of Jesuits and their emperorlike pope. Still, Ruth did not panic. She thought of a compromise. "Ask the Catholic if she'll convert," she wrote back to her son. When her son wrote back to say that the Catholic wouldn't, Ruth again thought of a solution: they could be married in the campus chapel, which was safely Baptist. But again, her son wrote to say the Catholic insisted that the wedding take place in her church, a full mass, or she wouldn't marry at all. Ruth sighed; she knew all about stubbornness as well. "The Catholic can be married in her church," Ruth said diplomatically, "but why not ask the Baptist minister to perform the service?"

In those days ecumenical services uniting Catholics and Protestants were still rare and certainly had never been performed in the small town of Redlands, California, but the Catholic monsignor and the local Baptist preacher happened to be friends, and with permission from Rome, both men officiated at the wedding of Ruth's firstborn son.

There, she thought, everyone can be reasonable after all.

By 1968, Ruth was a grandmother to two Americans. She and Charles went to visit and discovered the grandchildren couldn't understand their English and she couldn't understand theirs.

Old age, she thought. The dentures. Charles had a former student who was now a dentist. He'd given them a special deal and pulled out all their teeth. Sounds slipped out of her mouth now before she could bite them into English words. At least she and Charles could still laugh about it.

Ruth's youngest son married a Czech-American musician and moved to New Jersey. Only the middle son lived in New York City, caring for his parents.

How long had it been since everyone lived in the City, every weekend a salon conversation at Dr. Hu Shih's apartment? Dr. Hu and his wife had returned to Taiwan in 1958 and then a few years later Dr. Hu had died of a heart attack; Ruth remembered receiving the memorial notice in the mail. It seemed a century ago. Now everyone was moving, friends drifting to the suburbs. To be with children, grandchildren. Moving from Manhattan to the vast hinterland interior of the United States.

~

Ruth watched the Vietnam War on television, watched the few reports about the Cultural Revolution in China, the world in turbulence. Her brothers sent her letters from China, asking for help. They
were stranded in the countryside. Afraid. It was then that she came
up with her *Life* magazine scheme to send them money, but it didn't
work. Then for a period, their letters ceased altogether. She could
think of nothing to do to save them. A terrible thing to admit, she
who had always thought of ways to do just about anything.

A letter arrived from the son of the kind aunt who had been head of
obstetrics at Bethany Hospital in Shanghai. This generous woman,
who had let Ruth stay in the hospital for three months after the birth
of her first son, had been attacked by the Red Guards. After the civil
war, Ruth's aunt had not fled to Taiwan. Instead she had opted to stay
in China and worked as head of the teaching hospital of the prestigious
Peking Union Medical College, which had been founded with a grant
by the Rockefeller Foundation in 1915. Now despite her patriotism,
this aunt was being persecuted for her Western ties and education.

Ruth thought of a clever plan to help her. She bought warm flannel
pajamas, long winter underwear, thick wool socks for her aunt and
washed them all until they appeared so old that no one in their right
mind would want to steal them. She sewed American money into the
hems of the pajamas, into the waistband of the underwear. Then she
shipped the whole package to China, with a folksy note about "keeping warm in the Beijing winter." But the box was returned to Ruth,
with a letter written in an unfamiliar calligraphy, not her aunt's. The
official letter from the customs office proclaimed rather haughtily:
"China does not need old clothes!"

Ruth heard no news from her niece, the one she'd left behind.

All her life Ruth had been an important person, essential, a savior.
But what good had it been to be so strong when she was young?
Ruth needed her strength now. She felt as though she moved through
water, through mud, her limbs heavy.

In 1972, her eldest son, the firstborn, the one she named after her
alma mater, betrayed her, visiting her devious brother-in-law. Ruth
was devastated. Didn't he remember who tried to steal his youngest
brother?

She wrote to Winberg long, anguished letters in Chinese—her English wasn't so good anymore. She used to be a professor of English, she'd been Lady Mountbatten's interpreter, but who'd know now? She only spoke to the ladies at the temple senior center and she wasn't sure their English was standard either, so many immigrants lived in the City.

Ruth felt old now, in her late sixties. She hadn't had a paying job since Taiwan and her hips hurt, not to mention the problems with her eyes and her hearing and her gums. She didn't enjoy eating anymore. What a fate for a Chinese.

She wrote all her sons frequent, urgent letters offering them advice on how to raise their families, how to navigate their lives, advice she wished she'd had when she was their age.

She suspected she had become an embarrassment to them, with her Old World ways, her thrift. They didn't listen to her advice, they wanted her to spend her money, "enjoy life," they called it. Take a trip, they said. She complained at the senior center that her children didn't understand, they had no idea how hard life could be. If she had one regret, perhaps this was it, that she'd hidden too much of the difficulties, of her sorrows. She wrote more letters.

In 1973 her eldest son moved back to the East Coast; at least his wife, the Catholic, was sympathetic. Ruth told the Catholic the story of her hard life, her mother's sad life; she wanted someone to listen to her.

Her sons still visited every weekend for dinner. She had three grandchildren now, two girls, one boy. Ruth talked to the children about television because it was the only thing they had in common. She predicted that the singer known as Cher would become a really big star, forget about that Sonny. Cher can do anything, she insisted to her disbelieving grandchildren. She thought it was a big mistake for the Miss America pageant to dismiss that nice man Bert Parks, just because he was old. And he was younger than she!

Everyone at the senior center agreed. America, the nation of youth.

There was no denying it, Ruth thought. She was an extraneous woman now, no longer at the center of her family.

Her body was rebelling against her will. Cataracts clouded her eyes, her gums hurt. Smiling was a burden to her face. Her stomach had pains. She took a variety of pills every day.

Ruth knew what happened to old women. Hadn't she seen it all before? Her own mother? A vital woman who had made her husband's fortune, discarded like a used tissue.

She saw it all the time on the soap operas she loved to watch every day. In the movies too. That terrible film *The Sound of Music*. The world laughed at an older woman.

And hadn't she done the same? To her niece? She'd left her behind in China because she was a girl, because a girl is harder to protect.

"Don't let her wear pretty clothes. Put her in plain things. Otherwise she will be kidnapped," she told her daughter-in-law, warning her, trying to protect her oldest grandchild.

She remembered distant events in the past as if they had happened yesterday. Her sons were forgetful. She reminded them when she could, at dinner, when the family was together. Everyone acted embarrassed, but she persisted. The past must not be forgotten.

If they could forget the past, they could forget her.

She donated money to her alma mater, wrote a long letter to the president, recording her suffering during the war and after. Someone should know. She sent her will to her sons, reminding them what was important.

People who saw her now, in the mid-seventies, might say that she was "eccentric," this politely demeaning euphemism for an old woman who refused to be ignored. The apartment was filled with things she wouldn't allow to be thrown away because you never knew when the government would fall and it was every man for himself again, and things like paper and plastic bags and towels would become luxuries. But Ruth didn't care what people thought of her: she'd seen the unimaginable. She knew that anything was possible in life.

By the late 1970s, it certainly seemed as though anything was possible in this crazy new world. The North Vietnamese had defeated the Americans, who after World War II had seemed unbeatable. Her brothers had disappeared. The young people of China had lost their minds, denouncing their own parents during the Cultural Revolution. In America the young people had gone crazy, demonstrating in the streets. The world turned upside down. Heaven and earth had changed places.

Ruth was certain that Charles was planning to remarry. After all they'd experienced, after all they'd lived through together! She was no longer a beautiful woman, and she felt the loss in her heart. Her hair had thinned, a woman's beauty was her hair. She wore a nice wig, black and curly on top of her head, warm, good for cold days, but a wig was no substitute for her own hair, which was now the color of stone. She'd grown wide and slow; walking, she felt as though she were moving through water against a current. Ruth was suspicious even of her friends at the senior center.

"He's waiting for me to die," she told her first son's wife, the Catholic, when they were alone in the kitchen, able to talk freely.

Ruth wanted to be reassured. She wanted to be told:

No, it's not true. He loves you, only you. He will not remarry the minute you are dead. Your family will never forget you.

Because of her, she and her brothers were not cheated out of their inheritance, her mother was not ignobly forgotten and dishonored, her father didn't get away with treating her mother like a woman, like a wife, like someone of no consequence.

Because of her, her husband received his first official appointment.

Because of her, the family had a grand house to live in, her sons a private school to attend. Because of her connections, her savvy, her judge of character, her scrimping and saving, her will to fight, the family survived the war. She took care of her brothers. Because of her, the family escaped to America, her sons were educated, all Ph.D.s.

Her family should be grateful forever.

Ruth wanted to believe.

But because nothing had turned out in her life as she had wished, she decided to hedge her bets. She arranged secretly to change her burial plans. Better this way when it was still her choice to make and not a decision imposed upon her by a fickle husband. As she couldn't trust the eldest son anymore, she went against tradition and asked the youngest for help. He obeyed his mother, good son. Her legacy to the family was set in motion.

She hadn't lost it after all, her ability to think of a solution to any problem. Now Ruth could live the rest of her life in peace.

At last, she'd thought of a way to ensure that her family would remember her forever.

23

REUNION IN CHINA

A cousin, May-lee, Gu Fu, and Gu Mu in Beijing, 1985.

~ May-lee ~

I did not attend my grandmother's funeral.

When she died in 1981 when I was thirteen, we were living in South Dakota where my family had moved two years previously. It was difficult to travel to New York City. There were no direct flights from Sioux City, Iowa, our nearest airport. My mother and brother absolutely hated to fly and they certainly couldn't manage it now for such a sad occasion. So instead, only my father went back to New York to attend Nai-nai's funeral.

After the funeral, we all went to pick up my father from the airport, my brother and I insisting even though it was a school night. We wanted details about the funeral, fresh, uncensored, not tired and tidied up from the retelling.

"How was your father?" my mother asked. She was driving, watching the road. Her profile was stark against the windshield, the lights from the oncoming cars splashing around her silhouette like water.

"Not good," my father said wearily. "He wouldn't leave the coffin. Just refused to go."

"He didn't go home? The funeral home let him stay?" my brother piped up beside me in the backseat.

"Yes—no! He didn't stay all night. During the wake, he wouldn't leave. He just sat there and cried."

I poked my brother in the ribs, he squeezed my wrist, hard. I grunted but refused to give in. I didn't want my brother's questions to break our father's concentration, change his mood. Then he wouldn't say anything until he was alone with our mother, then we'd never learn what had happened.

"We tried to make him go. We had to take him by the arms and almost drag him out."

He told us then how Ye-ye had sat next to the coffin for hours, crying. It became embarrassing. All the family friends were there from long ago, from China, from before the war and immediately after. They came to pay their respects and Ye-ye could greet no one. He could not leave the coffin. He cried loudly, "I'm a bad husband. I should die first. Give you many hardships." My father didn't want people to think Ye-ye had lost his mind, but he could think of no way to console him.

"Ba," my father had pleaded, taking one arm as his youngest brother tugged on the other. "Mother would want you to sit down. Don't cry, don't cry." He said that he felt as though he were talking to my brother and me, when we were younger, when he still believed he could reason with us, keep us from publicly misbehaving.

"Ye-ye kept crying, 'I want my body to be creamed,' " my father continued.

"Creamed? You mean cremated!" I could never keep my mouth shut.

" 'I want to be creamed. Just throw my ashes into the ocean!' " My father grew more emotional, remembering.

"Cremated. He wants to be 'cree-mate-ed,' " I insisted.

"Calm down," my mother commanded. "We're not going to talk about this anymore. Your father needs to rest." My mother took charge, keeping the peace. My father was grateful, undoubtedly. He leaned back against the headrest, tried to close his eyes. I watched him as he turned to look out the window instead, observing the way the highway markers glowed in the headlights then disappeared as if they were matches extinguished by a gust of wind.

It was a long way home.

~

It was late. My father should have been tired, exhausted, but he was restless. He sat on the edge of the living room couch, his open suitcase at his feet. He wore his pajama shirt with his trousers, the belt still neatly buckled.

I sat at the dining room table, pretending I had homework to do yet.

My father bent over, plucked a balled pair of black dress socks from his suitcase. "I forgot I packed these. I had to wear my blue socks to the funeral. The thick ones."

"Unpack tomorrow," my mother called from the kitchen where she was making tea. "Aren't you tired? I always hate traveling. Can't sleep in a strange bed."

"No, no, no. I'm fine." My father rummaged past the program from the funeral service, his neatly folded dress shirt, his plastic bag of dirty laundry. "Here, I saved the shampoos from the hotel for you. And the soap," he called to my mother. Then he passed some stationery to me across the table.

"Thanks," I said, enthusiastically examining the embossed sheets. "Did you get any towels?" I joked.

We had matches from every restaurant he'd ever been to, shampoos, lotions, combs, and shoeshine kits. He kept them in a big box in our closet, "for guests," he said. "I'm not like some people. I only take souvenirs from first-class hotels, the best." When he first came to America, there was another Chinese student who'd taken all the used toothpaste tubes that he'd found in the bathroom of his dormitory. He had thought nobody wanted them, why else would they be left out like that so anyone could take them? "We had to make him put them back. Some people don't understand anything!"

This is the kind of story from his past that my father liked to tell. The other stories, which would have explained why he flew into a rage every time he heard the sound of drums, why my grandmother would suddenly bring up the past in the middle of a family gathering and everyone would fight, why no one would discuss the war—these stories, he never discussed with us.

That night he didn't talk about the funeral anymore. He and my mother went to bed, and soon I could hear him snoring through their bedroom door.

I stayed up late, later than anyone in my family. I enjoyed being alone, the silence of the house, the wind in the tall grass of the fields around us, the blue light of the moon falling like gauze across my skin. Now I sat at the table, thinking about my grandparents. I wanted to tell my grandfather what I was thinking, how startled I was to learn Nai-nai had died, to ask him how he felt about the burial, all these impolite questions. I wanted to talk to him but he had become very hard of hearing and could not hear my voice on the phone. Sometimes when he called, if I picked up the phone, he would continue to say, "Hello? Hello?" and then hang up because he couldn't hear me talking to him at all.

I tried to write him letters but he rarely wrote to me directly except at holidays. Usually he would tell my father when he received my letters and sometimes my father remembered to tell me what he'd said and sometimes my father didn't think of it until weeks and weeks later, and by then, he'd forgotten exactly what it was Ye-ye had told him.

I hated this. I suspected that if I could speak in Chinese, a forceful language, my grandfather would be able to hear me. I could ask him everything. But there were no opportunities to learn Chinese in our town and our father never wanted to teach us, my brother and me, although we periodically begged him to.

But my father always said he was too busy. "I'm not a language instructor," he'd say.

I stayed up very late that night, worrying about all this, my inability to speak to my grandfather anymore, my grandmother's death and funeral, my father's reluctance to speak about the past. But try as I might, I couldn't imagine how I would solve these problems.

A few weeks after the funeral, my grandfather called to tell my father about his vision, how Nai-nai had come back to tell him that my middle uncle needed to be married. After he made arrangements with his relatives in China to fix up my uncle with a bride, Ye-ye waited patiently for more messages, but it would be years and years before she would visit him again.

In 1985, when I was eighteen, my father had an opportunity to go to China for an academic conference and he decided to try to look up the members of the family that were still living. He was extremely high-strung, thinking about this trip, his first back since he'd left at age sixteen in 1949. He wanted all of us to go with him, but again because my mother and brother were afraid of flying, they decided not to go. So by default, only I accompanied my father to China.

In preparation for our trip, I bought a book called *Learn Chinese in Ten Minutes a Day*. It promised miraculous results if the reader studied the book's bright graphics and well-organized lesson plans: Shopping, Eating, Checking into Your Hotel, etc.

Mandarin Chinese, the language of the text, is a tonal language. The first tone is flat and high, the second rises in tone as if the word were a question in English, the third dips in the middle, and the fourth is a falling tone, roughly equivalent to a word written with an exclamation point after it. I learned about these tones after I went to college and studied Mandarin formally. A word's meaning was completely dependent on its tone. For example, *ma* pronounced in the first tone meant "Mama," in the second, "hemp"; in the third tone *ma* meant "horse" and in the fourth tone it was a verb meaning "to curse." Tones are everything in Chinese.

In the front of the book was a diagram of curving lines to show what the four tones looked like if they were written on paper instead of spoken. There was no accompanying tape.

Needless to say, I did not learn how to speak Chinese by studying this book even for an hour or two a day. But I did bring the book in my suitcase because I thought the pictures might prove to be useful.

I also prepared for China by reading every book I could find on Americans traveling to China. I was especially taken with Barbara Tuchman's vividly written memoir, about Nixon's historic trip in 1972, *Notes on China*. I was struck by one event she had described in particular, which many of the guidebooks also mentioned: the Chinese propensity to form a circle around any Americans they encountered and then to stare. Sometimes they clapped to show their friendliness. She recommended clapping back. This was the polite response in Chinese culture, she said.

How fascinating, I thought.

In those days nearly all the travel books on China assumed "American" meant "white" and prepared tourists accordingly.

But of course, nothing prepared me for China.

~

The Beijing airport was humid. I was used to air-conditioning in summer, everywhere indoors. Here the air was unprocessed. It was warm, moist, and smelled faintly like garlic mixed with exhaust. Men lay stretched out along the plastic benches, resting through the extremely long layovers that were commonplace in China in those days. As we made our way to customs, we passed through a long, brightly lighted corridor lined with a sparse series of plastic advertisements: an expensive brand of liquor, a Swiss watch company, cigarettes. China in 1985 was only beginning to embrace a market economy and advertisements were still relatively rare. One sign for Chinese-made cosmetics depicted a soft-faced Asian woman surrounded by flowers. I was not used to seeing Asian faces in advertisements and wanted to take a picture, but my father urged me along. "Don't waste time!" Then he took off down the corridor, his thick black eyebrows like warring caterpillars on his forehead, his tense look. I had to run to keep up with him.

Young men and women in baggy green cotton uniforms with gold buttons and militarylike epaulettes, and wearing white short gloves, directed us toward customs with stiff hand gestures as if we were jets that needed guidance on the tarmac.

Customs was very strict in those days, with many restrictions on what could be brought into China; all gifts had to be declared. "Overseas Chinese" bearing gifts for relatives could bring only a limited number of articles of clothing, a set number of meters of cloth, one TV, one refrigerator per person, for example.

We had brought no large consumer goods and were soon waved along to the baggage carousels. Here a lot of very young girls, dressed in baggy green uniforms that seemed much too big for them, waited to help passengers with their luggage. I thought they looked about thirteen or fourteen years old at most.

"How old do they look to you?" I asked my father. "Children wouldn't be working here, would they?"

My father asked one of the girls her age. "She said she's nineteen," he reported.

"My goodness," I said.

Then several of the girls clustered around our luggage cart, giggling. They covered their mouths with their hands but were nearly bent over double with their mirth. They said something to my father.

"What's so funny?" I asked him.

"They're laughing because they're surprised you don't speak Chinese," he said.

We were staying downtown right on Chang An Avenue at the Beijing Hotel, next door to the Forbidden City. In those days, when China was just opening up to the West, the hotel was dark, dingy, in need of repair. Today the Beijing Grand Hotel—as it's now known—is a five-star hotel, a luxurious place with marble floors and giant fountains, but back in 1985 when we checked into our room, we found watermelon seeds littering the carpet.

My father grimaced. "China is so poor," he said. Then he took a shower for twenty-five minutes.

When we went down to the lobby again, Ye-ye's sister and her husband—Gu Mu and Gu Fu—were waiting for us. They'd come all the way from Lanzhou in western China, three days' journey by train. Now they were all smiles. "Welcome!" Gu Fu said, in his perfect British accent. Gu Mu nodded at me happily. Although four years had passed since I'd last seen them at my uncle's wedding, they looked exactly the same. Gu Fu was dressed nattily in a crisp cotton shirt and creased trousers, his gray hair combed straight up from his forehead like a brush; petite Gu Mu was smiling behind her thick glasses.

Gu Fu wanted to know what kind of gifts my father had brought. My father had brought only money because he wasn't sure what anyone would want. He explained that he hadn't had any time to convert it to Chinese money yet.

In those days, there were two different currencies in China, *renmin bi,* the "people's money" and Foreign Exchange Currency or FEC. Ordinary Chinese shops could not accept FEC and foreigners were not supposed to carry any of the "people's money." Foreigners were technically permitted to shop only in so-called Friendship Stores that accepted the special money. In 1985 the Communist government was still unsure as to how much China should open up to the rest of the world. This elaborate system of currency was meant, in part, to limit foreigners' access to the people and vice versa. However, the end result was that a thriving black market arose to change money at twice the government rate. Everyone wanted American dollars.

Gu Fu assured my father that he knew where to convert the money on the black market and he'd take care of that for the family.

For a mild-looking man in his seventies, I thought he was very savvy.

The next morning we took a taxi to meet my grandmother's only surviving brother, her second brother, the one whose daughter she had refused to take to Taiwan.

The Family had gathered, waiting for us, in my great-uncle's apartment. The walls were painted a bright blue on the bottom half, white on the top. There were two tiny windows and two standing electric fans. I was surprised by the severity of its sparseness, the rough wooden table, the crooked wooden stools, the sagging gray sofa.

Once upon a time my grandmother's second brother had been a wealthy man; he'd married into the illustrious Yen family, a clan who could trace their lineage to imperial tutors. He'd been a surgeon, educated in Germany, renowned and respected. He'd stayed behind in China after the Communist victory because he thought he'd be fine, because he thought everyone in the world needed a doctor, because he thought he had nothing to do with politics. He'd been wrong.

He was a very angry man.

~ *Winberg* ~

I did not recognize him, this elderly stranger before me, but I remembered him immediately. In his prime, my second uncle had been extremely handsome, like a matinee idol. He'd had a self-confident air, which some people mistook for arrogance. He was still very tall, over six feet, a fact that had made my mother very proud, but now my uncle's movie-star looks were gone. He limped. The self-confidence had been replaced by bitterness.

My uncle paced, leaning on his cane. He'd been injured during the Cultural Revolution, he said, when as a foreign-educated surgeon he'd been sent down to the countryside for reeducation. His wife was dead. I was introduced to my cousins, whom I'd never met, and then their children, a tall thin young man nicknamed Little Tiger and his younger sister, a girl of fifteen. My uncle was very proud of his grandson, who'd been admitted to the medical school of Beijing University, the Chinese equivalent of Harvard.

More of my cousins were here waiting to greet us, including my uncle's eldest son, who'd been put in an insane asylum for ten years because he refused to renounce his faith in God. He'd been released finally in 1982. He'd been an engineer, a graduate of China's top science school, Qinghua. "Useless," he said now, meaning his education, his training. He'd been in the asylum too long; his skills were outdated. But to make amends for his suffering, the government had assigned him to a new work unit: he was head of a poultry production factory. I translated his position in English as "CEO" for my daughter's sake. "Like Purdue," I said, wanting to show him that I wasn't looking down on him. "A very big company."

"Oh, how nice," my daughter said to him.

My cousin shook his head. "Useless now," he said in Chinese.

My uncle and his family had prepared a lunch for us, a banquet in their apartment. It was too hot to eat, there was no air, I couldn't breathe. I was sweating all over my body. "It's not necessary," I called to them as they began to bring out platters of meat. "I'm inviting you. Come to my hotel. You're all invited."

But of course they had to have a banquet for me in their home, it would have been rude otherwise. I knew I'd have to eat. I wanted a cold drink. They offered me hot tea and warm beer.

They had me sit against the wall, the seat of honor: even though I was not the oldest member of the family present, I was representing my father. I couldn't argue with them. I sat trapped against the wall, my uncle and his son seated beside me. They both spoke to me at once, in both ears, shouting about the past, the Cultural Revolution, how terrible it had been. My mother's number one brother, my uncle Shou-tao, and his wife were both dead. She'd committed suicide during the Cultural Revolution; he'd managed to survive for a while. I couldn't imagine my uncle dead. In my mind he was still a robust man, the same as when he'd taken me to spit on the Japanese soldiers in Nanjing after the war. A tall man with jet-black hair, so proud of his starlet wife that he'd sold his land to buy her a fancy foreign car. Their only son was still alive; he was a geologist at Beijing University. During the Cultural Revolution he'd taken in other members of the family, protected them, fed them when they had nothing to eat. My mother's aunt, the woman who had been head of obstetrics at Bethany Hospital and who had allowed my mother to stay there for three months after I was born, was dead. All her fingers had been crushed by the Red Guards, to punish her for being an educated doctor. Her son had been denied an education, sent down to the countryside, unable to get a Beijing city resident permit even today.

After a while I couldn't concentrate. I couldn't listen to these stories. I remembered my mother's family as I had known them, rich and proud, patriotic enough to stay behind after the civil war. "We are Chinese, we will stay in our country," my number one uncle had said proudly. "What do I care about politics? I'm a doctor. China will always need doctors."

Little Tiger was translating for my daughter. My ears were ringing from the languages, English and Chinese blending into an incomprehensible stream, the three voices shouting at once, bouncing off the close blank walls. My ears rang. My cousin's wife put the thickest slices of pork on my rice bowl. I ate without tasting. I felt as though I were trying to swallow my own tongue.

I looked around me, trying to focus on anything but my uncle's ravaged face. Someone had pinned to the chalky wall a crisp new calendar bearing the image of the Holy Family, drawn as if they were Chinese. Living in America, I'd grown accustomed to the image of a blue-eyed Jesus; here Christ had black straight hair and narrow eyes. Mary was dressed like the Buddhist Goddess of Mercy, in a flowing robe that recalled images of Guan Yin in Song dynasty paintings. Joseph similarly looked more like a Mongolian herdsman than a Jewish father.

How long had it been since I'd seen such pictures? They reminded me of my mother, which was probably why my secular uncle and his family had prominently displayed this picture. So obviously new in the dusty room, it must have been purchased for my visit.

"So you can buy these religious things now? No problem?" I asked, pointing to the wall.

My relatives were startled. I'd interrupted someone. My uncle shrugged. "You can buy all kinds of things nowadays."

My cousin's wife brought out glistening slices of watermelon, signaling the end of the meal. Thankfully, I bit into the sweet, cool fruit.

The table erupted with laughter. "You still like watermelon," my cousin's wife smiled. "You're still Chinese, not too Americanized."

My uncle and cousin seemed sated of their need to talk about the past; silently they spat the seeds into their hands. No more horror stories. I was thankful.

I thought I should say something. "I'm very happy that we can be together again. Family shouldn't be separated. My mother would be very happy today. But she never lost her faith in God. She knew someday China would be open again and the family reunited."

Everyone smiled politely.

Then I said, "And from my father, I have brought some small gifts for the family."

"A refrigerator? You're allowed to bring one refrigerator each time you come, you know." One of my cousins was very excited. "We could all use an American refrigerator."

"No, no, no. A refrigerator's too big, how could I bring one?"

"A classmate of mine has a new refrigerator. He has cousins in Hong Kong," my nephew Little Tiger added.

"You can come back in a few months," someone else suggested. "In the fall, the weather's beautiful. It's too hot now. You can bring one then."

"I can't bring a refrigerator. The voltage is different. It wouldn't work here." My head throbbed. My chest felt tight. Everyone was so poor. My mother's family had been rich. They were surgeons, engineers, professors. My mother had had her own school. She built our house. A huge house, brick, Western-style, indoor plumbing, central heating. She built a house for her brother. I remembered. Our family had been rich. We had a house full of servants. Our servants dressed better than other families' servants. We were like royalty.

Today everyone was dressed in the same loose cotton pants, the wrinkled cotton shirts. Everyone was poor.

"I'm inviting you to a banquet. At the Beijing Hotel. A special banquet. You're all invited," I said. "The whole family. Tell everyone."

They offered to take me sightseeing, but I was exhausted. I needed to take a shower. I said I needed to rest, jet lag. I lied and said I had to prepare for the academic conference that I would be attending the next day. I suggested they take May-lee sightseeing while I was at the conference.

My daughter took pictures of us in front of my uncle's shabby concrete apartment building, all of us squinting into the setting sun. Then May-lee and I went back to our hotel and I took a sleeping pill.

~ May-lee ~

The next morning, before I left for my grand tour of Beijing, a woman arrived at our hotel. She was waiting in the lobby when we headed down for breakfast. She rushed toward my father, apologizing. She'd taken the train, seventeen hours, she'd missed the reunion at her father's apartment. She was sorry. She hadn't slept at all. She handed him a bag of bananas, she'd carried them on the train with her, a gift of fruit, a good gift in those days in China.

My father's face wore the grim, worried expression that had settled there since he'd stepped off the airplane into the sticky night air. He couldn't say a thing.

"I was like a daughter to your mother. She always said that." The woman looked anxious, her eyes focused on my father's without blinking, unwavering, intense. Survivor's eyes. She turned to me and repeated everything in clear English. But she seemed unsure of her language ability and smiled nervously.

"I recognized you." My father nodded. "You look exactly the same."

Then all at once the woman laughed, an amazing laugh, light, effervescent with surprise. It seemed impossible that it came from the slight woman before us. It was a girl's laugh. "Oh, no, no, no," she protested, covering her mouth with one hand. "I'm so old."

And then I recognized her too. She was the girl with the fashionably bobbed hair, in a plaid *qipao* and high-top sneakers. She stands with my father and his two brothers by statues of winged animals and minipagodas on Purple Mountain outside Nanjing. It's a family outing, after the war, after the Japanese defeat but before the Communist takeover. Four teenagers being forced by my grandmother to pose nicely in front of these cultural treasures on a hot day, they scowl into the camera lens.

It was the last picture from Nanjing. Soon, my grandmother would decide they must leave Nanjing, leave China. She'd leave this girl too, although her second brother begged her to take the girl to Taiwan, and the girl cried and cried.

Later Nai-nai regretted the decision in the way that you can only regret the past, without knowing what would have been better to do, knowing only what was done.

"I recognized you immediately," my father said to his cousin as they stood face to face in Beijing. "You were always like my sister."

~ Winberg ~

On our last day in the capital, as my father had instructed me to do, I held a banquet for both sides of the family together, the Tsaos and the Chais. I invited them all to come to the restaurant in our hotel and then suddenly a wave of sadness came over me. My father had always ordered the food at the banquets that our family had hosted in New York. Imperial affairs. He consulted with the owners and the chef, he knew exactly what was appropriate for any occasion. He was sure to order food the children would like, soft food that my mother could chew easily, something special and symbolic in honor of our guests. We had to have at least two soups, one mid-meal to change the palate, one at the end to soothe everyone's stomach. A fresh fish was essential. It was brought out on a platter, cooked whole, head still intact. It was important to point the head at the guest of honor. Sometimes when one of his former classmates joined us, they would fight over this issue. My father would point the fish head at his friend, his friend would protest and turn the platter so that the head pointed to my father. They could argue like this for some time until someone relented, saying, "Okay, okay, I will only accept because I don't want the fish to get cold," and then he'd select the choicest bit of meat with his chopsticks and give it to the other man.

Chinese banquets are an elaborate ritual. Non-Chinese sometimes have mistakenly thought that Chinese banquet tables have no hierarchy because they are round, with no head or foot. But in fact, seating is extremely important. The most honored guests should sit closest to the wall, the host with his back to the door. My father explained to me that this custom had begun centuries earlier when a devious general had invited his enemy to dine with him, a fake bid for peace. His guest sat with his back to the door and mid-meal one of the general's soldiers quickly slipped in the door and stabbed the unsuspecting guest in the back. Ever since that time, the host always sits with his own back exposed, the guests' backs safely to the wall.

It felt strange to be hosting this "family" banquet, when my father was so far away and my mother buried, four years now. I was supposed to be my family's representative, the firstborn son returned to China to honor my parents' family, but I felt like a child, playacting like an adult.

I let my uncle choose the courses. He was the senior male relative and besides, I wasn't sure what food to order. I had no idea what would be appropriate anymore. Fortunately he knew exactly what to do.

There were seven different plates of hors d'oeuvres, hot and cold, twelve main courses, and three different desserts as well as fresh tea, Coca-Cola, sweet hawthorn wine, and clear rice wine.

Everyone seemed to enjoy the food although they complained the prices were too high. "These hotels for foreigners, they really know how to make money!" one of my cousins sighed.

"The service isn't very good. That's what communism has done to this country!" My uncle shook his head.

Gu Fu called across the table to me. "Why didn't you teach that daughter of yours any Chinese! All she can say is 'I don't understand,' 'Thank you.' It's a disgrace." Then he nodded at my daughter and said in English, "You should take some pride in your heritage!"

"I'm going to study Chinese in college," she responded.

"I should bloody well hope so!" he sniffed.

Everyone acted as though we got together like this every weekend for dinner. They argued with each other, complained about prices, the difficulty of finding good appliances. No one talked about the past that I remembered or the family fights that my mother remembered. Perhaps all had been nearly forgotten, supplanted by the events of more recent history. Perhaps my relatives were only being polite, deliberately concentrating on the neutral present. I had no way of knowing, but gradually I began to relax in this atmosphere of congenial, familial bickering.

"I want to propose a toast," I said, picking up my glass. "First I want to toast my families in China. To my mother's beloved brother, who had to endure much suffering."

My mother's only surviving brother nodded enthusiastically. "That's right. I really suffered."

Everyone lifted a glass now and took a sip.

"And to my father's sister, a scholar in her own right, and her distinguished husband, who has done so much to keep track of the family." I turned to Gu Mu and Gu Fu.

"To my brother's son!" Gu Mu tipped her glass at me and then gave it to her husband to drink for her.

"To my mother's daughter!" I said, raising my glass to my cousin, who blushed now, smiling.

Soon everyone was a little tipsy and the toasts grew more effusive.

"To the glorious advancement of Sino-American relations! To the ten thousand points of cross-cultural exchange! To the eternal prosperity and happiness of the Chinese and American masses!" shouted one of my more distant cousins, who had joined the Communist party in his youth and was quite practiced at giving toasts.

Finally even my daughter raised her glass. *"Xie xie,"* she said carefully. *"Xie xie."*

"Well, at least she pronounced 'thank you' correctly," said Gu Fu, mellowed now from the wine.

24

RETURN TO PURPLE MOUNTAIN

Winberg in front of
his childhood home,
Nanjing, 1985.

~ May-lee ~

Going to China when I was eighteen changed my life. I'd grown quite depressed living in South Dakota and my grandmother's sudden death when I was thirteen, less than two years after we'd left the East Coast, had come as a blow to my sense of self. One more link to my happier childhood had disappeared.

When I was twelve, my father had decided to leave New York. He was tired of the rat race of working in the city, and he thought the heartland would provide a safer, more wholesome environment for his family. He was wrong.

As we were the only mixed-race-Asian family living in our town, we became the scapegoats for a community suffering during the height of the family farm crisis. People shot at our house; three of our dogs were shot and killed over the years; one was run over by a truck in our yard—the tracks in the mud showed where the driver had left the road to chase her into our field, hit her, then backed up over her head. Dead snakes were surreptitiously placed in our mailbox. My parents were sent hateful, anonymous letters. Too often when I walked down a street in town, a pickup truck would pull up beside me and a grown man would shout out his window, "Jap!" before speeding off. My brother learned to survive with his fists.

It was the eighties, the era when our national media nightly reported alarming stories of the Japanese Threat: Japanese businessmen buying up American landmarks, *kereitsu* carving up the business world into their own spheres of influence, America's burgeoning trade deficit. I learned the hard way how irresponsible media reports affected public opinion, and how an isolated community suffering hard times could project its rage onto racial stereotypes.

We were not Japanese, of course, but I learned that prejudice is not rational. After all, even if we had been Japanese, we would not have been responsible for the economic woes of the region. Furthermore, the verbal abuse I suffered from adults was inexcusable. As a twelve-year-old child, how could I have hurt them?

The years I lived in South Dakota were painful because I experienced racial hatred on a daily basis. I lived in fear. I learned to distrust people. Sometimes I hated myself.

I also came to be absurdly sentimental about my childhood. Growing up in a mostly Italian-American town in New Jersey, I had never felt any prejudice directed toward me. I remembered only happy times, a family that loved me, visiting with my grandparents in Manhattan every weekend. My cousin, brother, and I were all mixed race but we were never treated as though race mattered.

But after living in South Dakota, I felt like a strange, odd-looking creature with my brown-black hair and my largish eyes but low-bridged nose and high cheekbones. I felt that I could not call myself Chinese as I didn't know the language and had never been to China, but I was not considered "American" by the people I encountered. I was a freak.

But in China, no one cared. My father's family had far greater problems to worry about than my racial mix. They wanted me to understand what they had suffered under the Cultural Revolution and they wanted me to have pride in my Chinese heritage. Who cared what some people in an isolated town in an isolated region of America thought?

The day that Gu Fu and Gu Mu took me sightseeing around Beijing, Gu Fu instructed me to be very quiet when he went to buy our tickets to the various parks and monuments. There was a two-tier pricing system, one price for Chinese citizens and a much higher price for foreign tourists. So long as I didn't say anything, the ticket sellers assumed I was completely Chinese too, and let Gu Fu pay the cheaper price.

Gu Mu laughed happily at this clever trick.

As I walked in the streets, people would frequently come up to me to ask me directions. Although I sported a space shuttle *Columbia* T-shirt and French braids, not exactly common in those days, they assumed I was just another trendy Beijing teenager. Gu Fu and Gu Mu looked more like tourists, visiting from the provinces, with their sunglasses and sun hats. I remember one elderly woman, who'd asked me how to get somewhere, burst into startled laughter and clapped her hand over her mouth when I had to try to explain that I didn't speak Chinese. Apologizing, Gu Fu explained to her that I was from America.

"She doesn't look like a foreigner," the old woman said, shaking her head. As she walked away, she turned back to get one more look at me and then laughed again.

Years of anxiety peeled away each day. I felt lighter and more giddy at each new revelation. Everything was new and familiar at the same time. The sounds of Mandarin, the smell of *cong you bing* onion cakes frying, the sight of grandparents walking their one grandchild, all filled me with nostalgia for my happy weekends with Ye-ye and Nai-nai.

I enjoyed exploring the twisting, narrow alleys of Beijing by myself, observing the women bargaining with the farmers who sat before piles of fresh peppers and oranges and ten-foot-high mountains of watermelon. I watched old men taking their caged birds for walks then hanging the bamboo cages in the low branches of pine trees so that the birds could "enjoy nature" while the men sat around stone Chinese chess tables. Nai-nai had accidentally killed my mother's canary, I remembered suddenly, because she'd insisted upon opening the window behind its cage at dawn and it caught cold; she'd been certain a bird couldn't be happy living indoors all the time.

Bicyclists whizzed past me, carting live chickens in their baskets or a new television strapped on the package rack. Every sidewalk was crowded with people of all ages, buying things, carting things away, arguing and joking and calling to friends at the tops of their lungs, silently munching a steamed *baozi* or a stick of candied haw-thorn apples, noisily slurping noodles in front of one of the new privately run businesses that were just beginning to take root in the city. And everywhere I went, no one stared at me or called me names.

For the first time in nearly six years, I felt like a human being again.

At the end of my stay in Beijing, my fifteen-year-old cousin Xiao Mei gave me a white cardboard box, lined with thick cotton batting. It was the kind of box that, in America, would have contained jewelry. However, inside I found six jagged rocks, unpolished, their scientific names in Chinese and English written beneath them with a blue felt-tip marker.

"So you will not forget China," she said.

"Don't worry," I said. "That's impossible."

However, although I grew more delighted with each passing day, my father grew more moody. From the beginning, he refused to translate anything our relatives said, and when I insisted, he shouted once, "What's the matter with you? How come you don't speak Chinese?"

On our final day in Beijing when I said that I wanted to go out sightseeing while he was at his conference and so I needed to know when I should be back for the family dinner, he snapped, "What? You didn't hear what they said? How come you're so dependent?"

By the time we left for Nanjing to try to find my grandmother's house, he was taciturn, grim-faced, and irritable. He refused to say what was the matter.

In order to go to Nanjing, we first flew to Shanghai then transferred to a train for the three-and-a-half-hour ride to my father's former hometown.

In the dark, smoky Shanghai station long wooden benches bespoke the elegance of a bygone era, but everything else revealed the poverty of contemporary life. The concrete floors were littered with cigarette butts, fruit peels, and other tatters of trash. Families with the ruddy cheeks and patched clothing that revealed their country origins lay curled around their plastic luggage. A voice hissed on the tinny PA system above the dull roar of the crowd. Somehow we found our way to the proper gate.

I blinked, blinded by the sudden sunlight as we left the station to stand outside on the crowded platforms. Women in bright kerchiefs hawked bags of cookies, dried cuttlefish, and preserved fruits for the train ride ahead. Their voices rose above the din shrilly, but most of the hundreds of waiting travelers ignored them, instead focusing upon the doors to the big black coal-driven train that would take us to Nanjing.

Suddenly the conductors unlocked the doors and the crowd rushed forward in a great stampede. A few of the fleet-footed slithered up the steps and in the door, rushed into the cars, then leaned out the windows as their friends and family members handed up their baggage. Children were passed above the heads of adults and slid in through the open windows. Everyone else was forced to wait in the great, throbbing bottlenecks before each entrance.

We had purchased tickets in the first-class section, which meant that we were allowed to enter a car without fighting our way to the door. Here the seats had cushions and there were little tables with white tablecloths. Peering through the glass door that separated the cars, I could see the masses packed together in second class on wooden benches, their luggage perched precariously above them on the metal racks. A third-class ticket meant the bearer stood in the aisles.

Despite the seemingly endless number of passengers who were boarding, the train got off to a surprisingly swift start. The whistle blew in warning and the peddlers who had been conducting sales to passengers via the open windows now stepped back from the train. The station slowly drifted away from us, we passed shanties and dilapidated shops that lined the railroad tracks for a few more miles and then quickly we picked up speed and headed toward the countryside.

Soon a young woman dressed in a boxy white jacket, army-green pants, and dainty white gloves arrived carrying an iron kettle. She poured us glasses of hot tea.

Outside the windows, the countryside rolled by: paddies green with young rice shoots, water buffalo grazing in the ditches, women with kerchiefs balancing baskets on a pole across their shoulders as they trod along the narrow pathways between the mirrorlike fields.

"Look, Papa!" I pointed out the window, but he only scowled.

Halfway to Nanjing, the temperature heated up considerably.

Though all the windows were open, the cross-breeze was unbearably hot. Not for nothing was Nanjing known as one of China's four furnaces (the other three being Chongqing, Nanchang, and Wuhan). I'd never felt heat like this, the humid air like boiling water in my lungs.

At this point, my father turned a bright red. "I'm dying," he groaned. "I'm having a heart attack." Usually an impeccable dresser, even when traveling, he shed his button-up shirt and sat now in his sleeveless undershirt.

"Don't you have cold drinks?" he asked the tea girl as she came by again.

She smiled. "Hot water is good for you. It makes you sweat." She filled his teacup to the brim.

"I'm going to die," my father gasped. "I should never have come back. Why did you want to come?" He looked at me now as if this trip were my idea.

I remembered the can of Coke in my bag and took it out now, handing it to my father. I'd been delighted by the Coca-Cola cans with the famous logo written in Chinese characters, *Ke kou ke le,* literally "Tasty and Enjoyable." I'd tried to slip an empty can into my suitcase to take home, but my father had seen me. "What are you doing?" He grabbed the can. "Don't take trash." He thought it was unseemly, his daughter behaving like a crazy, and threw the can away. But when he wasn't looking, I had tucked a new can, still full, from the minibar into my camera bag just before we checked out of our hotel.

The Coke was warm by now, of course, but he was thrilled.

"I took it when you weren't looking," I explained.

He gulped down half the can before he came up for air.

"It's a good thing you never listen to anything I tell you," he said finally.

When we arrived in Nanjing, more relatives were already waiting for us at at our hotel: a man and a woman, apparently in their early forties. My father was embarrassed by their greeting because he didn't remember them. It was quickly made clear that he'd never met them before, but they'd heard through the grapevine that family from America was coming and didn't want to miss us.

These ersatz cousins now offered my father a mesh bag of mandarin oranges then launched into business. They knew where my grandmother's house was. Another member of their family had in fact set up in a shanty across the street, just to keep an eye on it, the man said. Although the government, officially Communist, did not recognize private property or the ownership of land, Overseas Chinese could reclaim a building that they'd had built prior to the 1949 revolution. They wanted my father to do exactly that.

There were apparently three families living in my father's old home now. "The government divided it up, we can't get these people out," the man sighed.

"But now that you've come back to China—" The woman smiled.

"You can reclaim the house and give it to us," the man finished excitedly.

"We can all go today to kick those squatters out!" the woman said.

"I don't know," my father said. "I wasn't sure it was still standing. I didn't bring the deed."

They looked very disappointed.

My father made his "cousins" wait in the lobby while we went to our room and he changed out of his sweaty clothes. Then he telephoned down to the lobby and told them we'd all get together later for dinner perhaps, for dessert, but he was too exhausted after his train trip to be sociable at present.

They said they didn't mind waiting.

"No, go away," he said gruffly. "Come back later."

However, they disregarded his command and instead followed us to look for Nai-nai's house.

To look for my grandmother's house, we used a guide and official driver connected with the local party office for overseeing visits with Overseas Chinese. The levels of bureaucracy in China never failed to amaze me—there seemed to be an official office for everything! But I was very happy to have this guide, a trim woman in her fifties, because she spoke very good English and was willing to translate what everyone said for me.

My father gave them the address to his old house, and she and the driver thought they knew where it was located.

My father grew more and more alarmed as the driver approached his old neighborhood near the Nanjing Drum Tower, a Ming dynasty watchtower whose drums had been used centuries earlier to warn the populace of impending attacks. In the era of the republic it had been a popular meeting place for student protesters when organizing their marches urging the government to reform. Now, the neighborhood was much run-down, the alleys near the Drum Tower rutted and narrow, crowded with small shacks with tin roofs and worse. People dumped their refuse directly into the street.

Fidgeting in his seat, my father grimaced.

Our driver had to circle the alleys over and over, he couldn't find the address anymore. "People keep building these illegal structures," he said, pointing to the shacks. "Someday the government will tear them all down."

We hit a major pothole and his dashboard ornament, a yellow dog with a bobbing head, rocked so violently that the head popped off. The driver swore.

Suddenly we heard a car honking behind us. Our driver abruptly stopped the car and rolled down the window to shout at the car behind us. However, it turned out to be my father's cousins. They'd followed us, after all, in a taxi.

"It's here! Here!" the man was shouting, gesticulating broadly.

Indeed, we'd nearly missed the house, which was set back away from the shacks, behind a wall. Our guide now ran ahead to inform the inhabitants of our visit.

"You see! It's still here!" My father's cousins smiled happily, pointing.

My father didn't answer.

Our guide returned to say that we could look through the house if we wanted to, but she made the cousins wait in the alley. I found my heart beating rapidly. All my childhood I'd heard of this house and I was expecting a mansion, something exotic and spectacular. As we entered the courtyard, I felt confused then disappointed. The gray brick house before us looked old and neglected. The yard was very tiny now, no signs of Nai-nai's American-style playground anymore. The lawn had returned to dirt and trash was piled in the corners.

Nevertheless, I convinced my father to pose for a picture.

Standing before the open door, our guide hurried us along, so I had no time to linger and try to take in the full structure. My father dashed inside now, and I rushed in after him. Inside it was too dark to see properly. I remember an elderly woman pacing in the shadows, afraid we'd come to reclaim her home. My father rushed through all the rooms anyway, shaking his head, as if he were looking for something important, something lost. I had to run to keep up with him. Finally, he strode outside again, to the dirt yard that was once a lawn. He scowled in disgust and rushed through the listing metal gate, into the alley, where he continued walking, although it was ninety degrees with ninety-percent humidity, a typical Nanjing summer day, and the taxi with the air-conditioning was waiting behind us.

Racing away from his mother's house, he shouted down the street, "Everyone is poor! Everything is ruined! The country is ruined!"

I ran after him.

He paced one way then the next, evading me, as he shouted some more, in Chinese now. His face was dripping with sweat. He waved his arms as if to ward off a giant bird in a Japanese monster film. "Filthy! Dirty! Ugh! Everything is dirt!"

"You're going to have a heart attack!" I warned.

Finally, I persuaded him to get back into the car. He ranted and raved the entire way back to our hotel. "China is ruined!" he said again. I felt embarrassed. I thought our guide would be horrified, the driver ashamed or angered, but instead they fell silent, nodding. They seemed to agree with him, in fact.

By afternoon my father was strangely calm. I couldn't tell if he was feeling better or merely exhausted.

At our guide's suggestion, we decided to head to the mountains, to enjoy the scenery and relative coolness. Even in the car, with the air-conditioning going full blast, my skin was burning, sticky from the viscous heat.

Perhaps alarmed by my father's outburst, the cousins had decided to stay in the city.

As we weaved our way through the crowded streets of Nanjing, the car competing with the sturdy black bicycles and screeching buses packed to the bursting, arms and heads poking from the windows, I admired the broad French sycamore trees that had been planted along the main boulevards at the beginning of the century. Their leafy branches stretched above the streets and sidewalks like enormous parasols. Families sat in their shade on tiny wooden stools, fanning themselves. Laundry hung limply from the branches like so many tangled kites. Street vendors squatted beneath them on the shady curbs, their harvests of fresh watermelon, peaches, green beans, and ginger root piled into minimountains.

As we left the city and entered the surrounding hills, tall pines replacing the sycamores, the road narrowing as we climbed higher and higher, the air cooled somewhat. Busses gasped and puttered up the hills behind us; half the population of Nanjing seemed to be heading out of town this afternoon, everyone trying to escape the heat.

Our guide decided to take us first to a newly opened coffee shop. "This is very modern," she promised my father.

A pink neon sign over the door announced, using the new post-1949 spelling system, "Meiling's Bar." According to a placard, Soong Mei-ling, Chiang Kai-shek's wife, used to spend many a hot Nanjing afternoon in a nearby mountain retreat. To set the mood there were a series of enlarged black-and-white photographs on the pastel walls: women in soft gray *qipaos,* close-up shots of bound feet in embroidered slippers, young men with queues sporting long silk robes, blurry rickshaws, and wizened old men fingering opium pipes. A fake sedan chair was propped up in the corner next to a potted plastic fern. It was all quite exotic.

My father paced agitatedly. "You shouldn't do this," he said to no one in particular. "It's not respectful."

The young wait staff seemed perplexed. They obviously enjoyed working in a chic coffee shop; they found the references to the old "feudal days" before the revolution hip, daring even. But I think my father felt like an anachronism. He was the only one present who remembered Soong Mei-ling and the days when Nanjing was the capital of all China.

I convinced my father to have a seat.

"Do you have any cold drinks?" he asked the waitress.

She appeared shocked by this request. It was only 1985 after all, people hadn't quite adapted to Western tastes yet, like drinking cold carbonated beverages when everyone knew that cold drinks were bad for the stomach.

So we drank piping hot tea, the leaves floating thickly along the surface. The waitress also recommended a sweet dessert and brought out a pudding of sorts made from lotus seeds and crushed sweet red beans.

"A Nanjing specialty," our guide said.

"Sure, sure," my father said. He hadn't been able to eat lunch due to the heat and was growing hungry now.

The waitress gave us each a glass bowl decorated with bright pink dragons.

My father grumpily took a bite. Suddenly his face changed, softened. He bent over the bowl and greedily slurped down spoon after spoonful of the pudding.

"I remember this!" he cried out. "I had this when I was a child." He scraped the bowl clean. "I remember, I remember!"

Now the waitress came back to the table and brought him another bowl. She laughed to see him so happy. "So you really are from Nanjing!" she said.

My father was rapturous. Memories tumbled out, mixing events and locations from his childhood travels during the war. "We lived in the countryside. The floors were made of dirt. The servants used to take me to watch cockfights. My mother was so angry." He giggled, a naughty little boy again.

Then he said something to the waitress, something unusual I could tell because it sounded different from his regular Chinese, and she clapped happily. "How can you speak Sichuan dialect?" she asked.

He beamed proudly. "I grew up speaking Sichuan dialect in the war!"

Then he told me how during the war while fleeing the Japanese army, his family had lived in a village. He told the story about Ye-ye being nearly thrown off the boat on the Yangtze River. He talked about hiding in caves while Japanese fighter planes bombed some city. I'd never heard him speak like this before.

My father acted as though a tight cord inside him had been cut. "Let's go up to Purple Mountain!" he said as if the idea had just occurred to him. "We used to go every weekend in the summer. The servants brought cots, we used to lie under the pine trees." He sighed. "It was so cool under the trees."

Now my father, who had refused to go to any of the tourist sights in Beijing, wanted to visit every sight on the mountain. We went to see Sun Yat-sen's mausoleum, climbing all hundred-plus steps to visit the tomb of the first president of the Republic of China. Then we went deeper into the pine forests and visited the Ming dynasty Beamless Hall, so-called because its vaulted ceiling had no beams, its stones were fitted together using only a mortar made of rice paste. We visited the nine-story Linggu Pagoda, which was actually designed in the 1930s by an American architect as a memorial to dead Kuomintang members.

Finally we went to the tomb of a minor Ming dynasty emperor. It was believed that the soul of the deceased left its tomb to walk the earth occasionally, but that if it could not find its way home, the soul would be forced to wander endlessly, perhaps causing mischief in its unhappiness. To ward off this possibility, the ancient architects erected a series of large stone statues to mark the way leading back to the tomb. This traditional-style Sacred Path was lined on both sides with pairs of auspicious animals, elephants and camels, mythical beasts with a single horn and wings, lions with scales and hooves, as well as turtles with giant steles on their backs that outlined the prince's illustrious deeds in life. We posed for pictures before the elephants.

I remembered these statues from the album my father had made of my grandmother's life. He had posed here as a boy with his brothers and cousin in the final months before they left Nanjing. Until I saw them for myself, I had somehow never believed that such things really existed. The photos seemed like an illustration to a fairy tale. Now I could touch these statues with my own hands.

That evening when it was cooler, we returned to the city. The cousins returned after dinner and my father invited them both and our guide for dessert at our hotel's nightclub. In those days, such clubs played only classical music—rather than rock or Western pop music—despite the presence of a disco ball and strings of colored lights.

While the guide and I had glasses of cool watermelon juice, my father and his cousins shared a tall, warm bottle of local Jinling beer, chatting happily now.

One of the barmaids, dressed in a fluttery chiffon floor-length ballgown, came to our table. There were not many people in our hotel, and we were the only foreigners in the club.

"Do you want to dance?" she asked me. Because Chinese people were still shy after the enforced years of prudery under Mao, women danced with women and the men stood in clumps around the dance floor, smoking and watching the women waltz. Only the boldest men and women danced together.

"Go ahead," my father urged me.

"I don't know how to dance this way," I said, glaring at him.

"It's okay. We'll show you," the barmaid said.

"Why don't you dance?" I asked our guide.

"Oh, no," she said. "I'm much too old for dancing."

"Go on," my father said. "Have some fun!"

Now I felt as though everyone would think I was being rude if I refused, so I got up to join the three dancing barmaids while everyone else stared at us. The canned music, an instrumental version of "How Much Is That Doggie in the Window," blared tinnily. While the Chinese women floated daintily across the polished wooden floor, I awkwardly tried swaying in some semblance of rhythm. My father, the guide, and his cousins waved at me encouragingly.

Mercifully, the song ended after a few minutes, and I ran back to the table before I could be sucked into a new dance routine. My father, quite the jolly man now, applauded loudly.

"Did you have fun?" he asked.

Now I was the surly one.

As our sweet desserts arrived—only Western-style cakes this time, no traditional Nanjing specialties—my father waxed philosophic. He spoke of the remarkable transformations occurring in China, how just a decade ago, the country had been completely closed to the West, who then could have imagined this trip would be possible?

"China has really changed," he sighed, thinking of the past, his childhood, the wars.

"Not enough," said our guide.

"Not enough," said the cousins, shaking their heads.

The next year, 1986, my father and I traveled to China again and this time he enjoyed everything. Together we went to the Summer Palace, Tiananmen Square, and the Forbidden City where my father dressed up in a fake imperial robe for five yuan and had his picture taken seated on the throne. We went to the Great Wall and my father posed for pictures with me and a camel. Everything made him laugh cheerfully.

By this time, I'd had a year of Mandarin in college. I could bargain

over prices. I could read the maps. I could leave the hotel room with
impunity, riding the city buses.

I was no longer dependent. No longer a source of embarrassment
for him.

"So you're really learning to speak Chinese," my father said, as if
he were still surprised by the very idea.

Our relatives all had refrigerators and color television sets now.
The women were wearing skirts and high heels. My father's cousin,
the daughter Nai-nai had left behind, had received a visa to work in
New York at Columbia University. We celebrated with a seventeen-
course banquet.

After dinner, my father and I took a walk through downtown
Beijing. Everyone was healthier looking, more solid, more fashionably dressed. Only elderly men still wore Mao suits. Instead of watermelon carts, there were ice-cream vendors on every street corner.

My father and I bought two bars. I don't like the taste of milk
generally but I liked this ice cream because it wasn't milky at all. We
both agreed it was delicious.

"China's really changing," my father told my grandfather when we
came back to the United States. "Do you want to go with me next
time and see for yourself?"

But Ye-ye's health had taken a turn for the worse, and in October
he died without ever returning to his old home, without visiting the
family, without seeing what China was becoming.

25

THE VISITATION

(Left to right) Winberg's son Jeff, Charles, and Winberg celebrating Charles's birthday, around 1970.

~ May-lee ~

When I was nineteen, before my grandfather died, Ye-ye called my father to say that my grandmother had visited him in a dream again. She'd been silent all these years since my uncle's wedding, and he'd grown despairing. But now she'd come in his sleep. She was a little girl, with two pigtails and apple cheeks, dressed in pink silk pajamas. She had wings and flitted about him.

"Don't go!" he called, trying to catch her, but she flew away, laughing, just as his fingers touched the hem of her shirt, the tips of her embroidered slippers.

"Come here! Come play with us," she giggled. Then she rolled him a piece of fruit. My grandfather didn't know the word for this fruit in English and my father didn't recognize the term, but it was round and hairy, a Chinese fruit.

"I'm going to die," Ye-ye told my father.

"Don't talk like that," my father said. "You're fine."

But two days later, my grandfather died in his sleep.

My father said Ye-ye had been very happy about the dream because Nai-nai was young and pretty again. Plus she'd forgiven him.

My father told me all this the way someone else might say that Ye-ye had decided to spend the winters in Florida. All my family's stories unfolded in this manner.

"He knew, he knew," my father said, over and over, after Ye-ye's funeral. "He knew and I wouldn't believe him."

~ *Winberg* ~

I was fifty-four when my father died, too old to be considered an orphan really. But that's how it felt, that I'd been suddenly orphaned.

Before he died, he called to tell me about his premonition. Then he said that he wanted me to dedicate a room in my house to him and my mother. It should be their room forever. With their pictures and a bowl of fresh fruit. He was insistent about the fruit. "Not plastic. Real." He knew that if the fruit were real, I'd have to change it regularly, I couldn't forget about my parents that way. "Chinese are very practical," he said.

I told him, of course, I'd do that if he really wanted me to, but it was silly, because he was fine. He could come to visit me, stay in my house for real, a room for him anytime he wanted. "Don't worry," I said. "You're fine. You're not going to die at all."

"I'm not worried," he replied.

Then we hung up.

Had I known, had I believed him, I would have said a million other things. That he didn't need a shrine in my house to be remembered, I would never forget him, never forget my parents. I would have told him all the things that I remembered about their life, their sense of honor, their struggle, their pride, their intelligence, their fights, their great love.

But I was tired, and I didn't want him to grow emotional and me with him, and so I ended our call without saying any of these things.

I hadn't thought it possible, my father mortal after all.

Perhaps everyone who has ever lived thinks this way.

I cannot remember my father's funeral. I read the eulogy that my wife had written for me because I had been too distraught to write

one myself. Because my father had moved out of the city to the suburbs to live with my middle brother and his wife, he was not taken
to a Chinatown funeral parlor as my mother had been. Instead the
service was entirely Western. Perhaps that is why I don't remember
the service, because it was plain and Protestant. There was no large
portrait surrounded by flowers before the casket, no procession of
mourners bowing before the open casket to express their condolences
to the family. There was the usual sinister-sounding organ music and
a minister who rambled, everything orderly and proper.

My wife had a photograph of my father printed up on good bond
paper to be distributed to all the friends who came. In the picture,
my father's seated in one of his New York classrooms, in a suit and
tie, a calligraphy brush in his hand, the blackboard just visible behind
his head. A dignified photograph. I have no idea how old he is in
the picture. He looked the same way the entire time he lived in America, an older man, but not an *old* man, not someone who could die.

My voice broke while reading the eulogy. I couldn't continue.

I can't remember anything else. It's a confusion of faces and dark
suits, families from China, from New York.

Afterward my father was buried in the plot he'd chosen, beside a
tree, outside my mother's mausoleum. He told me that he had chosen
this plot so that he could be like that strong tree, standing guard
outside my mother's tomb forever. The physical distance between
their graves would be a sign of respect like the space he always left
before my mother's name in his letters.

The gravestone wasn't ready yet for the interment, of course. I
didn't see it until the next year when I visited his grave. He'd chosen
the epitaph with care. It read:

DR. CHU CHAI,
HUSBAND OF RUTH MEI-EN TSAO CHAI

26

THE STONE BODHISATTVA

Winberg in front of his parents' former apartment building, 220 West 71st Street, New York City, 1999.

~ *Winberg* ~

I went with my daughter this summer to New York, to visit with old friends. It'd been years since I'd last been in the city. She suggested we visit my parents' old neighborhood, and without thinking, I agreed.

I didn't recognize their building at first. My daughter had to point it out. West Seventy-first has really changed, gentrified. I remember the building next to my parents' was a cathouse, the prostitutes used to sit on the stoop in the summer, their pimp parading down the sidewalk in his rooster-colored finery. Now the only people scurrying in and out of the buildings are yuppies carrying gym bags and bottles of designer water. The Christian church on the corner that had been so unfriendly to my mother is gone. I remember we could see it from the window of my parents' eighth-story apartment, but it's been razed, replaced by a generic, brick health-care facility. Gone, too, is my mother's senior center. Instead there are two new synagogues just around the block. I guess there's no longer the need to provide subsidized lunches for elderly Jewish immigrants. This neighborhood's affluent.

My daughter insists upon taking a picture. Obligingly, I stand in front of this building that used to be my home, my parents' home, this strange place where young athletic couples now live.

"Yep," I say to my daughter, "everything's changed."

She looks disappointed, but I have to admit, I'm relieved. Now I don't have to feel that I've returned home only to be reminded that my parents are gone. Because this is not the neighborhood I remember, I do not feel as though my parents are missing. I do not feel their loss all over again.

In my mind's eye, my parents are always in their cluttered apartment, surrounded by their China antiques, the sofa under sheets, the Oriental carpet I gave them for Christmas one year rolled up in a corner "to keep it nice." They're walking arm in arm down the street, slowly, my father exercising after his heart attacks, on their way to the senior center, both dressed for the outing, my father in a three-piece suit, my mother in her wig and a silk dress, both their dentures firmly in place. They're waiting for me to come from the suburbs in Jersey, waiting on the curb because they know there's no parking to be found, waiting for me to take them to their favorite restaurant, my kids and wife in the car.

But in this new, sanitized version of their neighborhood, this movie-set version of New York, I don't expect to find them and so I cannot miss them when I stand outside their apartment building of thirty years, knowing that they won't be momentarily coming out of the glass doors to greet me, my mother's plastic shopping bags on their arms, their voices rising on the air, both of them speaking at the same time, both eager to tell me the latest gossip, my mother's latest investment scheme, my father's latest idea for a book.

I can only stand on the pristine sidewalk while my daughter takes a picture in this neighborhood of strangers, feeling vaguely disoriented, wondering how it's possible that time has passed so quickly, so definitively.

Once upon a time, when they'd first come to the city, my father liked to attend the auctions of Chinese antiques—missionaries' collections, American advisors' booty—that were held in a small auction house on West Sixty-ninth. Usually the prices were too high for his meager salary, and my father sat shaking his head as he watched a particularly nice Ming vase or a Qing scroll skyrocket out of his reach, while my mother put a consoling, perhaps restraining, hand on his arm. But one miraculous Saturday, he was able to bid upon and win a stone bust of the bodhisattva Guan Yin, the Goddess of Mercy.

Charles chortled gleefully, as pleased as if he'd stolen it from some temple himself, rubbing his hands together and thumping his cane on the ground triumphantly. Ruth smiled then, too, to see him so happy. But after they paid their money, they realized they'd have to carry it home. Spending more money on a cab was out of the question and the subway with all its steps wasn't an option obviously.

"It's only half a dozen blocks," Charles said optimistically.

Ruth gripped the shoulders of the bodhisattva so that Charles could take the head. Fortunately, its elaborate hairstyle formed a perfect handle so that he could still walk with his cane and hold the hairpiece with one hand. The first block they shuffled along, trying to match their steps. By the second block, they had found their gait. By the fourth block, Ruth's shoulders ached, Charles thought his fingers were going to fall off, and they didn't care who stared at them or what those kids on the stoops were shouting. By the time they made it home, they were drenched in sweat. Once safely inside the apartment, Charles let his cane drop so that he could take the statue in both hands, but then he lost his balance and they careened across the apartment, reaching the sheet-draped sofa just in time to loft the bodhisattva onto its cushions. While Charles massaged his left arm, Ruth sat on the floor, facing the reclining statue.

"You've been cheated," Ruth said, panting. She brushed a damp strand of hair from her forehead. "This isn't the Goddess of Mercy. It's hell's gatekeeper."

This struck them both as hilarious, and they laughed out loud, in a free and easy kind of way, the way they used to laugh when they were young, before the wars. Exhausted, they lay down on the floor on their backs on the throw rug, laughing until tears stung their eyes and they couldn't breathe and still they couldn't stop.

"The Goddess of Mercy has killed us!" they roared.

Ruth sighed finally, wiping her eyes, then laid a hand across her forehead. Charles rolled onto his side to watch her.

"We're old," she sighed. "That's the problem."

"No, I'm old," he said. "You're still just a girl. You haven't changed at all."

"And you still can't tell a lie. That's always been your problem."
She sighed. "But that's why I wanted to marry you. Because you had
an honest face." Then Ruth laughed again.

I know this story because my parents told me after I came home from
classes at NYU and wondered where the Buddhist statue had come
from. Later they gave the bust to me when I left for California, for
my first tenure-track teaching position. At first I hadn't wanted to
take it. I was shipping my things across the country, and I had
enough to pack as it was, what with all my books. But they persisted.

"It'll remind you of us," they said.

I'd acted offended then and insisted they keep it. But when the
movers arrived in California with all my books, I found the bodhisattva packed in a box, cushioned with a hundred balled-up Chinese
newspapers. A note was taped to the nose: "For Winberg, Love
Mother and Father." I recognized my mother's calligraphy.

My mother, she didn't leave anything to chance.

ACKNOWLEDGMENTS

The authors would like to thank the following people: our family in America and China; Dr. Gene Swanger and Mrs. Caroline Swanger for their hospitality and generosity in showing us around Wittenberg and Springfield; Mrs. Louise Romig Haas, whose friendship with Ruth and family has endured three generations; Dr. John Kuan and Mrs. Grace Kuan for their hospitality in Taipei and conversations on Buddhism; Professor S. C. Tony Leng and Mrs. Nora Leng for sharing their memories of life in China during the war years and for traveling companionship; the Grinnell-Nanjing Fellowship Program; Professor Andrew Hsieh; Professor Jan Berkowitz-Gross; Howard Goldblatt for great classes and great books; Lani Kwon Meilgaard, woman warrior, whose faith and encouragement made this book possible; Marilyn Krysl, in whose inspirational classes this book began; Linda Hogan, teacher and friend; Janet Hard, guardian angel; Li Li, Howard Choy, and Shelley Chan for encouragement; Deborah Baker for editorial genius; Professor Robert Scalapino; Keiko Hjersman and the Institute of East Asian Studies at the University of California-Berkeley; Jane Dystel and Miriam Goderich for believing in the manuscript; Melissa Jacobs, our insightful editor, for her brilliant guidance; Sally Kim, Pete Wolverton, and Carolyn Dunkley for taking care of us at St. Martin's; Elizabeth Catalano for her conscientious copyediting; Jeff Chai for sharing memories, and Virginia Chai for her proofreading skill.

We found innumerable books useful for providing background and filling in historical details, including: Iris Chang, *The Rape of Nanking* (New York: Basic Books, 1997); Jerome Chen, *The Highlanders of Central China* (New York: M. E. Sharpe, 1992); *China Handbook, 1937–1945*, compiled by the Chinese Ministry of Information (New York: Macmillan, 1947); *Historical Statistics of the United States: Colonial Times to 1970* (Washington, D.C.: Government Printing Office, 1975); *History of the Sino-Japanese War: 1937–1945*, compiled by Hsu Long-hsuen and Chang Ming-kai, trans. Wen Ha-hsiung (Taipei: Chung Wu Publishing Co., 1971); *The Holy Bible: New King James Version* (Nashville, Tenn.: Thomas Nelson Publishers, 1994); John Israel, *Lianda: A Chinese University in War and Revolution* (Stanford: Stanford University Press, 1998); T. Christopher Jesperson, *American Images of China: 1931–1949* (Stanford: Stanford University Press, 1996); Harry H. L. Kitano and Roger Daniels, *Asian Americans: Emerging Minorities.* 2nd ed. (Englewood Cliffs, NJ: Prentice Hall, 1995); Theodora Lau, *The Handbook of Chinese Horoscopes* (New York: HarperCollins, 1995); Howard S. Levy, *Chinese Footbinding* (New York: Walton Rawls Publishers, 1966); Ichisada Miyazaki, *China's Examination Hell: The Civil Service Examination of Imperial China*, trans. Conrad Schirokauer (New York: Weatherhill, 1976); *The Rape of Nanking, an Undeniable History in Photographs*, edited by Shi Young and James Yin (Chicago: Innovative Publishing Group, 1997); Sterling Seagrave, *The Soong Dynasty* (New York: Harper & Row, 1985); Jonathan Spence, *The Search for Modern China* (New York: Norton, 1990); Te-kong Tong and Li Tsung-jen, *The Memoirs of Li Tsung-jen* (Boulder, CO: Westview Press, 1979); Barbara Tuchman, *Stilwell and the American Experience in China, 1911–1945* (New York: Macmillan, 1970); *Wartime Capital, Chongqing Today* (Chengdu: Sichuan People's Publishing House, 1991).

August, 2001